T0105279

THROUGH EUROPE
WITH A JUG OF WINE

OTHER BOOKS BY MORRISON WOOD

With a Jug of Wine (1949)
Fisherman's Wharf Cookbook (1955)
More Recipes with a Jug of Wine (1956)

THROUGH EUROPE
with a jug of
WINE

By Morrison Wood

FARRAR, STRAUS AND GIROUX

NEW YORK

To

BEATRICE

My Wife

A beloved comrade and a fun-loving traveling companion
who explored, tasted and sipped with me with great enthusiasm.
Her voluminous notes have been the basis
for much of the material in this book.

CONTENTS

ACKNOWLEDGMENTS

I would like to express my very deep gratitude to the scores of people throughout Europe who have been so kind and generous and helpful and friendly in assisting me not only to gather information and recipes for this volume, but to smooth the way in traveling some ten thousand miles through the British Isles, France, Italy, Switzerland, Germany, Holland and Belgium. Hotel owners, restaurateurs, heads of local tourist offices, guides, and officers on the both the Cunard liners, the Queen Elizabeth and the Queen Mary—all went out of their way to give courteous service and inestimable help, so often beyond the line of duty.

I particularly want to thank Mr. Peter ffrench-Hodges, of the British Travel and Holidays Association in London, England, Mr. Ian F. Anderson, of the Scottish Tourist Board in Edinburgh, Scotland, Mr. T. J. M. Sheehy, of the Irish Tourist Board in Dublin, Ireland, Miss Maeve Fitzgibbon, Press and Public Relations Manager, Shannon Free Airport at Shannon, Ireland, Monsieur Georges Normand, Chef de Service d'Accueil, Commissariat General au Tourisme in Paris, France, Mlle, Andrée Antonetti, of the French Tourist office in Nice, France, Conte Dr. Sigmund Fago-Golfarelli, Chief of the Press and Public Relations Department, Ente Nazionale Italiano per il Tourismo in Rome, Italy, Dr. Dante Frigerio, Director, Swiss National Tourist Office in Milan, Italy, Mr. Fred Birman, Director, Press and Public Relations Department, Swiss National Tourist Bureau in Zurich, Switzerland, Herr Hans C. A. Seelemann, Director of the German Tourist Bureau in Zürich, Switzerland, Herr F. F. Schwarzenstein, Director of the Press Department, German Central Tourist Association, in Frankfurt, Germany, Mr. Charles J. Belmon, Director, Netherlands National Tourist Office in Cologne, Germany, the San Francisco and Paris offices of the

Cunard Line, and the American Express Company, especially the offices in London, Paris, Nice, Rome, and Zürich.

Finally, I am particularly grateful to my highly efficient and competent secretary, Maxine Joyce, who typed and helped proofread the manuscript, and who made it possible for me to meet what appeared to be an impossible deadline.

INTRODUCTION

In keeping with my first two cookbooks, *With a Jug of Wine* and *More Recipes With a Jug of Wine,* this volume is, in my considered opinion, another damn good cookbook. It contains recipes for some of the most delicious and unusual dishes that skilled and inspired European chefs and cooks could produce.

First of all, I'd like to set forth briefly some details of Mrs. Wood's and my journey to Europe in search of the finest and most unusual foods we could find in the glittering cuisine of the several countries we planned to visit.

We sailed from New York on the *Queen Elizabeth* April 11, 1962. We spent four months living in London. Then we bought a Humber Super Snipe Sedan and toured England, Scotland, Ireland and Wales.

After a three weeks' rest, we drove down to Lyyd, and flew across the English Channel with our car. After some time in Paris we motored through France down to the Riviera. The weather in France (and all over the northern hemisphere, according to the newspapers) was cold and stormy, so we rented a lovely apartment in St.-Jean-Cap-Ferrat, right on the Mediterranean. We remained there three months, making many trips to the interior of Mediterranean Provence. Next we set out for Italy, and quite thoroughly covered that wonderful country. From Italy we crossed the Alps and toured Switzerland, first with Lausanne as our base, and then Zürich. There we rented an apartment for two months and spent much of our time in the surrounding country. Then we went into Germany, and toured up and down and across that fairyland of beauty. From Germany we went into the Netherlands, then into Belgium, and finally back to Paris. On December 6, 1963, we sailed for America on the *Queen Mary.*

From the time we arrived in London until we sailed from

Cherbourg we visited 156 cities and towns, and by "visiting," I don't mean we just passed through. We explored every community, saw the best that it had to offer historically, architecturally, culturally, and gastronomically.

We were very fortunate in having the aid of the various national and local governmental tourist offices. In almost every city we had guides, we had letters to hotels and restaurants, and were advised about, or taken to, the best eating places. I think that I am safe in saying that not one American in one hundred thousand has ever seen western Europe as Mrs. Wood and I saw it.

I cannot praise too highly the people of the British Isles, France, Italy, Switzerland, Germany, the Netherlands and Belgium. Everywhere we went we encountered nothing but courtesy, friendliness, and helpfulness. Everyone seemed to be very interested in us, and in our mission. I was a bit fearful about the language barrier in all the European countries except France. But it was a fear without basis of fact. English is spoken in all the hotels, in practically all the restaurants, by guides, by governmental representatives and tourist bureaus, by shopkeepers, and by many officers of the law. Oh, occasionally, an Italian policeman would bawl me out (I think), gesticulate wildly, shake his finger at me, then finally move on, giving me up as an impossible job. I'd feel sort of sorry for them, though. A tongue lashing is so ineffective when the lashee doesn't understand what is being said!

I was really amazed at the prices in the British Isles and on the Continent. By American standards I found hotel rates to be far from expensive, and the cost of meals to be most reasonable. For instance, the perfectly wonderful table d'hôte dinners at the Park Lane Hotel in London cost about $2.75 per person. At most of the top restaurants the bill for our dinners would run about $12 or $13 for the two of us, and that would include two cocktails, a fifth of fine wine, coffee and two liqueurs, and the tip. And, as you can see by many of the recipes in this book, we didn't have ordinary entrees.

Of course in France and Italy, the bistros and trattorias are much less expensive than the starred restaurants. In Paris, for example, there are hundreds of restaurants serving excellent food (sometimes better than the expensive restaurants) at prices that seem almost ridiculous to Americans. We had a perfectly delicious and expertly cooked dinner one night at the Restaurant René, with a bottle of local wine, and the bill was $4.80. The place was not swanky, but very plain. The table coverings were paper, with simple china and glassware. But the food was perfection.

I collected hundreds of recipes during our travels. A number of them are not included in this volume for one or two reasons. First, they may call for comestibles that are not available in America. Second, they would be impossible to prepare in American kitchens, because of the lack of a great many specialized utensils, or stoves with several burners, or spits, or charcoal ovens.

However, the recipes that have been included can be made in almost any American home, and the ingredients called for can be obtained in almost any American grocery store or meat market, or, in some cases, in specialty food shops. Some of the recipes have been adapted for American preparation, some hard-to-get ingredients have been changed so that the American housewife or amateur cook can use the recipes.

Parenthetically, it is amazing the number of American food products, or reasonable adaptations, that can be found in European stores. There is a huge supermarket in Paris on the Avenue de l'Opera called Monoprix. They have a large assortment of frozen foods, and all sorts of products that one sees on the shelves of American Supermarkets. I found similar stores in Nice and in Zürich and in Rome, and in Berlin.

One final word about this volume. In a very limited way I have tried to make it a sort of gastronomic guide book. I have gone into some detail about hotels at which we stopped, and about restaurants in which we ate. If you go to Europe, I feel sure that you will never go wrong in patronizing the same hotels and restaurants; in fact, I believe that they will enhance the pleasures of any European trip.

But whether you do go to Europe, or whether you follow our

European travels in the comfort of your armchair (and kitchen), I do hope that you will have as much fun, and enjoy as much good eating, as Mrs. Wood and I did.

Morrison Wood

Nice, France
Zürich, Switzerland
San Mateo, California

THROUGH EUROPE
WITH A JUG OF WINE

1 ⚡ WINE

The subject of European wines, particularly the wines of France and Germany, is so vast, and so complicated, that it would be futile for an amateur oenophile such as myself to attempt, in a few pages, to even scratch the surface of the subject, fascinating though it is.

During our travels in Europe Mrs. Wood and I drank innumerable bottles of wine. We never ate a meal (except breakfast, of course) that was not accompanied by at least one bottle of wine, and in many instances two half bottles, when different wines were called for. We drank many of the very great red and white wines of France, and the great white wines of Germany. Occasionally, we took part in wine tastings where four or five or six wines were sampled.

Our usual practice in hotel dining rooms and in restaurants would be to select our dinner, and then ask the captain or waiter to recommend a wine that would be appropriate. In the great majority of cases this proved to be a wise procedure, and we were seldom disappointed in the wine served to us. Rarely did a wine steward or waiter try to foist off a bottle of inferior wine, or a very expensive wine that did not go with the food.

In the provinces we always announced that we were not interested in American or Continental food. What we wanted, we said, and what we insisted upon, was not only the *vin de pays* (wine of the country or locality), but the best of the local food specialties prepared in the local way. And it was usually a delight to see the smile of pleasure that would spread over the proprietor's or waiter's face.

Throughout Europe there are scores and scores of wonderful wines that are obtainable only in the locality in which they are produced. Such wines, as a rule, do not travel well; they must be drunk while young and fresh.

You can't drink a great wine every night. If you did, your taste buds would become surfeited, and your pocketbook would soon have a lean and hungry look. So you vary your wine menu, only occasionally studding it with stars.

The two greatest wines of Germany are Rhines and Moselles. The Rhines come from the valley of the Rhine River from about Karlsrue to Koblenz, and the Moselles come from the valleys of the Moselle river and its tributaries, the Ruwer and the Saar. The important Rhine districts are the Rheinpfalz (Palatinate), Rheinhessen, and Rheingau. The finest of the Rhine wines come from the Rheingau district. The wines from the other two districts are not as great as those from the Rheingau, but they are wonderful wines.

We drove up the Rhein valley as far as Mainz, and the names of the towns read like an expensive wine card—Deidesheim, Oppenheim, Nierstein, Nackenheim, Bodenheim, Laubenheim, and Hockheim (it is from the town of Hockheim that the British get the term "Hock," which they apply to Rhine wines). We sampled most of the wines of this region, and they were exquisite, fruity and fragrant.

Personally, I prefer the Moselles to the Rhines. They are always made from the Riesling grapes, and they are light, fresh and flowery. When you drink a fine Moselle, it is like tasting the scents of a flower garden.

Wherever you go in Germany you will find delightful wines. In Würzburg we tasted Franconian wine, which comes in squat flasks called *Bocksbeutels.* Of course, people in the region of Franconia think their wine is unsurpassed, and there is a saying, "Franconian wines, to be precise, are a foretaste of Paradise."

We had an unusual experience when we were in Mainz. Our German Tourist office guide, Horst Wirbelauer, took us for a drive across the Rhine into the heart of the Rheingau. We stopped at a little *weinstube* in Eltville, a village not far from Rüdesheim. There they make a specialty of serving three-ounce bottles of various Rheingau wines of old vintages. We had a 1911, a 1917, and a 1937. It was really amazing—after 52 years the 1911 was still delicious, just a fraction down from its peak. The 1917 was not good, but the 1937 was absolutely marvelous. If you are ever in Mainz, don't fail to go to Eltville, across the river.

If you want an authoritative book on German wines, Alfred Langenbach (who owns the Langenbach vineyards in Worms, which makes the only fine Liebfraumilch obtainable) has written two or three excellent books. No living person knows as much about German wines as Alfred, who happens to be an old and dear friend.

Switzerland has no very great wines, but we found a number of very pleasant and delightful wines in that country, and enjoyed them during our stay there. Among the best of the whites are Fendant, of sterling quality and rich in sugar without being sweet, Neuchâtel, a dry, rather sparkling wine, Dézaley, St. Saphorin, and Aigle. The best reds are Dôle (of which we never tired), the dark red Veltliner, and *Oeil de Perdrix,* a lovely rosé.

There is so much wine made all over Italy that I wouldn't have been surprised if I had turned on a faucet in a particularly luxurious hotel, and found a luscious red wine coming out!

The great red wine of Italy is, of course, Chianti. *Chianti Classico* comes from the district roughly between Sienna and Florence, and is the true Chianti, the name protected by law. The finest Chiantis are Brolio, Villa Antinori, and Ruffino. Incidentally, if you see the word *vecchio* on a bottle of Chianti it means that the wine is "old," having matured for two years; *stravecchio* indicates that the wine has been aged for some years.

The second great wine of Italy is Orvieto, which is white. It comes from the province of Umbria, has a delicate bouquet and a delightfully sharp aftertaste.

Two of the most delightful wines we drank very frequently were Soave, a white wine with a delicate bouquet and velvety flavor, made in the district east of Verona, and Valpolicella, a dark ruby-red wine of great charm, with a light bouquet of bitter almonds, which also comes from a district near Verona.

Another delightful red wine is Lambrusco, which is dry, yet sparkling. We first encountered it in Bologna, at the final dinner of the Food Fair. It is the perfect wine to drink with rich food.

In Rome, the Frascati can be excellent, and sometimes not so good. We were fortunate, the bottles we had were excellent.

In Liguria we enjoyed two wines, Cinqueterre, a white wine with a somewhat aromatic bouquet, and Portofino, a rather dry white wine with a tart, pleasing flavor.

In Parma we liked the Sangiovese, a dark, ruby-red wine, dry, with a trace of flint in its flavor. Its delicate bouquet reminds one of violets.

In Naples we had both the red and white Falerno. The white is a "brut" wine, with plenty of body and a delicate bouquet. The red has a distinctive bouquet, reminiscent of flowers, and its flavor is dry but fruity. This latter is the most famous wine of Roman antiquity, and is mentioned by Ovid, Virgil, Pliny, and others.

Two wines we will never forget were the Caruso wines, the red and the rosé. These wines are perfectly delicious, and come from the vineyards of Signor Caruso, near Ravello.

I will not attempt to extol the virtues of the great French wines. I must confess that I do not believe that the great French white wines surpass or excel the great white wines of Germany. But there can be no doubt that the Burgundies of France are the greatest red wines on earth.

During our travels in France we thoroughly enjoyed such wines as Châteauneuf du Pape, Beaujolais, and Puilly Fuissé for everyday drinking. In Mediterranean Provence we frequently had such wines as Bellet, Côtes de Provence (both red and white), Salvernes, Blanc de Blancs, Château St. Roseline, Château de Selle Clos Mireille, and Cassis.

If you would really like to learn about French wines, I would suggest that you buy Alexis Lichine's splendid book, *Wines of France*. It is, to my mind, the most comprehensive and readable book on French wines ever published.

In closing this chapter I would like to quote a delightful passage from Alexis Lichine's book* about how wine came to Cassis.

Once upon a day, God was up in heaven, taking a vacation after creating the world. Gabriel came over to Him to report that people were complaining, down on earth. "What's the matter down below?" God asked, and Gabriel began polishing the

---

* *Wines of France* by Alexis Lichine, copyright 1951, © 1955, 1963 by Alfred A. Knopf, Inc. Reprinted by permission of the publisher.

mouthpiece of his trumpet with his thumb. "Well, they're complaining that everything is too flat and smooth down there. Oh, they like it, mind You, they think it's a wonderful world, but they're just a bit bored with it all." God scowled and looked hard at Gabriel's trumpet for a long moment, and then He smiled. "I've put so much time and effort into the world, it seems a shame to end it all. Listen, Gabriel, take a big sack of hills and crags, and boulders and alps, and sprinkle them around. But do it neatly, mind. I don't want the world all messed up, even if the mortals do."

So Gabriel loaded up a big sack and went down to spread some roughness around. It took him all day, and by quitting-time he was pretty tired, and he still had a lot of mountains left. There was nothing to do but carry the leftovers back up the Highway that leads to Paradise. Now, as everybody knows, the earthly gate of the Highway that leads to Paradise is at Cassis, and as Gabriel started up, he gave the big sack on his shoulder a hitch. The sack had been in for some pretty rough wear during the day, and that last extra hitch was too much for it. The bottom tore open and all the left-over hills tumbled down on Cassis.

Gabriel went up the Highway that leads to Paradise and reported his day's activity to God. But he didn't tell Him about the torn sack.

The next day God heard the sound of weeping coming up from the earth below, and, listening closely, He could hear the bawling of children, and the dry, hard sobbing of bitter men. He jumped up straightway and went down to find out for Himself.

As He came through the earthly gate of the Highway that leads to Paradise, which, as everybody knows is right at Cassis, a terrible sight met His eyes. A bent and twisted man was hacking at the hard, steep earth with a wooden hoe, sobbing bitterly; and seated on a rock beside the road was a humped and crooked woman, holding a skinny baby to her shriveled breast. They, too, were crying as if their hearts were cracked.

"What's this?" God bellowed, and the noise made the baby wail even harder. "Are you the fine creatures I put on this fine earth? What's happened to you? Why are you so crooked and lean, and, man, why are you grubbing at that poor earth while your wife and baby sob?"

The man looked up at God and rubbed the back of a dirty hand across his nose. "Look at this earth," said the man. "Every day I work it, trying to raise a few poor olive trees and tend these miserable grapevines. But the trees bear no fruit, and all we get from the vines is thin, sour wine."

God looked at the thin vine the man had been hoeing and then at the huddled woman and the bony child. He was deeply touched, and a tear rolled down His cheek and fell on the withered vine.

And suddenly, as God's tear splashed on it, the vine began to grow, strong, green leaves to sprout along its length and bunches of golden grapes to form under the leaves. And as the vine grew, its strength spread to the other vines, and in an instant the entire slope was covered with a fruitful vineyard. In another moment the entire valley was a mass of emerald vine leaves and ruby grapes. And that is how the glorious wine of Cassis, which, as everyone knows, is at the gate of the Highway that leads to Paradise, came to be.

2 ≈ HORS D'OEUVRES

Whenever I read of, see, or eat hor d'oeuvres the memory of a luncheon given for Mrs. Wood and me while we were in Florence, Italy, will come flooding back, and a mouth-watering picture will appear in my mind's eye, as vivid as it was on a day in May of 1963.

Dr. Boninsigne, from the Florence office of the *Ente Nazionale Italiano per il Turismo,* picked us up at our hotel at ten in the morning for a drive through the countryside surrounding Florence. We visited a number of points of interest, and it was one-thirty when we drove into the courtyard of a magnificent villa about 12 miles from Florence.

This was the Villa Borromeo, a 15th century feudal villa which originally belonged to the family of Cardinal Borromeo. It looked out over the hills of the beautiful Chianti district, and is an outstandingly beautiful example of antique Florentine architecture. The old stables have been transformed into a most charming and picturesque dining room of very large proportions, with great arched ceilings. Signor Annoni, the manager, seated us at a window table, and we were served paper-thin slices of prosciutto ham, and a lovely Chianti. Then we were led over to three large tables in the center of the dining room, to select our antipasti!

Mrs. Wood and I almost gasped with amazement as we contemplated the loaded tables. Never have I seen as beautiful and as many different hors d'oeuvres. I counted over forty when I realized that I was holding up the rest of the party. There were small fish, anchovies, prawns, scampi, calamaretti, oysters, crabs, clams, mussels, tunny fish, cold sturgeon in oil, all kinds of vegetables, artichoke hearts, various kinds of beans, mushrooms, pimentos, peperoni, eggs, tongue, all kinds of olives, and so on and so on and so on. Heavens only knows how many I sampled—

7

my plate was heaped with the delicacies, and I could have gone back for a second sampling, but my host warned me there was more to come (that was the understatement of the year—we had ravioli, quail and rice, fresh asparagus, steak Florentine, french fried artichokes, and assorted fruits in assorted liquors!).

In European restaurants and hotel dining rooms hors d'oeuvres are quite as popular as they are in American eating establishments. As in the United States they range from the very simple to the rather elaborate; from very inexpensive to very dear. Surprisingly enough, some of the most delicious hors d'oeuvres are to be found in the little French bistros and Italian trattorias.

Caviar and smoked salmon are almost always present on the menus, and, in season, oysters. Seafood cocktails are popular (and expensive). Potted shrimp seem to be a favorite English hors d'oeuvre; France is famous for its pâtés and throughout Europe assorted hors d'oeuvres (antipasti, really) are featured and ordered with great frequency.

I never thought that I would savor an appetizer that could even approach the intriguing deliciousness of Quiche Lorraine, and of caviar pie. But that was before I visited Ashford Castle in Cong, Ireland, and got to know Noel Huggard, the owner and very active managing director.

Ashford Castle is, to my mind, the most beautiful and fascinating hostelry in the British Isles. Originally a medieval castle on the shores of Laugh Corrib, it was rebuilt and enlarged by the Guinness family, of brewing fame. In 1939 Noel Huggard bought it, modernized it, and turned it into a hotel. He personally supervises every meal, and the food served gives evidence of his culinary skill and attention. He even carves a fine roast himself for his guests. Lobster Lorraine is one of his masterpieces.

LOBSTER LORRAINE

Unbaked pie crust shell	*3–4 eggs*
White of 1 egg	*1–2 cups rich milk*
Cooked lobster meat	*1 tbsp. chopped parsley*
1 smallish onion	*Salt*
1 tbsp. butter	*Grated nutmeg*

Line an 8-inch pie plate with flaky pastry, and brush the entire surface with white of egg. Dice enough cooked lobster meat to cover bottom of pie shell. Finely chop a smallish onion and sauté it in a tablespoon butter until tender. Then add diced lobster meat to onions, and when cool, spread over bottom of shell.

Beat 3 eggs with 1 cup rich milk (or 4 eggs with 2 cups milk for deeper tart), together with 1 tablespoon chopped parsley and salt to taste. Pour this custard over layer of lobster and onions in pie shell. Sprinkle with grated nutmeg, and bake in a 400-degree oven for 15 minutes. Then reduce temperature to 325 degrees, and bake 30 minutes longer, or until knife comes clean from custard. Serves 6.

The celebrated appetizer of Nice and its environs is *pissaladiera*, which is somewhat akin to the famous Naples pizza. It is a large, round, pastry shell filled with cooked onions, and sometimes leeks, garlic, anchovy filets, pitted Italian black olives, and sometimes tomato purée. It is so popular that in addition to being served in most Nice restaurants, it is a feature of many bakeries, being sold in small, individual pastry shells. The only objection I have to the Niçoise *pissaladiera* is that the pastry is a little too thick and heavy. When we have this delectable my wife makes her marvelous light and flaky pie crust, and the tart is then wonderful. This is the way it is done.

PISSALADIERA

Unbaked pie crust shell	1 *egg*
Cream	½ *cup cream*
2–3 *large onions*	*Salt and pepper*
½ *clove garlic*	*Grated nutmeg*
1½ *tbsp. butter*	*Grated Parmesan cheese*
1½ *tbsp. olive oil*	*Anchovy filets*

Pitted Italian black olives

Make a rich pie shell from your favorite recipe, and when it is in an 8-inch pie tin, pat the bottom of the pie shell with cream (this seals the bottom) and chill.

Slice 2–3 large onions finely and sauté them, together with half a clove of garlic in 1½ tablespoons each olive oil and butter until transparent. While the onions are cooking bake the pie shell in a preheated 400-degree oven for 2 minutes. Remove the pie shell from the oven, and when onions are cooked place them in in the pie shell. Spoon over the onions a well-beaten egg mixed with ½ cup cream. Season with salt and pepper to taste and a dash grated nutmeg. Sprinkle the top with grated Parmesan cheese, then put a lattice pattern of anchovy filets over the top. Place pitted Italian black olives in diamonds of the anchovy filets, and bake in a 350-degree oven for 30 minutes until golden brown, and custard is set.

A very popular first course hor's d'oeuvre in Germany is broiled mushrooms, which are usually served on toast. But we found an exceedingly delicious variation on this theme in a quaint restaurant in Zürich, just off the Parade Platz. It is called the Zeughauskeller, and, as its name implies, it was a famous old arsenal, built in 1487. In 1927 it was turned into a German beer hall, and is most popular today. Nothing fancy, but wonderful food and beer.

An interesting note on the preparation of the mushroom tarts: The pastry for the tart shell is rolled out very thin, and tartlets are cut out with a buttered pastry cutter. Then the tart shells are baked in the oven, the edges being propped up with dried peas, until done. If you are adventuresome, you can try this method, using your favorite pastry dough. If not, line individual containers with the pastry, and bake until done.

CREAMED MUSHROOM TART

Baked tart shells	1 *tbsp. flour*
1 *lb. fresh mushrooms*	5 *oz. cream*
1½ *oz. butter*	*Salt and pepper*
2 *tbsp. finely chopped onions*	*Juice 1 lemon*

Wash and coarsely chop the mushrooms, and cook in the butter, to which has been added the chopped onions, and gently sauté for 6 to 7 minutes. Then dust the mushrooms with flour, stir, and add the fresh cream. Season with salt and pepper to taste, add the lemon juice, and simmer for about 5 minutes. Take pastry shells from oven, fill with the mixture, and serve very hot.

The French word *pâté* means a pie, or pastry, or a sort of loaf made from poultry, meats or game, firmly compressed, and sometimes surrounded by a *croute* (crust) of puff pastry. A great many of the superlative French pâtés are very difficult to make. *Pâtés en croute* require a special mold which have hinged, removable sides. The preparation and cooking require a great deal of work, and the process is quite complicated. The filling may consist of chicken, or pork, or game, such as pheasant, venison or rabbit.

During our European travels I gorged on pâtés. And, believe it or not, some of the most delicious were listed simply as *Pâté de Maison* in French bistros, and little country inns or restaurants. The recipes for these pâtés are practically impossible to obtain, for each chef seems to have his own secret formula which he jealously guards.

My quest for unusual recipes in the European countries we visited was not limited to professional chefs or maître d'hôtels in restaurants. Sometimes our guides, or members of the tourist office staffs, or acquaintances we made in various cities would, upon learning that I was a cookbook writer and gathering material for another cookbook, offer pet recipes.

In Amsterdam we made a tour of the canals that lace the city in a luxurious sight-seeing motor canal boat. The guide was a charming young woman, speaking excellent English (as all of the guides in European countries do). After we left the canals and started on a tour of the harbor the guide came over to chat with us. We got to talking about food and before we disembarked I had her recipe for a curried chicken pâté which, she said, "I have never before given to anyone."

CURRIED CHICKEN PÂTÉ

1 *lb. chicken livers*	*Pinch dried marjoram*
6 *tbsp. rendered chicken fat*	*Pinch ground cardamon*
1 *tbsp. curry powder*	4 *oz. dry vermouth*
Salt and freshly ground pepper	1 *tsp. dry sherry*
Pinch dried basil	2 *tbsp. sweet sherry*
Pinch dried thyme	3 *tbsp. sour cream*

Clean 1 pound chicken livers and cut them into small pieces. Sauté them slowly in 6 tablespoons rendered chicken fat, for about 15 minutes, mashing them with a fork all the time they are cooking. Then turn the flame down to its lowest point and mix into the mashed chicken livers 1 tablespoon of your finest curry powder, salt and freshly ground pepper to taste, a generous pinch each dried basil, thyme, marjoram, and a pinch ground cardamon. Remove pan from the fire and add 4 ounces dry (French) vermouth, 1 teaspoon dry sherry, and 2 teaspoons sweet sherry. Continue to mash the whole until a fine paste results. Correct the seasoning, if necessary, as to the salt and curry powder (possibly add 1 scant teaspoon more of curry powder if you desire). At the last, stir in about 3 tablespoons commercial sour cream. Blend everything well, put the paste into a covered crock, and refrigerate at least three days.

Two other chicken liver pâté recipes were given me by Madam Nicole, who owned the grocery store in Beaulieu-sur-Mer, where I traded during our stay in St.-Jean-Cap-Ferrat. Nicole spoke very good English, and we both shared the hobby of unusual cookery. Sometimes she had to grope for the right English word, but she would give me the French word, and I could usually help her out.

The first recipe she said was *"Très Francaise."*

CHICKEN LIVER PÂTÉ I

1 *lb. chicken livers*	4 *oz. sweet butter*
Water	1 *tsp. salt*
1 *bay leaf*	1 *tsp. prepared French Mustard*
Pinch dried thyme	3 *oz. brandy*
1 *tbsp. chopped parsley*	3 *tbsp. grated onion*

In a saucepan put 1 pound of chicken livers, enough water to cover, and add 1 bay leaf, a pinch of dried thyme, and a tablespoon chopped parsley. Bring water to a boil, then simmer for 20 minutes. Drain livers, chop coarsely, then put through finest blade of food chopper. Next mix the liver paste with 1 cube sweet butter, and 1 teaspoon each of salt and a French prepared mustard. Then add 3 ounces of good brandy and 3 tablespoons grated onion. Mix well (in a blender if you have one). Put in a buttered small casserole, cover, and store in refrigerator to chill. Serve with crackers or Melba toast.

This pâté is amazingly similar to imported *pâté de foie gras.*

CHICKEN LIVER PÂTÉ II

1 *lb. chicken livers*	2 *tsp. seasoned salt*
1 *cup finely chopped onions*	1 *tsp. dry mustard*
¼ *cup rendered chicken fat*	1 *tsp. prepared French mustard*
4 *hard-cooked eggs*	1 *medium onion*
2 *tbsp. rendered chicken fat*	

Wash and dry 1 pound fresh chicken livers carefully. In a covered skillet cook the livers and 1 cup finely chopped onions in ¼ cup rendered chicken fat about 10 minutes. Then drain and cool, reserving cooked onions and juices. Grind chicken livers and 4 hard-cooked eggs, using medium blade, and blend thoroughly. Add 2 teaspoons seasoned salt, 1 teaspoon dry mustard, few grains cayenne pepper, 1 medium onion, finely ground, 2 tablespoons rendered chicken fat, and reserved cooked onions and their juices. Mix thoroughly and well. Refrigerate in crock or bowl covered with wax paper for at least 24 hours before serving. This makes 3½ cups. Serve on crackers or Melba rounds.

In the magnificently beautiful English Lake District we stopped overnight at the Windemere Hydro Hotel. High on a hill, Windemere is not far from Morecambe Bay, which is famous for its shrimps. As a matter of fact Morecambe Bay shrimps are practically identical with the tiny Bay shrimps on California's coast, and they are equally as sweet and succulent.

While I believe that the shrimp pâté we had for dinner at the Windemere Hydro was made from the Morecambe Bay shrimps, it can be made from other varieties of shrimp.

SHRIMP PÂTÉ

½ lb. shrimp	Pinch dried tarragon
1½ oz. dry white wine	Freshly ground black pepper
Pinch salt	Dash lemon juice
	Olive oil

Put ½ pound shelled, cleaned and cooked shrimp through the finest blade of food grinder twice. Add 1½ ounces dry white wine, pinch salt, pinch dried tarragon, freshly ground black pepper to taste, a dash lemon juice (or lime juice), and mix well. Then gradually add enough of the finest olive oil to make a creamy paste. Put in a covered crock and refrigerate for at least 24 hours.

In Italy the trattoria is the counterpart of the French bistro. The décor is negative; the waiters are usually in shirt sleeves; the china and glassware are quite ordinary. But the atmosphere is often intriguing, and the food is frequently better than in the higher priced *ristorantes*.

Mrs. Wood and I thoroughly enjoyed the Trattoria Sostanza in Florence. In a long narrow room packed with tables seating six to eight, you really rub elbows with fellow gourmets. Two amazing waiters perform miracles of service, dashing to and from the small kitchen, where a charcoal grill gives out aromatic smoke, and simmering kettles add their mouth-watering aromas.

A most unusual and delicious appetizer was served to us, and Mario scrawled out the recipe for us.

CROSTINI DI FEGATINI
(Chicken Livers on Toast)

1 *tbsp. butter*	2 *tbsp. condensed chicken*
2 *tbsp. minced onions*	*bouillon*
2 *tbsp. minced ham*	*Dash lemon juice*
½ *lb. chicken livers*	1 *tsp. drained capers, chopped*
	Bread rounds fried in butter

In a skillet over low heat melt 1 tablespoon butter and add 2 tablespoons finely minced onions. When they are soft and golden add 2 tablespoons finely minced ham. Let ham brown a bit, then add ½ pound chicken livers that have been diced fine and dusted with flour. Cook gently until livers have changed color yet are rather firm (do not overcook). Add 2 tablespoons condensed chicken bouillon and a few drops of lemon juice. Cover pan and cook gently for 10 minutes. Remove from fire and add about a generous teaspoon drained chopped capers. Allow mixture to cook, then store in refrigerator until ready to serve on rounds of bread lightly fried in butter.

In Antwerp we dined one night at one of the most fascinating restaurants we encountered throughout our European travels— Sint Jacob in Galicie, on a narrow street just off the Stadhuis Platz.

The restaurant dates back to 1577, and is composed of three magnificent old guildhouses made into one establishment. The façade remains exactly as it was originally. The interior has been changed only slightly—partitions removed, and the necessary modern conveniences added. The whole place is filled with treasures of another age. The owner, J. Doyen, and his son took us on a tour of the place, pointing out historic paintings, rare old furniture, and other treasures of glass and porcelain.

The dinner was magnificent, with old world service. But what particularly intrigued us was the hors d'oeuvre, *cocktail de Homard*.

A freshly boiled baby lobster, split in half, was brought to the table on a wooden board. The maître D carefully removed all the meat, cut it into bite size pieces, and placed them in a glass bowl set in crushed ice. Then it was gently mixed with a delectable dressing, or sauce. Finally, two rather large chilled compotes lined with crisp lettuce leaves were brought to the table, and they were filled with the lobster and dressing.

COCKTAIL DE HOMARD
(Lobster Cocktail)

1 *boiled baby lobster*	½ *tsp. Dijon mustard*
½ *cup mayonnaise*	2 *tsp. chopped chives*
1 *tbsp. tomato catsup*	1 *tsp. chopped parsley*
1 *tsp. Worcestershire sauce*	2 *tbsp. brandy*

Salt and freshly ground pepper

Combine the above ingredients (except the lobster) and chill. Prepare as directed above.

The city of Zürich, Switzerland, has a great many very fine restaurants. Some of the best are housed in ancient guildhalls that still stand on the banks of the River Limat, such as Ruden's, Zimmerleuten's, and Saffran's. Others are tucked away on narrow side streets, often difficult to find, but so rewarding when you do find one, and are comfortably seated.

One of the latter is the Veltliner Keller, tucked away on a little winding street up near the Lindenhof Platz, in the old part of Zürich. The restaurant is six hundred years old, with beautiful maple paneling, and the waitresses were dressed in native Swiss costumes.

A very delicious dinner started off auspiciously with *Crêpes à la Mode du Patron,* a specialty created during the war by the owner, Willy Kessler, to cope with meatless days. It is a delectable first course hors d'oeuvre.

CRÊPES À LA MODE DU PATRON
(Cheese-Filled Pancakes)

Little thin pancakes (3 per
    person)
Grated Emmentaler (Swiss
    cheese)
Grated Gruyère cheese
Grated Parmesan cheese

Melted Emmentaler cheese
Paprika
Melted butter
Diamond-shaped pieces of
    canned pimento

Make your pancakes according to your favorite recipe, but use
no baking powder. Pour a couple of tablespoons of batter in a
small frying pan greased with butter, and then tilt the pan with a
circular motion so that the batter covers the entire pan before it
cooks. The cooked pancakes should be very thin.

The cheese filling is ⅓ grated Emmentaler, ⅓ grated Gruyère
and ⅓ grated Parmesan, well mixed together without heating.
Each little pancake is spread thickly with this mixture, and then
rolled up.

For each serving put 3 of the cheese-filled crêpes in a flat,
greased pan and cover them entirely with melted Emmentaler
cheese. Brush with melted butter, sprinkle with paprika, and broil
for 3 minutes. Take out and decorate with little diamond shaped,
flat chips of Emmentaler and alternate strips of pimento. Place
under broiler again for 1 minute, then serve immediately.

There is one item that is on the menu of almost every restaurant and hotel dining room in France, from three-star establishments on down to the most unpretentious auberge, or inn. You
have probably guessed that the item is *escargots* (snails).

I devoured escargots with unadulterated delight from the north-
east coast of France to the southeast coast. There were small
ones, medium ones, and the succulent giants from Burgundy that
feed on vine leaves. Usually they are served in their shells,
bubbling hot. But at the excellent Grand Hôtel du Louvre,
where we stayed both times we were in Paris, the escargots were
served in tiny earthenware casseroles, just big enough to hold a
single escargot and its perfumed butter. Incidentally, it was this

method of serving escargots that won my wife over to them. In America Mrs. Wood absolutely refused to eat escargots, but now she is an avid devotee of this magnificent hors d'oeuvre.

There are a number of ways of preparing escargots, but it is hard to beat this recipe, which I obtained in Provence.

ESCARGOTS PROVENÇALE

48 *cooked escargots and shells*	¼ *tsp. freshly ground pepper*
1 *cup softened butter*	*Pinch grated nutmeg*
4 *large cloves garlic*	*Few grains cayenne pepper*
1 *shallot*	1 *tbsp. minced pitted Italian*
8 *tbsp. chopped parsley*	*black olives*
1 *tsp. salt*	1 *tbsp. dry white wine*

Combine and blend thoroughly 1 cup softened butter, 4 large cloves garlic and 1 shallot (or little green onion, bulb and top) both finely minced, 8 tablespoons chopped fresh parsley, 1 teaspoon salt, ¼ teaspoon freshly ground pepper, pinch grated nutmeg, a few grains cayenne pepper, 1 tablespoon very finely chopped pitted black olives, and 1 tablespoon dry white wine.

Have ready 4 dozen escargots and their shells. Place a nugget of the prepared butter in the bottom of each shell. Then put in an escargot, and seal the opening with more of the butter mixture, pressing it down well so that the shell is filled to the brim. Place the escargots in their shells in muffin tins and set them in a 400-degree oven for 7 or 8 minutes, or until they are thoroughly heated through and bubbling. Serve immediately to 4 or 8.

The cocktail hour at the Wood ménage is one of the most pleasant periods of the day. It is a time for complete relaxation, good conversation, perhaps listening to the news on television, and leisurely reading the evening paper.

We vary the cocktails to suit our whims, and we also vary our "nibbles," which are a most important part of the occasion. Usually the accompaniment is a bit of unusual cheese, or a dip of some sort, with assorted crackers. And always, a dish of peanuts, or cashews, or almonds, or assorted nuts.

Naturally, I am always on the lookout for something a little different to go with our cocktails. On this trip I picked up three that we have found delicious and different. The first is an Edam cheese spread, which was suggested to me by our guide in Amsterdam as we were watching two men carrying a board of Edam cheeses.

EDAM CHEESE SPREAD

Small Edam cheese   *Few grains cayenne pepper*
½ tsp. Worcestershire sauce   *1 tbsp. chopped chives*
¼ tsp. dry mustard   *1 tbsp. chopped pimento*
                  Beer

Cut the top from a small Edam cheese and scoop out the center, leaving a thin wall to maintain the shape. Mash the cheese thoroughly then add ½ teaspoon Worcestershire sauce, ¼ teaspoon dry mustard, a few grains cayenne pepper, 1 tablespoon each chopped chives and chopped pimento, and enough beer to make a spreading consistency. Replace the seasoned cheese in the shell, refrigerate, and serve chilled.

The next one was served at a small cocktail party in Nice. The cheese that was mixed with the Roquefort is not obtainable in America, but my hostess said that a fine English Cheddar would do very well.

ROQUEFORT CHEESE SPREAD

1 cup grated Cheddar cheese   *1 mashed clove garlic*
    (about ¼ pound)   *1 tsp. Worcestershire sauce*
¾ cup crumbled Roquefort   *Dash Tabasco sauce*
    cheese   *¼ cup beer*
½ tsp. fennel seeds

Combine the Cheddar and Roquefort cheese, the garlic, the fennel seeds, the Worcestershire sauce, the Tabasco sauce, and the beer. Beat well until well blended and smooth. Refrigerate, then serve chilled on assorted crackers.

The third is really an hors d'oeuvre for a cocktail party, rather than two people. We had these cocktail sausages in rum fixed in a chafing dish in the bar of the Three Tuns Hotel in Durham, England, where we were informally entertained by the manager before dinner.

COCKTAIL SAUSAGES IN RUM

2 4-oz. jars small pork cocktail   ½ cup dark brown sugar
        sausages   ½ cup soy sauce
                    ½ cup rum

Sauté two 4-ounce jars small pork cocktail sausages on one side in the blazer of a chafing dish. Pour out the grease. Add ½ cup dark brown sugar and ½ cup soy sauce, and simmer the other side of the sausages in that mixture. When sausages are brown add ½ cup of heated rum and ignite. Serve from chafing dish with a toothpick in each sausage.

3 ⚡ SOUPS

From Marseilles to Menton, along the French Mediterranean Coast, there are three great fish soups—*Bouillabaisse, Bourride,* and *Soupe aux Poissons.* Each is superlatively good, but Bouillabaisse is, of course, the most famous of them all, known and imitated all over the world.

There are many who say that Marseilles is not only the Bouillabaisse capital of the world, but that the absolute best Bouillabaisse is made there. However, such a statement will be disputed from Toulon to Menton, probably most vigorously in the Niçoise area. The truth is that each locality has its own variation of the dish, and, as Waverley Root says in his excellent book, *The Food of France,* "Almost every cook has his own variation of the variation!"

Bouillabaisse uses a variety of Mediterranean fishes which are unknown in America. Lobsters and crab may be included, but a fierce argument rages about putting shellfish into a Bouillabaisse. Chief among the other ingredients are onions, leeks, tomatoes, garlic, parsley, thyme, bay leaves, olive oil, fennel, and saffron. When the cooking of the Bouillabaisse is completed the bouillon is poured over slices of bread, and the fish are served in a separate dish, as are the shellfish, if used.

In my search for a recipe for Bouillabaisse that would closely approximate the Mediterranean I tried a number of restaurants in Nice and its environs. One night we had dinner at Raynaud's in Nice.

Restaurant Reynaud is one of several restaurants on the Quai des États-Unis, literally just across the street from the Bay of Angels. In the summertime you can eat on the outdoor terrace in front of the restaurant, and in the colder season you eat in a very luxurious dining room. The atmosphere is charming, the guests cosmopolitan, the service excellent, and the food magnificent. Here one can be served an authentic *salade Niçoise* which I shall detail in a later chapter.

Mrs. Wood and I had Bouillabaisse, and it was regal. Afterwards, over our coffee and cognac, Monsieur Raynaud came over and sat with us. I told him I would like to work out a Bouillabaisse that could be prepared in America, with American fishes. He said he would like to give it a little thought, and suggested that I drop by the restaurant in a couple of days, well after lunch time, and we'd talk it over.

I think that the following recipe will closely approximate the Mediterranean Bouillabaisse, except for the unusual flavor of the Mediterranean fishes. Personally, I don't believe there is a great deal of difference.

BOUILLABAISSE

2 *lbs. firm-fleshed fish*	5 *tbsp. olive oil*
2 *lbs. tender-fleshed fish*	2 *onions*
1 *large live lobster*	2 *leeks (white part)*
1 *lb. shelled shrimp*	2 *tbsp. flour*
2 *lbs. raw fish trimmings*	4 *fresh tomatoes*
including heads and tails	3 *cloves garlic*
2 *oz. minced onions*	1 *bay leaf*
Several stalks parsley	1 *tbsp. chopped parsley*
12 *peppercorns*	*Stalk celery*
1 *qt. dry white wine*	*Pinch fennel seeds*
2½ *pints water*	*Pinch powdered saffron*
Pinch salt	*Generous pinch dried thyme*

Slices stale French bread

There should be about 5 to 6 different varieties of fish used, such as fresh cod, haddock, red snapper, bass, whiting, red fish, sea trout, rockfish, etc.

First, make the fish *fumet,* or essence. Put bones, heads, tails, trimmings, chopped up, in a buttered pan with 2 ounces minced onions, several parsley stalks, and 12 peppercorns. Let this stew for a while with the lid on. Then add 1 quart dry white wine and a little over 2½ pints water. Add a pinch salt and boil gently for 25 minutes. Then strain through a very fine sieve and reserve liquid.

In a deep saucepan or Dutch oven heat 5 tablespoons olive oil, then add 2 onions and the whites of 2 leeks, both chopped, and cook for 5 minutes. Sprinkle in 2 tablespoons flour and let it brown a little. Then add 4 peeled, seeded and chopped fresh tomatoes, 3 cloves garlic crushed, 1 bay leaf, 1 tablespoon chopped parsley, a stalk celery, cut up, a pinch each fennel and saffron, and a generous pinch dried thyme. Arrange over this the lobster, cut crosswise into pieces, and the shrimp, split lengthwise. Next add the 2 pounds firm-fleshed fish, and pour in 3½ pints reserved fish fumet, adding salt and pepper to taste. Bring to boil and boil for 5 minutes. Then add the 2 pounds tender-fleshed fish, bring to a boil, and boil another 5 minutes.

Remove fish to a deep platter, and shellfish to another deep platter and keep hot. Bring stock to a boil again then pour into a large, hot soup tureen.

To serve place 2 slices slightly stale French bread about ½ inch thick in each soup dish, and pour over them the bouillon. Also aportion to each person the fish and shellfish, served in another soup dish. This recipe should serve 6.

One of the most celebrated seafood restaurants in Paris is Drouant's. It is on the Place Gaillon, quite near the Opera. It is a two-star restaurant, and is run by the third generation of the Drouant family, Jean Drouant. The chef des cuisines is Jules Petit, who was head chef at the French Pavilion during the New York World's Fair of 1939.

Incidentally, it is at Drouant's that the ten members of the Academie Goncourt meet once a year to award the top literary prize, the Prix Goncourt. This is a great event in Paris, and the Place Gaillon swarms with reporters and photographers awaiting the result of the voting.

Our first meal in Paris was at Drouant's, and it was a memorable one. We started out with *Bisque de Homard,* which surpassed any bisque I have ever tasted. Jules Petit wrote out the recipe for me meticulously, and this is the translation.

BISQUE DE HOMARD
(Lobster Bisque)

2 ¾-lb. live lobsters	2 cloves garlic
5 oz. butter	6 tomatoes
2 onions	1 small bay leaf
2 carrots	¼ tsp. dried thyme
2 oz. brandy	1 tbsp. chopped parsley
1 cup dry white wine	Salt and pepper
6½ cups bouillon	1 cup cream
⅓ lb. raw rice, washed	3½ oz. butter
	1½ oz. brandy

Put 5 ounces butter in a large skillet, and when hot add 2 onions and 2 carrots, coarsely chopped, and cook slowly until vegetables are clear. Then add to the skillet two ¾ pound live lobsters which have been cut in half lengthwise (be sure to remove the dark veins and small sacs back of the heads). Let contents of skillet continue to cook for a few minutes until lobsters turn red. Then set alight 2 ounces warmed brandy and pour over contents of skillet. Put out flames by adding 1 cup dry white wine, then add 6½ cups bouillon, ⅓ pound raw rice, well washed, 2 cloves garlic, split, 6 tomatoes which have been peeled, seeded and chopped (or 3½ ounces tomato purée), 1 small bay leaf, ¼ teaspoon dried thyme, 1 tablespoon chopped fresh parsley, and salt and pepper to taste. Cook slowly for 15 minutes.

Remove lobsters from skillet, take out the meat and cut it in small pieces, and keep warm. Continue cooking the contents of skillet another 15 minutes. Then strain the broth through a coarse sieve into a saucepan. Put remaining solids through a fine sieve, pressing them through to obtain a sort of cream, into the saucepan containing the strained stock.

To the saucepan add a generous cup fresh cream, and whisk in 3½ ounces butter cut in small pieces. Then add the lobster meat, and 1½ ounces brandy. Heat through thoroughly, correct seasoning and serve.

I have never driven on finer roads that the autostradas in Italy and the autobahns in Germany. They are beautifully kept up, pass through gorgeous country, and frequently there are gas stations just off the road. In Italy there are a chain of restaurants which operate at various places along the autostradas, and often they offer delightful respites when you want a drink or a snack, or even a full meal.

On our way from Salerno to Rome, not far from the Monte Cassino Monastery (where some of the fiercest fighting of the Italian campaign took place) we stopped at one of these restaurants. It was as pretty a restaurant as one could imagine. There was a large outdoor dining terrace furnished with white wrought-iron tables and chairs, and a view as far as one could see of the lovely green countryside. It was a warm day in May, and after an apéritif I had a chilled tomato soup that was perfection. The head waitress was pert and pretty in her starched uniform, and spoke excellent English. When I expressed a desire for the recipe, and showed my credentials from the National Italian Tourist Office, she went into the kitchen, and a short time later came back with the recipe written out in English.

MINESTRA FREDDA DI POMIDORO
(Cold Tomato Soup with Sour Cream)

6 *ripe tomatoes*	2 *tbsp. tomato paste*
6 *little green onions*	3 *tbsp. flour*
1 *clove garlic*	2 *10½-oz. cans chicken*
¼ *tsp. dried oregano*	*bouillon*
½ *tsp. salt*	1 *cup sour cream*
⅛ *tsp. freshly ground pepper*	1 *tsp. curry powder*
3 *oz. dry vermouth*	1 *tsp. finely grated lemon rind*

Crostini

In a saucepan combine 6 ripe tomatoes, thinly sliced, 6 little green onions (bulbs and tops) finely chopped, 1 minced clove garlic, ¼ teaspoon dried oregano, ½ teaspoon salt, ⅛ teaspoon freshly ground pepper, and 3 ounces dry Vermouth. Cook over gentle flame until tomatoes are tender, about 10 minutes. Then add 2 tablespoons tomato paste and 3 tablespoons flour. Blend everything well, then gradually add two 10½ ounce cans condensed chicken bouillon, stirring constantly while adding, and continuing to stir until mixture comes to a boil.

Into a glass bowl strain the mixture through a wire sieve, forcing solids through. Allow mixture to cool, then refrigerate for at least 3 hours. Before serving stir in 1 cup chilled commercial sour cream to which has been added 1 teaspoon each fine curry powder and finely grated lemon rind. Serve very cold.

Crostini are simply rounds of bread fried in olive oil or butter, and spread with grated Parmesan cheese. They are put under the broiler for a few moments until cheese begins to melt.

In the internationally famous spa of Baden-Baden, Germany, the Casino is naturally the focal point of the world of fashion, with its sparkling gatherings, and the excitement of the gaming tables. It is set in the Kurpark, with its colorful flower beds which change from season to season. Adjoining the Casino is the Kurhaus Restaurant, where the food is on a par with the view—magnificent. We stopped there for luncheon on our way to Heidelberg, and I shall never forget our first course, a cold lobster bisque. Here is a translation of the recipe given me.

COLD LOBSTER BISQUE

1 *medium onion*	½ *tsp. paprika*
3 *tbsp. butter*	*Pinch cayenne pepper*
3 *tbsp. flour*	1 *cup diced cooked lobster*
1½ *cups milk*	*meat*
1 *cup chicken consommé*	2 *oz. brandy*
½ *cup dry white wine*	1 *cup heavy cream*
1 *tsp. salt*	*Minced chives*

Sauté 1 medium onion, chopped, in 3 tablespoons butter until soft. Stir in 3 tablespoons flour and blend well. Then gradually add, stirring constantly, 1½ cups milk, 1 cup chicken consommé, and ½ cup dry white wine. Season with 1 teaspoon salt, ½ teaspoon paprika, pinch cayenne pepper, and cook until thickened.

Put 1 cup diced lobster meat in a saucepan and pour over it 2 ounces warmed brandy which has been set alight. Heat lobster meat gently, then add it and the juices of the pan to the white sauce. Cook over a low heat for 15 minutes. Then strain the mixture through a wire sieve, forcing the solids through. Allow to cool, then refrigerate for at least 3 hours. Before serving add 1 cup chilled heavy cream, whip the whole with a rotary beater for a minute or two, and serve, garnished with minced chives.

One of the outstanding experiences of our European trip was our visit to the Shannon International Free Airport, on the River Shannon in County Clare, Ireland. This was the world's first duty free airport, and besides being a marvel of construction, with luxurious facilities for the traveler, it is in the center of some of Ireland's loveliest and most historic regions.

It was in the vicinity of the airport that Mrs. Wood and I had an amazing "day and evening out of the past" at Bunratty Castle, which we wrote about in the Chicago *Tribune* in the fall of 1962. Later, we stayed at the lovely Old Ground Hotel in Ennis, a short distance away from the airport, and we were so entranced with the airport restaurant and its superb food that we went over there to eat three or four times. It was there that we first tasted some of Ireland's wonderful duck, and Aran scallops.

Thirty miles out in the Atlantic from Galway, Ireland, lie the three Aran Islands, immortalized by J. M. Synge in *Riders to the Sea,* and the setting for that memorable film, *Man of Aran.* These islands are rugged and barren in character, and many of the 1,700 inhabitants are fisherfolk who still speak Gaelic. For the antiquarian the islands are a treasure trove of ancient stone forts and early Christian churches; for the traveler there are excellent beaches and fascinating walks; and for the gourmet there are Aran scallops!

I have never tasted a more delicious soup than Aran scallop, as prepared by André Fernon, chef at the Shannon Free Airport restaurant. This is his recipe.

ARAN SCALLOP SOUP

4 *oz. fresh pork or unsmoked bacon fat*	1 *pint fish stock*
¼ *lb. potatoes*	6 *scallops*
1 *oz. butter*	*Juice of scallops*
¼ *tsp. dried thyme*	4 *tomatoes*
1 *tbsp. chopped parsley*	*Broken crackers*
⅛ *tsp. salt*	1 *oz. butter*
Pinch pepper	3 *oz. hot cream*
2 *oz. chopped onions*	*Ground mace*
	Chopped parsley

Sauté 4 ounces fresh pork or bacon fat (unsmoked) and ¼ pound potatoes, peeled and diced, in 1 ounce butter until golden. Then add ¼ teaspoon dried thyme, 1 tablespoon chopped parsley, ⅛ teaspoon salt, pinch pepper, 2 ounces onions, chopped, 1 pint fish stock, and the juice of 6 scallops. Bring to a boil, then lower flame and simmer gently for 20 minutes. After blanching the 6 scallops dice them, and add to soup, and cook for another 15 minutes. Then add 4 tomatoes, peeled, split and diced, and continue to simmer gently for 10 minutes or so. Next, add broken up crackers to soup until it has thickened slightly. Finally, beat in 1 ounce butter and 3 ounces hot cream. Sprinkle each serving with pinch ground mace and chopped parsley.

Galway Bay is noted for its lobsters and oysters, and nowhere are they better prepared than in the Great Southern Hotel, at Galway, Ireland. We were too late to attend the annual Galway Oyster Festival, held in September, but the charming manager of the hotel gave me the unique menu used by the Great Southern during the festival. Both Mrs. Wood and I drooled over the dishes listed, and I was given the recipe for the Great Southern Hotel's celebrated Galway Bay Oyster Broth.

GALWAY BAY OYSTER BROTH

30 *oysters and shells*	*Juice 1 lemon*
3 *pints cold water*	2 *tbsp. tomato catsup*
1 *pint dry white wine*	*Salt and pepper*
3 *large shallots*	*Pinch saffron*
2 *oz. butter*	6 *tbsp. butter*
10 *oz. cream*	4 *tbsp. flour*
3 *dashes Tabasco*	2 *tsp. chopped parsley*

Remove beards. Open 30 oysters, and carefully retain all juices. In a large saucepan poach the oysters in their juices for about 6 minutes. Then strain, reserving juices. Chop oysters finely.

Wash oyster shells thoroughly, place in a large saucepan, cover with 3 pints cold water, 1 pint dry white wine, and boil briskly for 30 minutes. Strain the liquid through cheesecloth.

Sauté 3 large chopped shallots (or 6 little green onions) in 2 ounces butter until tender. Add chopped oysters, oyster stock, and liquid, 10 ounces cream, 3 dashes Tabasco, juice 1 lemon, 2 tablespoons tomato catsup, salt and pepper to taste, and a pinch saffron. Bring to a boil, then thicken with 6 tablespoons butter creamed with 4 tablespoons flour. Stir well, then simmer very gently for 3 minutes, then add 2 teaspoons chopped parsley, and serve. This recipe makes about 10 servings.

The following recipe is one of two or three in this book which are not European, but inasmuch as they were part of our journey to Europe, I'm including them.

There was a time when dining car cuisine on the country's crack trains was something to write home about. Travelers between New York and Palm Beach, between New York and Chicago, and between Chicago and Los Angeles were offered rare delicacies, cooked to perfection and served with a flourish.

But this happy state of affairs began to fade away, and in time meals on even the finest trains became far from outstanding, and rather commonplace, scarcely worth the tedious standing in line waiting for a table.

I am happy to report, however, that the pendulum is now

swinging back. On our trip from San Francisco to Chicago on our way to Europe, Mrs. Wood and I enjoyed superlatively delicious food, expertly cooked and graciously served, aboard the California Zephyr. And advance dinner reservations eliminated waiting in line for a table.

On our first night out we had as a first course a Green Turtle soup, Anglaise, that surpassed any I have ever tasted before. This is the way Chef Walter Blockman prepared it in his compact but efficient galley.

GREEN TURTLE SOUP, ANGLAISE

1 *onion*	1 *No. 2 can green turtle meat*
1 *carrot*	3 *hard-cooked eggs*
3 *stalks celery*	2 *segments lemon rind*
4 *oz. butter*	*Few drops Worcestershire*
1 *pint Espagnole (or brown)*	*sauce*
sauce	2 *oz. dry sherry*
1 *pint consommé*	*Salt and freshly ground pepper*
1 *pint purée of tomato*	*Finely chopped parsley*

Slice 1 onion, 1 carrot, and 3 stalks celery and sauté in 4 ounces butter until tender, but not brown. Add 1 pint each Espagnole (or brown) sauce, consommé, and purée of tomato. Lightly boil for 1 hour, then skim and strain. Add a No. 2 can green turtle meat, diced, 3 hard-cooked eggs, diced, and 2 segments of lemon rind free from pulp and skin, finely diced. Finally add a few drops Worcestershire sauce and 2 ounces dry sherry. Season to taste with salt and freshly ground pepper, and sprinkle with finely chopped fresh parsley when served.

Chez Garac, in Nice, is not only one of the best seafood restaurants along the Côte d'Azur, but one that has some unusual characteristics. It is a pleasant and well-appointed restaurant located in the old town of Nice, facing the busy port with its kaleidoscopic panorama of fishing boats, large and small yachts, and occasionally Mediterranean cruise ships.

The restaurant is owned and very efficiently run by Madam

Pauline Garac and her sister-in-law, Madamoiselle Madeleine Garac, two charming hostesses. Madame Pauline speaks excellent English, always a great advantage for Americans when eating in a foreign restaurant.

The food is superb, and no attempt is made to dilute or weaken the fragrance and virility of Niçoise cooking. But most amazing of all, to me, are the elegant and ambrosial cakes and pastries, which are personally prepared by Madame Pauline. I have never tasted desserts anywhere that can equal the exquisite flavors and textures of Madame's chocolate "Fallen Leaves" cake, her raspberry roll cake covered with toasted almonds, and her orange cake.

Madame gave me the recipe for one of the specialties of Chez Garac, *Soupe de Poisson,* one of the three great fish soups of the Mediterranean Coast.

SOUPE DE POISSON
   (Fish Soup)

3 *tbsp. olive oil*	*Bit of orange rind*
2 *leeks*	*Pinch saffron*
2 *onions*	2 *quarts water*
2 *tomatoes*	2 *lb. fish*
2 *cloves garlic*	*Salt and pepper*
Pinch fennel seeds	4 *oz. large vermicelli*
1 *bay leaf*	2 *oz. grated Parmesan cheese*

Heat 3 tablespoons olive oil in a soup pot or large casserole, and add 2 leeks and 2 onions, both finely chopped. Let cook until vegetables are limp, then add 2 tomatoes, finely chopped. Let cook 1 minute longer, constantly stirring with a spoon. Then add 2 cloves garlic, crushed, a pinch fennel seeds, a bay leaf, a bit of orange rind, finely shredded, a pinch saffron, and last, pour in 2 quarts water.

You will need 2 pounds fish, such as whiting, perch, red snapper, sea bass, and fresh cod. Clean the fish and cut into pieces across the bone. Salt and pepper them to taste, then add them to the pot with the vegetables. Let contents of pot cook briskly for about 30 minutes.

Now pour the contents of the pot through a fine sieve into another saucepan, pressing the vegetables and fish through the sieve with a wooden spoon until only the bones of the fish remain in the sieve. Then put the thickened bouillon in the saucepan on the fire, and bring to a boil. Next add about 4 ounces large vermicelli, or other large pasta. Let cook slowly until the pasta is done. Finally, mix in 2 ounces grated Parmesan cheese and serve.

If you want *Soupe de Poisson* to reach its absolute peak of flavor perfection, you can add to each plate a generous tablespoon of *rouille*. This is a very hot and garlicky sauce, but it does unbelievable things to fish soups. Here is how it is made.

ROUILLE
(Fish Sauce)

2 *large cloves garlic*	1 *tbsp. fine breadcrumbs*
2 *chili peppers*	2 *tbsp. olive oil*
	3½ *oz. fish bouillon*

Pound finely in a mortar 2 large cloves garlic and 2 chili peppers. Add about a tablespoon fine breadcrumbs and 2 tablespoons olive oil. Mix well, then dilute the mixture with about 3½ ounces of the fish bouillon. These amounts can be varied. The more of the chili peppers, the hotter the *rouille*. It should have the consistency of mayonnaise, and the color of reddish mustard.

We were very happy at the Century Hotel in Antwerp, Belgium. Mr. de Bradaner, the charming manager, installed us in a most distinctive suite on the eleventh floor, with a magnificent view of the city, and the living room table was loaded with beautiful fruit. The main dining room, called the Restaurant des Ambassadeurs, was beautiful in its décor of red, blue and gold, and it was one of the few hotel dining rooms in Europe that had an orchestra playing dinner music. The food, naturally, was wonderful, and it was there that we had one of Belgium's national dishes, *Le Waterzoie,* a glorified chicken soup that is served as a main course.

LE WATERZOIE
(Belgian Chicken Soup)

1 5-lb. stewing chicken	Butter
1 lime	¼ cup chopped parsley
Water	1 bay leaf
2 onions	1 tbsp. salt
4 cloves	15 peppercorns
¼ cup cut celery	Pinch dried marjoram
3 leeks	Pinch dried thyme
1 carrot	1 fifth dry white wine

1 cup scalded cream

Rub a 5 pound stewing chicken well, inside and out, with a cut-up lime, then cut the chicken in serving sections, put the pieces in a pot, and pour in enough water to about half cover the chicken pieces. Bring to a boil, skim, then add 2 peeled onions, each stuck with 2 cloves, ¼ cup celery, chopped, 3 leeks, sliced, 1 carrot, sliced and previously sautéed gently in a little butter, ¼ cup parsley, 1 bay leaf, 1 tablespoon salt, 15 peppercorns, pinch each of dried marjoram and thyme, and a fifth of dry white wine. Cover the pot, and cook gently until the chicken is tender, about 3 hours.

At the end of the cooking time remove the chicken from the pot. Keep the two breasts intact, and reserve, keeping them warm. Cut the meat off the other chicken parts and dice it, reserving this meat also. Strain the stock through a sieve into another pot, pressing as much of the vegetables as is possible through the sieve. Then add the diced chicken meat to the strained stock, and reheat. Correct the seasoning, if necessary, then add the scalded cream. Mix well, and just before serving add a boned chicken breast to each deep soup plate, and pour the stock over them.

On our first night in Bologna Mrs. Wood and I were the guests of the president of the *Festival Della Cucina Italiana* (the Italian Food Fair) in the lovely indoor and outdoor restaurant on the fair grounds. It was the last night of the fair, and a very gala and interesting evening. We had a magnificent dinner, with wonderful

Italian apéritifs, wines, and cordials. After dinner we were privileged to attend the presentation of diplomas and awards to the cooks, and others who had contributed to the success of the festival.

While every item on the six course dinner was delicious beyond words, the soup that we had was one of the most unusual I have ever tasted. It was called *Minestra di Cubetti* (Broth with Cubes), and it really was an appetite whet rather than a heavy soup. The *cubetti* were small cheese cubes.

MINESTRA DI CUBETTI
(Chicken Broth with Cheese Cubes)

10 *oz. ricotta cheese* (*or cream cheese*)	*Pinch freshly ground pepper*
	Pinch powdered basil
2 *eggs*	*Pinch grated nutmeg*
Salt	1 *tsp. minced parsley*
1 *tsp. chopped chives*	1 *cup grated Parmesan cheese*

Chicken consommé

Make a paste with about 10 ounces well beaten ricotta cheese (or cream cheese), 2 beaten eggs, the chopped chives, a pinch each freshly ground pepper, powdered basil, salt and grated nutmeg, 1 teaspoon minced parsley, and a scant cup of the grated Parmesan cheese. When everything is well blended place the mixture in a buttered baking dish, place baking dish in a pan of hot water, and cook in a 300-degree oven until the paste is firm. Remove from oven and allow paste to cool. Then cut the paste into small cubes about a quarter of an inch in size. Place these in a soup tureen, and pour over them boiling chicken broth of good strength. Serve at once.

We were very fortunate in going to Scotland during the grouse season. Whenever the opportunity afforded we ate grouse. Usually it was roasted, but one night at the North British Hotel in Edinburgh we had grouse *Chez Soi,* which was a delicious ragout of grouse, with a rich dark sauce. I tried to get the recipe, but it was no go. We also had a marvelous soup made with grouse and pheasant at the Alexandra Hotel in Fort William. Mr. Nicholson, the most engaging proprietor, got the recipe for this soup from the chef, but it was quite vague in many respects. So I had to do the best I could with it, but the following recipe (part of which is my own) is most delectable. Inasmuch as grouse is not obtainable in America, I have substituted duck for the grouse, although any game bird can be substituted.

GAME BIRD SOUP

¼ cup bacon drippings	Pinch grated nutmeg
1 young wild duck	Pinch dried thyme
1 small pheasant	1 bay leaf
2 onions	2 crushed juniper berries
1 clove garlic	Salt and pepper
2 carrots	2 quarts chicken broth with
½ cup chopped celery	rice
Pinch powdered cloves	1 cup Burgundy wine
Pinch powdered mace	1 cup sliced fresh mushrooms

In a soup kettle melt ¼ cup bacon drippings, and add the disjointed duck and pheasant. Sear them well over a bright flame, turning them frequently. Then turn down the flame and add 2 peeled and chopped onions, a crushed clove garlic, 2 diced carrots, and ½ cup diced celery until lightly browned. Season with a pinch each powdered cloves, powdered mace, grated nutmeg, and dried thyme, 1 bay leaf, 2 crushed juniper berries, and salt and pepper to taste. Then stir in 2 quarts chicken broth with rice. Gradually bring liquid to a boil, and simmer gently for 1 hour, skimming any scum that rises. Then add 1 cup Burgundy wine and 1 cup sliced fresh mushrooms. Cover the kettle and simmer gently for about 40 minutes.

With a long fork or skimmer remove the pieces of meat from the kettle. Pick the meat off the bones, reserving the two duck and the two pheasant breasts, and dice the rest. Pour the contents of the pot through a sieve into another pot, pressing the solids through the sieve. Add the diced meat, reheat, and serve, floating the breasts on the surface.

Chicoree Witloof is the Belgian name for the carefully cultivated roots of the chicory plant, which we call endive. In the area
around Brussels the chicory roots are planted in September about
a foot and a half in the ground, and are covered with straw and
heated cylindrical silos. About six weeks later a closely formed
head of ivory-tipped white leaves has risen six to ten inches above
the ground. These heads of endive are cut from their brown roots,
cleaned, and packed in boxes, and shipped by rail, sea and air to
markets in Europe and America.

While we were touring the port of Antwerp, we stopped for
a bit of luncheon at a most remarkable hotel and restaurant, the
Scheldpark Hotel Nautilus. It is an ultra-modern building, and
lies, as an advanced beacon, on the bank of the River Scheldt,
near the majestic Kruisschans and the Boudewijnsluices, which
form the gateway to the maze of Antwerp docks. The hotel section
is small, containing only twenty-two rooms, but the restaurant,
café, and tea room have wide viewing windows. We sat there,
entranced, watching huge white ships coming into Antwerp. Our
light luncheon consisted of a typical Belgium dish, endive soup
Flemish style with ham.

ENDIVE SOUP, FLEMISH STYLE

1½ *quarts water*	1 *medium onion*
1 *medium-sized ham shank*	4 *heads endive*
2 *stalks celery*	¼ *tsp. bruised peppercorns*
1 *carrot*	1 *cup pearl barley*

Buttered croutons

Wash and crisp thoroughly in very cold water 2 stalks celery,
1 carrot, 1 medium onion, and 4 heads of endive.

Pour 1½ quarts water into a large heavy pot. Add a medium-
sized ham shank, the celery, chopped, the carrot and onion sliced,
and 3 heads of endive, chopped. Season with ¼ teaspoon bruised
black peppercorns. Cook over a medium flame for 2 hours. Then
remove the pot from the heat and strain the broth into a deep
saucepan. Dice whatever ham meat there is, and add to broth.
Also add 1 cup pearl barley, and cook for 15 minutes. Then add

the remaining head of endive, which has been sliced. Cook for 15 minutes more, or until endive is tender. Correct for seasoning if necessary, and serve piping hot in preheated plates, garnished with buttered hot croutons, to 4.

The best known soup in Italy is *minestrone* (with the great number of Italian restaurants in America, I think it is almost as well known here). But unless you have it in an Italian home in America, it will never be the same as it is in Italy.

There are different versions of minestrone in Italy. In the north of Italy it is usually made with rice as an ingredient. In Genoa that delectable sauce, *pesto,* is added. Some cooks make it without meat. But this version, which we had at the Hotel Savoia, the very excellent and delightful hotel where we stayed in Rome, I liked best.

MINESTRONE

½ *cup kidney beans*	*Pepper*
2 *tbsp. olive oil*	*Pinch dried oregano*
¼ *lb. bacon*	2 *quarts condensed consommé*
¼ *lb. ham*	*Small head cabbage*
¼ *lb. Italian sausage*	*Handful fresh spinach leaves*
2 *cloves garlic*	*Handful fresh beet greens*
1 *onion*	1 *cup Italian red wine*
1 *carrot*	1 *No. 2 can Italian tomatoes*
2 *stalks celery*	½ *cup elbow macaroni*
1 *zucchini (Italian squash)*	1 *tsp. dried basil*
1 *leek*	*Grated Parmesan cheese*
Salt	

Soak 1 cup kidney beans overnight in cold water.

In a heavy skillet heat 2 tablespoons olive oil, and add ¼ pound each chopped bacon, chopped lean ham, chopped Italian sausage, and 2 crushed cloves garlic. Sauté gently until brown, and then add 1 sliced onion, 1 carrot, 2 stalks celery, 1 zucchini, and 1 leek, all diced, salt and pepper to taste, and a generous pinch dried oregano. Let simmer for about 10 minutes.

In a soup kettle heat 2 quarts condensed consommé. Put the contents of the skillet into the stock and add the beans, which have been drained, a small head of cabbage, cut into thin strips (after removing the hard core), a handful of well-washed spinach leaves, and an equal amount well washed beet greens, and a cup dry red wine (chianti type). Simmer until beans and vegetables are tender (about 1½ hours). Now add a No. 2 can Italian tomatoes, and ½ cup elbow macaroni. Cook about 15 minutes longer. About 3 minutes before the soup is to be served add 1 teaspoon dried basil and stir it in. If the soup is too thick for your taste it can be thinned out with hot consommé. But remember minestrone is a "one dish meal," and, as one Italian told me, "it should be thick enough so that the spoon will stand upright in it!" Grated Parmesan cheese should be passed in a bowl, and liberally sprinkled on each plateful.

One of the great soups of Provence is *"Pistou" Potage Provençale*. It is really a very fine vegetable soup, but it has an addition that makes it a gastronomic masterpiece. It is so popular in Provence that it is canned, so that it can be enjoyed when fresh vegetables are no longer available. And even this canned version is delicious.

I was talking about the Pistou soup with Madame Nicole, the owner of the grocery store in Beaulieu where I traded. A couple of days later when I came in, she produced an old cookbook, *La Cuisinière Provençale,* by J. B. Reboul, and showed me the recipe. Then she wrote out some additions which she used when she made the soup for her family, and between the two of us the following recipe was devised. I made it four or five times while we were living in St.-Jean-Cap-Ferrat, and, accompanied by the superb French bread that I got at the Beaulieu bakery, it was a magnificent meal.

PISTOU POTAGE PROVENÇALE
(Vegetable Soup from Provence)

2 *quarts water*	2 *leeks*
1 *lb. seeded French green*	3 *tomatoes*
beans	10 *spinach leaves*
4 *potatoes*	2 *zucchini*
½ *cup white beans*	*Salt and pepper*
2 *carrots*	3 *oz. large vermicelli*

PESTO

3 *tbsp. minced* fresh *basil*	*Pinch salt*
leaves	1½ *oz. grated Parmesan cheese*
3 *cloves garlic*	2 *oz. olive oil*

In a soup kettle put 2 quarts water, 1 pound seeded French green beans cut in 1-inch pieces, 4 potatoes, peeled and diced, ½ cup white beans, 2 diced carrots, the white part of 2 leeks, diced, 3 peeled, seeded and chopped tomatoes, 10 leaves well-washed spinach, 2 zucchini, diced, and salt and pepper to taste. Let cook for 1 hour, or until vegetables are tender. Then add 3 ounces (in weight) of large vermicelli, or other large pasta, turn down flame, and let cook another 14 minutes.

In the meantime make the pesto, which is the secret of the soup's marvelous flavor. In a mortar put about 3 tablespoons minced *fresh* basil leaves, 3 cloves cut up garlic, a pinch salt, and 1½ ounces grated Parmesan cheese (modern recipes add a tablespoon of pine nuts). Pound the mixture with a pestle until you have a thick purée, then add, a little at a time, 2 ounces olive oil, still mixing, until mixture has attained the consistency of creamed butter. Remove soup from fire, and mix in the pesto. Cover for a few moments, then serve.

The province of Tuscany, one of the oldest regions in north-central Italy, has a rich and varied background in art, in literature, in science, and in ancient history. Coming down to the mundane considerations of wine and food, Italy's most famous wine,

Chianti, comes from the countryside south of Florence. Tuscan beef is of high quality; an abundance of fish comes from the Mediterranean and the nearby Adriatic; and the white Tuscan beans are ever present in soups, with rice, and with game.

Pasta e Fagioli, a thickish bean soup with pasta, is a great favorite in Tuscany. We had it at the Grand Hotel Duomo, in Pisa, and this is the way it's made.

PASTA E FAGIOLI
(Bean Soup with Pasta)

1 *lb. beans*	2 *cloves garlic*
2½ *quarts water*	*Generous pinch minced parsley*
Pinch dried thyme	8 *oz. elbow macaroni*
¼ *lb. salt pork, cubed*	*Salt and pepper*
2 *medium onions*	*Grated Parmesan cheese*
	3 *tbsp. olive oil*

Soak 1 pound navy or kidney beans in cold water overnight. Drain them and put in a heavy iron kettle and cover with 2½ quarts boiling salted water. Add a pinch dried thyme, cover, and simmer about 2½ hours, or until beans are almost tender.

While beans are cooking cube ¼ pound salt pork and sauté it in a skillet with 2 medium onions, chopped, and 2 cloves garlic, minced, until onions are golden. Add all this to the beans during last half hour of cooking, along with a generous pinch minced parsley.

When beans are cooked and tender take out about half the beans and put them through a sieve, and return the resulting purée to the pot. Then add 8 ounces elbow macaroni, or shells, or bow ties, which have been cooked about 4 minutes in boiling salted water and then drained, and 3 tablespoons olive oil to the kettle. Let simmer about 10 minutes more (or until pasta is tender, or *al dente*), then salt and pepper to taste, and serve in soup bowls with grated Parmesan cheese. This should serve 4 to 6 people, depending on appetites. Accompany this soup with crusty French bread.

As everybody (well, practically everybody) knows, Switzerland's most famous food product is Emmentaler, or, as it is more popularly known, Swiss cheese. Although other countries make cheeses similar to Emmentaler, to my mind they are but imitations. To me, Emmentaler is the most delicious of all cheeses.

It is amazing the number of things that can be done with Swiss cheese. While we were in Switzerland we had it in many different dishes. One of the most unusual and delicious ones was *Kassuppe,* a specialty of the Canton of Schwyz. It is made with Gruyère cheese, which is almost identical with Emmentaler, only its holes are slightly smaller, the color not quite so rich, and it is more strongly salted, and its flavor is stronger.

KASSUPPE
   (Cheese Soup)

14 *oz. stale brown bread*	4 *pints boiling water*
19 *oz. Gruyère cheese*	1 *cup dry white wine*

Cut 14 ounces stale brown bread and 19 ounces Gruyère cheese into small, thin slices. Place in a soup tureen, alternating one layer of bread with one slice of cheese. Cover with 4 pints boiling water and let stand for 2 to 3 hours. Then pour mixture into a large saucepan, bring to a boil, and crush ingredients with a wooden potato masher. Stir vigorously, add 1 cup dry white wine, heat thoroughly, and serve.

4 ▮ FISH

I don't believe there is any spot on the globe where there are such great varieties and number of fishes as there are in Western Europe. The British Isles are surrounded by salt water; France is bounded on the west by the Atlantic ocean and on the south by the Mediterranean; except in the North, Italy has one vast coast line; Portugal borders on the Atlantic; Spain on the Mediterranean; Denmark, Holland, Belgium, and Germany border on various seas. Only Switzerland is landlocked, but its rivers and countless lakes are filled with delectable fishes. The other Western European countries abound with fresh water fish from countless lakes and rivers. Europe is indeed a fish-lover's paradise.

The piscatorial glory of England is Dover sole which is, I understand, found only in the English Channel. While it is shipped to America by air, you have to eat it in England to really appreciate its delicate flavor and texture. Flounder is plentiful in America, and is a most delicious fish, but if you were to eat a bit of flounder, then a bit of Dover sole, the difference would be easily discernable even to an uneducated palate.

There is scarcely any fine restaurant or hotel in London that does not feature Dover sole in some delectable form of preparation.

The same is true in Paris, and many other French cities not too far from the English Channel. Holland and Belgium too serve many fine Dover sole dishes.

One of the most unusual and delicious Dover sole dishes we had one night at a special dinner at the Park Lane Hotel where we lived for the five months we were in London.

The Park Lane, on Piccadilly, in London's smart West End, is one of those very fine hotels that not too many Americans are familiar with. One does not see hordes of bellboys dashing about;

43

the reception desks do not have a battery of important looking clerks who look down their collective noses at you when you come in; the service in all parts of the hotel is quiet and highly efficient; the rooms, each with a bath, are very comfortable and lovely; and the dining room is quietly elegant, and, to my mind, serves some of the best food in London. Incidentally, the American Bar is a charming place, and I never had better dry martinis anywhere.

I think the excellence of the hotel, and the smoothness with which it is run, is due to the owner and very active Managing Director, Guy Bracewell Smith, and his assistant, Major Fries. Guy studied hotel management on the Continent and in some of America's finest hotels. He is a dedicated gourmet, and a connoisseur of fine wines, as the extensive wine cellar of the hotel proves. His head chef, M. Viguers, is one of the best in London, and his restaurant manager, Mr. Stone, is not only efficient, but charm personified.

On the night of July 4, 1962, Mrs. Wood and I were guests at a small dinner party given by Guy Bracewell Smith in the dining room of the Park Lane Hotel. Guy had told me that he had devised a dinner that would feature fruits, but he wouldn't elaborate on the menu. So I couldn't imagine what to expect.

It turned out to be a most unusual and intriguing dinner. The first course, after champagne in the American bar, was filet of sole Caprice, and with it was served a Gewürtztraminer. The entree was *Suprême de Vollaille Hawaiienne,* accompanied by Duchess potatoes and little green peas, served with a Château Gruaud-Larose. The dessert was *Quartiers de Pêches Flambées au Kirsch.* An apricot brandy accompanied this, which was perfect as a flavor-mate.

FILET OF SOLE CAPRICE

8 *small filets of sole*	*Fine breadcrumbs*
Salt and pepper	*Olive oil*
Flour	4 *bananas*
Melted butter	1 *tbsp. A.1. Sauce*

4 *oz. softened butter*

Slightly flatten 8 small filets of sole, season with salt and pepper, lightly dust with flour, then pass the seasoned filets through melted butter, and finally coat them with fine breadcrumbs.

In one large or two smaller skillets pour enough olive oil to coat the bottom(s) about an eighth of an inch deep. When hot, sauté 4 bananas, each split in half lengthwise, until nicely browned. Remove and keep hot. In the same skillet and oil sauté the filets of sole quickly on both sides, about 5 minutes. Place them on a lightly buttered serving dish, and top each with a half fried banana.

In the meantime mix about 1 tablespoon A.1. Sauce (or an equal amount of the liquid part of Major Gray's Chutney) with 4 ounces softened butter. Chill it, then wrap it in wax paper in the form of a cylinder (about diameter of a half dollar), and let it get very cold. Slice and serve separately with filets. This recipe serves 4.

Overton's restaurant, on St. James Street, is one of London's finest restaurants specializing in seafood. It is quietly elegant, the service is excellent, and the food superb. The night we were there we had a Dover sole dish that surpassed any we had ever tasted—Filet of Sole Walewska. Its flavors were so exquisite that after dinner I went back to the kitchen and asked the chef, A. Volinsky (a White Russian) for the recipe. He sent it to me the following day. It is a party dish, but not at all difficult to prepare and serve.

FILET OF SOLE WALEWSKA

4 *filets of sole*	1 *bay leaf*
2 *lobster claws* (*meat*)	*Pinch salt*
1 *lb. potatoes*	*Pinch pepper*
2 *oz. butter*	1 *oz. butter*
2 *oz. flour*	1 *egg yolk*
1 *pint milk*	*Salt and pepper*
4 *oz. dry white wine*	2 *slices large mushroom caps*
2 *oz. water*	1 *egg yolk*
2–3 *onion rings*	2 *oz. cream*
2–3 *peppercorns*	2 *oz. grated Parmesan cheese*

Before starting to cook the fish and sauce, begin to cook 1 pound peeled potatoes (either boiling or steaming). Although the potatoes are principally for decorative purposes, portions may be served with the finished dish.

Begin the sauce first. Melt 2 ounces butter in a saucepan, and gradually work into the butter 2 ounces flour, until it is absorbed and smooth. Make sure the mixture does not brown. When smooth gradually pour in 1 pint milk, working it into the roux by stirring with a wooden spoon to avoid lumps. When sauce begins to boil, turn down the flame to lowest possible point to keep sauce hot.

Have ready 4 filets of sole, each weighing approximately 5 ounces. Fold each filet, secure with toothpick, and place in a lightly buttered saucepan. Also place in the saucepan the meat from 2 lobster claws. Cover sole and lobster with 4 ounces dry white wine and 2 ounces water, and add 2 or 3 onion rings, 2 or 3 peppercorns, 1 bay leaf, and a pinch salt and pepper. Cover the saucepan with greased paper and cook for about 5 minutes.

Now mash the cooked potatoes through a sieve until completely dry. Add to them 1 ounce butter and yolk of 1 egg, and season to taste with salt and pepper. Stir until all is well blended (use wooden spoon) and keep warm until ready to use.

When about ready to serve decorate a flame-proof serving dish with the mashed potatoes, piped on decoratively with a forcing bag and fancy tube. Brown potatoes lightly under broiler. Remove from broiler and coat the dish lightly with some of the sauce. Remove folded filets and arrange them on the dish, and lay the lobster claws and 2 slices truffles (or 2 slices of large mushroom caps which have been sautéed in butter) across the sole filets.

Reduce the remaining liquor the fish and lobster were cooked in by half, and strain it into the sauce. Then, with a wire whisk stir in 1 egg yolk which has been beaten together with 2 ounces cream, and about 1½ ounces grated Parmesan cheese. Correct the sauce for seasoning, if necessary, and pour over the filets and lobster claws, and sprinkle top with about ½ ounce grated Parmesan cheese. Put under broiler until cheese begins to brown, then serve very hot. This recipe serves 2. For 4 or 6, double or triple the recipe.

The Gresham Hotel in Dublin, Ireland, is a joy to live in and a joy to eat in. It is situated on O'Connell Street, and is very modern, having been built since the Irish Rebellion. Every lounge and the three dining rooms are beautifully done, and I have never seen so many exquisite crystal chandeliers. Fresh flowers were everywhere, and the food was truly gourmet. Mr. Toddy O'Sullivan, who heads the Gresham, is a charming Irishman, and has endless energy, for he is everywhere, and never misses a thing that is not up to tip top standard.

We had two outstanding dinners at the Gresham. One featured prawns with a lobster sauce, which I will detail later, and the other was filet of sole Gresham. Both were gastronomic masterpieces.

FILET OF SOLE GRESHAM

8 medium-sized filets of sole	2 cups cream
Butter	6 tbsp. butter
Juice 1 lemon	2 tbsp. flour
1 bay leaf	3 egg yolks
1 small onion	3 tbsp. water
6 mushrooms	8 asparagus spears
1 cup dry white wine	8 medium-sized pieces cooked
2 cups water	lobster meat
¼ tsp. salt	16 cooked shrimp

Lightly grease a large skillet or saucepan with butter, and in it place 8 medium-sized filets of sole. Squeeze the juice of 1 lemon over sole and add 1 bay leaf, 1 small, finely chopped onion, 6 sliced mushrooms, 1 cup dry white wine, 2 cups water, and ¼ teaspoon salt. Place the skillet on the fire and simmer for 7 minutes, or until sole is tender.

Remove sole carefully and place on a napkin to keep warm. Return skillet to fire and reduce stock by half. Then add to it 2 cups cream. Remove bay leaf, and add 2 tablespoons each flour and butter which have been mixed together until creamy, and whisk all the time until sauce is creamy. Then remove from fire.

In a small saucepan place 3 egg yolks lightly beaten and 3

tablespoons water and heat over a slow fire until thick and creamy. Add this to the sauce.

In another large skillet containing 4 tablespoons butter preheat 8 medium-sized pieces lobster meat, cooked, 16 deveined cooked prawns, and 8 asparagus spears, cooked if fresh, or canned. Finally, place the filets of sole on a heat-proof serving platter, and arrange the lobster, prawns and asparagus spears on the filet. Cover all with the sauce, and place under broiler for a few moments, until sauce is bubbly. Serve at once to 4.

In Saulieu, only a short distance from Dijon, we visited our third three-star restaurant, the gastronomically famous Hotel de la Côte d'Or. The owner-chef is Alexandre Dumaine, whom most French gourmets consider to be one of the topmost chefs in France.

Our dinner was a magnificent experience. The first course was a pâté of pheasant, whose flavor was beyond description. Our entree was a dish for which Monsieur Dumaine is justly famous— a *Quenelle de Brochet garni de filets of sole, Langouste de l'Ocean, champignons et truffés.* With this we had a lovely Meursault. Cheese, coffee, and an old Marc de Bourgogne completed a perfect meal.

Quenelles are a preparation of pounded and sieved fish blended with a paste, or *panade,* made with milk, eggs, butter and flour, and then gently poached. They are usually garnished with filets of sole and/or shellfish.

This recipe takes work, care, and time, but it is not beyond an intelligent and competent cook, and is well worth it. But it is not a recipe for a novice to attempt.

QUENELLES DE BROCHETTE, GARNISHED WITH SOLE AND LOBSTER

(1) Panade, or Paste

¾ *cup milk*	½ *tsp. salt*
¾ *cup dry white wine*	1½ *cups sifted flour*
4 *tbsp. butter*	4 *eggs*

(2) Quenelles

Fresh pike	*Creamed butter*
Panade (above)	*2 tsp. salt*
4 eggs	*½ tsp. white pepper*
2 eggs (whites only)	*Few grains grated nutmeg*

(3) Mushroom Sauce

1 *lb. sliced fresh mushrooms*	*3 oz. Madeira wine*
2 *oz. butter*	*2 cups cream*
1 *tbsp. flour*	*½ tsp. salt*

(4) Garnish

Filets of sole	*Nuggets cooked lobster meat*

White wine and chicken bouillon

Into a saucepan put ¾ cup each milk and dry white wine, 4 table-spoons butter, and ½ teaspoon salt. Bring to a boil, stirring constantly, then remove from fire and gradually stir in 1½ cups sifted flour. Then add 4 eggs, one at a time, whisking well after each addition. Replace mixture over fire and stir vigorously until it comes away from sides of pan. Spread mixture on a dish, let it cool, then weigh it.

Put the same weight as the panade of fresh pike, free from bones and skin, through a food chopper, then put fish into a mortar and pound it thoroughly. Then add the cooled panade to the fish, and continue to pound and blend. Put pounded mixture through a very fine sieve into mortar again and add 4 whole eggs, one by one, and the whites of 2 eggs. Next add the same weight of creamed butter as the original weight of the panade, and blend it thoroughly into the fish-paste mixture. Add 2 teaspoons salt and ½ teaspoon white pepper, and tiny pinch of freshly grated nutmeg. Blend, then chill mixture in refrigerator for 6 hours.

Roll out chilled mixture on lightly floured breadboard and shape into pieces like small omelets, making each quenelle about 4 inches long and 2 inches wide in the center, and about ¾ inch thick. Poach them very gently in salted water in a shallow baking dish for 20 minutes. Then very carefully drain them and arrange on a heated platter.

Make a mushroom sauce as follows—in a saucepan sauté 1 pound fresh mushrooms, sliced not too thin, in 2 ounces butter about 8 to 10 minutes. Then sprinkle in 1 tablespoon flour, blending it with the butter in the pan. Then blend in 3 ounces Madeira wine. Finally add 2 cups cream and ½ teaspoon salt. Stir over a low flame until smooth and thickened.

In the meantime poach 1 filet of sole and 3 nuggets of lobster meat, each about the size of a walnut, for each serving, in equal parts of dry white wine and chicken bouillon to cover. When fish flakes with a fork, they are done.

To serve the Quenelles de Brochette place a quenelle on each hot plate, a folded filet of sole, and 3 nuggets of lobster meat. Pour over all enough mushroom sauce to cover well.

Sole is to be found on the restaurant menus of a great many of Germany's cities. The dish I encountered most frequently on menus was called *Seezunge Müllerin Art,* or "sole in the style of the Miller's Wife," which, I guess, is similar to the great French dish, *Sole Bonne Femme,* which means "housewife's style."

With magnificent beers to be found everywhere in Germany, naturally German cooks are past masters in the art of cooking with beer. We had this delicious filet of sole cooked in beer at the Grand Hotel in Nürenberg.

ROLLED FILET OF SOLE IN BEER

4 *filets sole*	1 *tbsp. finely minced onion*
Salt	¼ *bay leaf*
Slices smoked salmon	¼ *tsp. powdered ginger*
4 *mushroom caps*	2 *tbsp. butter*
1 *cup beer*	2 *tbsp. flour*
¼ *cup whipping cream*	

Sprinkle 4 filets of sole lightly with salt, place a slice of smoked salmon on each filet, and roll firmly. Arrange the rolls in a buttered baking dish, and top each roll with a mushroom cap.

To 1 cup of beer add 1 tablespoon of finely minced onion, ¼ bay leaf, and ¼ teaspoon of powdered ginger. Pour this over the rolled filets. Bake in a 375-degree oven for 25 minutes, or until the fish flakes when tested with a fork.

In a saucepan melt 2 tablespoons of butter, add 2 tablespoons of flour and blend well. Strain the beer from the baked filets and measure, adding additional beer to make 1 cup. Add the beer to the blended flour and butter and cook, stirring constantly, until smooth and thickened.

Whip ¼ cup of whipping cream until it is stiff. Fold this into the beer–white sauce, and pour it over the filets. Place the filets under the broiler for about 3 minutes to glaze the sauce.

One of the finest mountain centers in Scotland is the village of Braemar. The scenery around it is among the grandest in the Highlands, romantic, picturesque and wild, and its streams and forest abound with fish and deer. Eight miles down the River Dee from Braemer is Balmoral Castle, the residence of Britain's Royal Family during the various Scottish game seasons.

We stopped overnight at the Invercault Arms Hotel, a charming old yet pleasantly modern hotel. And it was there that we had a most unusual sole dish, Filet of Sole Balmoral.

FILET OF SOLE BALMORAL

4 *large (or 8 small) filets sole*	1 *cup thin white cream sauce*
5 *oz. condensed consommé*	1 *tsp. Dijon mustard*
4 *oz. dry white wine*	1 *hard-cooked egg, chopped*
½ *cup grated sharp Cheddar*	½ *tsp. grated horseradish*
cheese	*Salt and freshly ground pepper*
2 *oz. butter*	1 *tbsp. dry sherry*

½ *cup dry white wine*

Poach 4 large or 8 small filets of sole in 5 ounces of condensed consommé and 4 ounces of dry white wine in a large iron skillet for 10 minutes over a low flame.

Meanwhile prepare the sauce. Melt 2 tablespoons butter in top of double boiler, then stir in ½ cup grated sharp Cheddar cheese. When cheese is melted add 1 cup thin white cream sauce, and cook over gently boiling water 15 minutes. Then add 1 teaspoon prepared French mustard (Dijon), 1 chopped hard-cooked egg, and ½ teaspoon grated horseradish (preferably fresh), salt and freshly ground pepper to taste, 1 tablespoon dry sherry, and ½ cup dry white wine. Stir frequently. When thoroughly heated and blended pour sauce over filets and fish wine "fumet" in skillet. Cover and simmer for 10 minutes longer.

There is a delightful little restaurant located just off the Rue de Faubourg–St. Honoré, in the 8th Arrondissement of Paris, called La Truite. It is run by the Dorin family (Papa does the cooking), and the food is very superior. Many of the specialties of the house are Norman, and particularly delicious is Sole Normande.

SOLE NORMANDE

2 tbsp. chopped fresh parsley	Pinch salt
6 little green onions	1 tbsp. lemon juice
1 small clove garlic	2 tbsp. butter
1 small bay leaf	1 oz. dry white wine
24 medium-sized shrimp	1 oz. Calvados (or applejack)
1½ cups dry white wine	6 filets of sole
1 tbsp. butter	1 cup cream
1 cup sliced mushrooms	1 egg yolk
2 tbsp. butter	

In a deep skillet or saucepan place 2 tablespoons chopped fresh parsley, 6 little green onions (bulbs and tops) finely chopped, 1 small clove garlic, finely minced, and a small bay leaf.

Clean, shell, and devein 24 medium-sized shrimp, and place them over seasonings in skillet. Add 1½ cups dry white wine and 1 tablespoon butter. Cook over low flame until shrimps are cooked, about 10 to 15 minutes. Remove shrimps and keep warm, and reserve cooking liquid.

Boil 1 cup sliced mushrooms in enough water to half cover them, to which has been added pinch salt and 1 tablespoon lemon juice, for 3 minutes. Remove mushrooms and reserve liquid.

In a skillet sauté the mushrooms in 2 tablespoons butter lightly, but do not brown. Then remove them to a hot dish. Rinse the skillet the mushrooms were cooked in with 1 ounce each dry white wine and Calvados (or applejack).

Into a large skillet strain the liquid the shrimps were cooked in, and the liquid and juices mushrooms were boiled and sautéed in. Bring to boiling point, seasoning to taste with salt and pepper. Place 6 filets of sole in the liquid and gently poach them until done (about 10 to 15 minutes). Remove filets to a hot serving platter, arrange shrimps and mushrooms around filets, and keep all hot.

Over a brisk flame reduce the liquid the fish were poached in to about ½ cup. Then let it cool slightly and add to it 1 cup cream mixed with an egg yolk and 2 tablespoons butter. Blend this well over low heat with a wire whisk until sauce is light and slightly thickened. Pour sauce over sole, shrimp, and mushrooms, and serve.

Throughout the German Rhineland, at the first peep of spring, people will be singing, *"Der Mai ist gekommen, Die Bäume schlagen aus"* (May is here, the trees are in bloom), and they'll be flocking into the woods to gather clusters of the white flowers of Waldmeister.

The aromatic Waldmeister, which is known in America as woodruff, is a sweet-scented herb. The Germans steep it in dry white wine, and the resulting beverage is called May Wine. It may be served chilled with meals, or may be combined with champagne and liqueurs to make a delightful punch.

To make your own May wine place ½ ounce dried woodruff in a quart mason jar, and pour over it a bottle (fifth) of a good German dry white wine, Riesling, or Paul Masson Emerald Dry wine. Seal the jar tightly and let step for 8 hours. Or you may purchase May wine in good liquor stores.

A delicious and unusual German dish is filets of sole with May wine.

FILET OF SOLE WITH MAY WINE

4 *filets of sole*	*Melted butter*
Salt and pepper	*Fine breadcrumbs*
3 *tbsp. butter*	*Flour and butter roux*
1 *cup May wine*	1 *tsp. drained capers*

Salt and pepper 4 filets sole. Melt 3 tablespoons butter in a large skillet, arrange filets in skillet, and sauté over low flame for 3 minutes, basting with butter. Then pour 1 cup May wine over filets, and continue basting with liquid until fish is tender. Pour off excess liquid in small saucepan. Brush filets with melted butter, sprinkle lightly with breadcrumbs, and place under broiler for 5 to 6 minutes. Meantime thicken excess liquid with flour and butter roux. Add 1 teaspoon drained capers to sauce. Arrange filets on hot platter and pour sauce over. Serve immediately to 4.

When Mrs. Wood and I were driving through Scotland in the fall of 1962 we passed through a small fishing village a few miles north of Aberdeen. The name of the hamlet was Findon, and, according to legend, it was the place where finnan haddie originated.

It seems that a quantity of wood was stored in a building that also contained a large daily catch of haddock, which the Scotch call "haddie." The building caught fire, and it was soon filled with dense smoke. When the fire was extinguished it was discovered that some haddock in the building had attained a rich, brown color, but were otherwise undamaged. The thrifty Scots took the smoked fish home and cooked it, and found that it had a very pleasant, piquant flavor. So they called it Findon Haddie.

The Caledonian Hotel in Aberdeen prepares a creamed finnan haddie that is wonderful, particularly for breakfast.

CREAMED FINNAN HADDIE

2 *lbs. finnan haddie*	½ *tsp. paprika*
Milk	*Pinch cayenne pepper*
3 *tbsp. butter*	½ *cup cream*
1 *tbsp. chopped onion*	2 *tbsp. chopped sweet red*
2 *tbsp. chopped green pepper*	*pepper*
3 *tbsp. flour*	¼ *cup dry sherry*

Soak 2 pounds finnan haddie in enough milk to cover in a saucepan for 2 hours. Then put the saucepan over a low flame, and let it simmer until the fish is ready to flake, about 30 minutes. Remove fish from the milk, flake, and reserve milk.

In another saucepan melt 3 tablespoons butter and add 1 table-spoon chopped onion, and 2 tablespoons each chopped green pepper and chopped sweet red pepper. When vegetables are limp but not brown blend in 3 tablespoons flour, and then slowly add the milk the finnan haddie was simmered in (if necessary add additional milk to make a total of 1½ cups). While adding the milk stir constantly and cook until the sauce is smooth and thickened. Add ½ teaspoon paprika, a pinch cayenne pepper, and the flaked finnan haddie. Bring to a boil, then lower flame and simmer for 1 minute, stirring constantly. Add ½ cup cream mixed with ¼ cup dry sherry wine, and reheat, but do not allow to boil. Serve piping hot over toast triangles to 4 or 6.

The old French province of Languedoc, bordering on the Mediterranean, is chiefly noted for 3 gastronomical glories—garlic, cassoulet, and *Brandade de Morue* (creamed codfish). Languedoc's most interesting and famous city is Carcassonne. The fortified old *Cité,* with its magnificent citadel, is unrivaled in the world. In Carcassonne one finds an authentic cassoulet, and also a very delicious cod creation, Cod Carcassonne.

COD CARCASSONNE

½ cup olive oil	1 tbsp. walnuts
2 onions	1 tbsp. hazelnuts
2 cloves garlic	1 tbsp. almonds
2 tbsp. chopped parsley	1 tsp. butter
3 lb. fresh cod filets	2 tbsp. fine breadcrumbs
½ cup dry white wine	1 cup fish stock

Watercress

Heat ½ cup olive oil in a heavy skillet and add 2 onions, chopped, 2 cloves garlic, minced, and 2 tablespoons chopped parsley. Sauté over a low flame until onions are limp, but not brown. Then add 3 pounds fresh cod filets, ½ cup dry white wine, and simmer gently for about 15 minutes, or until wine has evaporated.

Mince 1 tablespoon each of walnuts, hazelnuts and almonds,

and sauté in a saucepan with a tiny bit of butter for about 3 minutes over a low flame, stirring constantly. Then add 2 tablespoons breadcrumbs and continue to cook, stirring constantly, for 3 minutes more, or until crumbs are golden brown. Then add 1 cup fish stock, and stir constantly until sauce begins to boil.

Pour the sauce over the cod filets, which have been kept warm, garnish with parsley or watercress, and serve piping hot.

It seems strange that in that part of France that borders on the Mediterranean, with its vast numbers of all sorts of fishes, a favorite article of food should be salted and dried codfish imported from Norway!

The great specialty of the Nice region is *stockfisch,* which starts out as a dried salt codfish, stiff as a board, and ends up as a delectable stew. The average tourist never samples it, because Nice restaurateurs think it is too plebeian for foreign clients, but they make it for themselves. The *stockfisch* is soaked for 3 days in water. Then it is made into a savory stew with olive oil, potatoes, onions, tomatoes, leeks, garlic, sweet peppers, Italian black olives, and herbs.

Another salt cod favorite is *Brandade de Morue.* I believe that it originated in the province of Languedoc, which adjoins Provence, and it is often referred to as the "glory of Nîmes." But it is also a favorite in Mediterranean Provence. What it actually is is creamed codfish, but raised to the nth degree of deliciousness. Throughout my life I have always scorned the ordinary creamed codfish, but not *Brandade de Morue.* Here is the recipe, adapted from an old Provencal cookbook which I have mentioned before, *La Cuisinière Provençale,* by J. B. Reboul.

BRANDADE DE MORUE
(Creamed Codfish)

1 *lb. salt codfish*	*Juice ½ lemon*
Cold water	*Pinch grated nutmeg*
1 *cup lukewarm milk*	½ *clove garlic*
1 *cup lukewarm olive oil*	*Pinch finely minced lemon rind*
¼ *tsp. white pepper*	3 *tbsp. heavy cream*

Soak 1 pound salt codfish in cold water for at least 10 hours, changing the water twice. Drain, add enough cold water to cover the fish (or filets), and bring to the boiling point, then lower the flame, and let the cod simmer for about 15 minutes. Let fish cool, drain, and carefully remove all bones (you can also remove any skin, although in Provence they believe that the skin contributes to the flavor). Shred the fish very fine, or put it through the finest blade of a food chopper. Now, the following directions are a literal translation from *La Cuisinière Provençale*.

"Place the codfish in a casserole and place it on the corner of the stove, in order that it retains a gentle heat. Have some milk in a small casserole beside it, and in another olive oil, both lukewarm." (A cup of each is about right.)

"Commence by putting a tablespoon of olive oil in the codfish, working it strongly with a wooden spoon, and crushing the pieces of codfish against the sides of the casserole. Add from time to time and little by little spoonfuls of olive oil and milk alternately, but always stirring strongly with the spoon." (It is from this that the word *brandade* takes its name—"to stir vigorously.")

"When your preparation arrives at the creamy state, when it is impossible to distinguish a single piece of fish, your *brandade* is finished." But not quite, for seasonings are to be added.

Put the casserole containing the creamy codfish in a larger container holding simmering water. Stir in about ¼ teaspoon white pepper, the juice of half a lemon, a pinch grated nutmeg, a half clove garlic finely minced, a little lemon rind finely minced, and about 3 tablespoons warmed, heavy cream.

Serve the *Brandade de Morue* over triangles of French bread that have been sautéed in fine olive oil or butter. Baked potatoes are an ideal accompaniment, along with a chilled dry white wine, preferably a Chablis, or an Emerald Dry.

One of the most delicious fish dishes we have ever had was in Würzburg, Mrs. Wood and I had spent the latter part of the morning visiting a wonderful old castle high above the river. It was a sunny day, but the wind had a chill in it, and we were very happy to motor to an old and picturesque restaurant called the Schiffbäuerin, where the director of the tourist bureau, Dr.

Schneider, joined Mrs. Wood, Herr Trucksess, our most erudite guide, and me for luncheon.

Dr. Schneider had ordered the main course, which was carp cooked in beer. But before sitting down at the table we went into a room adjoining the kitchen, where there were huge tanks of water, in which were swimming two or three varieties of fish. We were handed a net, and we each removed a live carp, which threshed about in the net vigorously. Then we returned to our table, had a cup of delicious soup, and finally the carp came to the table. And what a dish it was. This is the way it was prepared, in typical German style.

CARP FILETS COOKED IN BEER

2 lbs. carp filets	1 bay leaf, crumbled
1 oz. butter	¼ tsp. dried thyme
2 medium onions	5 peppercorns
2 small carrots	Pinch ground cloves
Grated rind 1 lemon	1 tsp. paprika
Salt	½ cup gingersnap crumbs
Freshly ground pepper	Dark beer
	Butter

Have ready 2 pounds carp filets. In a skillet lightly sauté in about an ounce of butter 2 medium onions, finely minced, and 2 small carrots, finely minced. When onions become limp but not colored take out minced vegetables and spread over the bottom of a baking dish. Distribute over the vegetables the grated rind of a lemon. Season the carp filets with salt and freshly ground pepper to taste. Sprinkle over vegetables 1 crumbled bay leaf, ¼ teaspoon dried thyme, a few peppercorns, lightly crushed, a pinch ground cloves, 1 teaspoon paprika, and about ½ cup gingersnap crumbs. Then lay the carp filets over the bed of vegetables and seasonings, dot with butter, and moisten with just enough dark beer to cover them. Put in a 400-degree oven and bake for about 25 minutes.

To serve, drain the filets carefully and arrange them on a hot serving platter. Pour the cooking liquor through a sieve, heat it up, add a little butter, and pour over the carp filets. With this serve new potatoes covered with butter and parsley.

Switzerland, with its countless lakes and rivers, is a gastronomic haven for anyone who loves fresh water fish. In the areas along the Rhine delicious salmon is the specialty. In the vicinity of the lakes of Lucerne and Zug, giant pike are the favored fish. In Eastern Switzerland the lake of Constance and the Rhine River offer inexhaustible supplies of fresh trout, grayling and salmon. Lake Geneva is famed for its perch, and it is impossible to travel along the shores of the lake without being tempted to enter one of the enticing little inns and sample the fried perch, or filet of perch *au Madère*.

One of the most delightful of Lausanne's many restaurants is the Château d'Ouchy, in the Ouchy district on the shores of Lake Geneva. A great outdoor dining terrace faces a lovely park, and the decor, service and food is comparable to similar Parisian dining places. One night we had a simple, yet noble entree of fried salmon.

FRIED SALMON OUCHY

3 *lbs. salmon*	3 *oz. butter*
Salt and pepper	*Butter*
Dried basil	2 *shredded onions*
Flour	*Dry white wine*

For 6 servings have 3 pounds salmon. After cleaning and scaling the fish, cut it into slices ½ inch thick, dry with a clean cloth (do not soak or wash), rub with salt and pepper, sprinkle over the slices a little dried basil, and dredge in flour. Lay the slices side by side in a large, heavy skillet containing about 3 ounces butter, and fry quickly until slices are golden brown on both sides, turning once carefully to keep slices whole. When the fish begins to come away from the bones arrange the slices on a serving platter and keep in a warm place. Add a little more butter to what is left in the skillet, and fry 1 or 2 shredded onions in it. When onions are very lightly browned pour them over the fish slices. Deglaze the skillet with a little dry white wine, and pour that over the fish and onions, and serve with parsley potatoes.

On our first night in Rothenburg, a city that is an unspoiled fragment of medieval Germany, and midway along the "Romantic Road" that runs from Würtzburg to Augsburg, we had dinner in a very old restaurant, the Glocken Weinstube. There I had a delicious salmon steak poached in beer. This is an approximation of the German recipe.

SALMON STEAKS POACHED IN BEER

3 *lbs. salmon steaks*	2 *tbsp. butter*
1 *small onion*	3 *tbsp. flour*
4 *peppercorns*	½ *cup heavy cream*
1 *small bay leaf*	*Pinch cayenne pepper*
2 *whole cloves*	*Salt and pepper*
Beer	3 *tbsp. minced parsley*

Place about 3 pounds salmon steaks in a shallow, well buttered roasting pan. Add 1 small onion, sliced, 4 whole black peppers, a small bay leaf, 2 whole cloves, and enough beer to barely, but completely, cover the salmon. Simmer very gently on top of stove, or in a 325-degree oven, until salmon is done, about 20 to 30 minutes, depending on thickness of steaks. Remove salmon carefully to warm serving plates, reserving the cooking liquid.

Melt 2 tablespoons butter in a heavy pan and cook until butter is golden brown. Then add 3 tablespoons flour and blend well. Next add 1½ cups of liquid in which salmon was poached, bring to a boil, and cook, stirring constantly, until smooth and thickened. Finally, add ½ cup heavy cream, a generous pinch cayenne pepper, and salt and white pepper to taste. Heat, strain into a sauce boat, and sprinkle with 3 tablespoons finely minced parsley. Serve at once over the salmon steaks.

Halibut along with swordfish are often called the "beefsteak of the sea." Both have a firm, white, flaky-textured meat with a delicious flavor and a minimum of bones.

I enjoyed halibut twice during our trip through the British Isles. The first time was at the Blue Boar Hotel in Cambridge, where the steaks were grilled with an accompaniment of dry vermouth and little green onions.

BROILED HALIBUT STEAKS

4 *halibut steaks*	*Little green onions*
Fresh lime juice	*Salt*
3 *oz. melted butter*	*Freshly ground pepper*
1 *cup dry vermouth*	*Fine breadcrumbs*
	Grated Parmesan cheese

Place 4 halibut steaks in a broiling pan and sprinkle with fresh lime juice. Combine 3 ounces melted butter and 1 cup dry vermouth, and heat, but do not allow to boil, and then pour over steaks. Sprinkle steaks generously with finely chopped little green onions (bulbs and tops), and salt and freshly ground pepper to taste. Place pan under broiler, about 3 to 4 inches from source of heat, and cook about 10 minutes. Once or twice during latter part of cooking baste carefully, so that chopped onions will not be washed off surface of steaks. Then turn steaks, season as before with chopped onions, salt and pepper, and broil for about 5 to 6 minutes, or until lightly browned, again basting with vermouth-butter after seasonings have been "set" by heat. Then remove from broiler, sprinkle steaks with fine breadcrumbs mixed equally with grated Parmesan cheese, return to broiler and let cook 2 to 3 minutes more.

The Stork Hotel in Liverpool has an imaginative chef. His treatment of halibut steaks was with a ripe olive sauce, and they were delectable.

HALIBUT STEAKS, RIPE OLIVE SAUCE

2 *lbs. halibut steaks*	*Dash pepper*
¼ *cup melted butter*	¼ *cup melted butter*
1 *tsp. salt*	¼ *cup pitted ripe olives*
1 *tsp. paprika*	1 *tbsp. chopped parsley*
	2 *tsp. lemon juice*

Get 2 pounds halibut steaks, cut in pieces to serve 6. Combine ¼ cup melted butter, 1 teaspoon each salt and paprika, and a dash ground pepper. Place steaks on a greased broiler pan about

3 inches from source of heat. Brush steaks with seasoned butter and broil 4 to 8 minutes, or until lightly browned. Baste with seasoned butter and turn carefully. Brush turned side with seasoned butter and broil 5 to 8 minutes longer, or until fish flakes easily with a fork. Serve immediately with the ripe olive sauce, which is made as follows: combine ¼ cup each of melted butter and pitted ripe olives, sliced crosswise, 1 tablespoon chopped parsley, and 2 teaspoons lemon juice. Heat well, and pour over steaks.

5 ⚬ SHELLFISH

Lobsters are plentiful in most parts of Europe. But before some purist writes a nasty letter to the editors, I'd better elucidate.

The true lobster is found only in the waters of the North and Middle Atlantic and the Northern seas of Europe. It has five pairs of legs, of which the first pair are enormous pincers, or claws. One is heavier than the other, with blunt teeth, which is called a crusher. The small one is called a cutter.

The spiny lobster, also known as the rock lobster and crayfish, closely resembles the true lobster, but does not have the two large pincer claws, and the principal meat is in the tail. The French name for this crustacean is *langouste*. The French name for the true lobster is *homard*.

You'll find the true lobster in the British Isles. Inasmuch as the waters around Scotland are very cold, the Scotch lobster is highly prized among connoisseurs. In France the Brittany coast furnishes both the homard and the langouste. While as a rule the Mediterranean is not noted for its shellfish, one can find excellent langouste in many places. That part of the province of Languedoc which borders on the Mediterranean is noted for its lobsters. The finest lobsters of Germany come from Helgoland, in the North Sea.

With its vast coastline and hundreds of miles of bays and inlets, Ireland is almost unsurpassed with respect to shellfish. In the cold salt waters off its coast are to be found lobsters, oysters, crabs, scallops, and prawns. In fact, Dublin Bay prawns are famous all over Europe.

We stayed at the lovely Old Ground Hotel in Ennis, the capital of County Clare, for several days, not only to catch up on my writing, but to drink in the beauties of this beautiful Irish countryside. On one of our trips we drove over to Liscannor Bay, which is noted for its lobsters. In the little fishing village of Quilty we bought a beautiful lobster from one of the fishing boats and then went to a charming little restaurant in Ennistymon, 2 miles away and had it cooked for us. When it was served, the owner said, "This we call Quilty Lobster Celestine. We're known all over County Clare for it."

QUILTY LOBSTER CELESTINE

2–3 lb. lobster	Dash Tabasco sauce
2 medium onions	3 cups hot milk
2 shallots (or little green onions)	2 oz. dry sherry
	1 oz. butter
4 mushrooms	2 oz. flour
3 oz. butter	2 cups hot milk
¼ tsp. dried tarragon	1 cup puréed spinach
2 oz. flour	2 egg yolks
¼ tsp. dry mustard	Salt and pepper
4 oz. cream, whipped	

Boil a 2–3 pound lobster for 20 minutes in salted water. Split lengthwise, remove meat from tail and claws, and cut meat into 1-inch pieces. Save the coral. Sauté 2 medium onions, chopped, 2 chopped shallots (or little green onions), and 4 mushrooms, diced, in 3 ounces butter to which ¼ teaspoon dried tarragon has been added, until vegetables are golden brown. Sprinkle in 2 ounces flour, ¼ teaspoon dry mustard, and a dash Tabasco, and stir to make a smooth paste. Add 3 cups hot milk, and stir until thick and smooth. Add lobster meat, lobster coral, and 2 ounces dry sherry. Set lobster shells on rock salt on a tray, and fill with lobster mixture.

For the sauce melt 1 ounce butter, stir in 2 ounces flour, and when smooth add 2 cups hot milk and cook for 15 minutes. Then add 1 cup puréed spinach, 2 egg yolks, season with salt and pepper, and blend well. Then fold in 4 ounces cream, whipped. Cover lobster in shells with this sauce, brown in a 350-degree oven, and serve on dishes with sautéed potatoes.

Another place we visited was Lisdoonvarna, the premier spa and health resort of Ireland. It is only five miles from the sea, and lobster is a favorite delectable in the hotels. This dish we had there is truly Irish, and is called Creamed Lobster Pegeen.

CREAMED LOBSTER PEGEEN

2 oz. butter	3 egg yolks
½ lb. cooked lobster meat	Salt and pepper
3 oz. Irish whisky	1 tsp. chopped chives
½ pint fresh cream	Mashed potatoes
1 tbsp. chopped parsley	

Place 2 ounces butter in a hot pan. When sizzling hot add ½ pound cooked lobster meat cut in large pieces, and thoroughly heat. Then pour over lobster meat 3 ounces Irish whisky and light. When flame dies out cover and keep lobster meat warm.

Beat together ½ pint fresh cream and 3 egg yolks, put in a saucepan, and heat slowly until it thickens slightly, stirring constantly. Then add lobster meat and juices and heat well without letting mixture boil. Add salt and pepper to taste, a teaspoon chopped chives, and a tablespoon chopped parsley. To serve, pipe hot mashed potatoes around a hot serving platter, and fill the center with the creamed lobster.

At the Great Southern Hotel in Galway we had a third delicious Irish lobster dish called Stuffed Cleggan Lobster. This gets its name from a little fishing village near Galway.

STUFFED CLEGGAN LOBSTER

4 small live lobsters	1 tbsp. dry mustard
Butter	Pinch cayenne pepper
1 pint Béchamel sauce	Grated Parmesan cheese

Split 4 small live lobsters, clean thoroughly, butter them, and broil until cooked. Remove cooked lobster meat from shells and keep hot.

To 1 pint Béchamel sauce add 1 tablespoon dry mustard and a pinch cayenne pepper. Line lobster shells with part of this mixture, then place thin slices cooked lobster meat in the shells. Cover the lobster meat with remaining sauce and sprinkle with a thick coating of grated cheese. Place whole in a hot oven until well heated, then serve.

On that fabulous strip of land bordering the Mediterranean from Marseille to Menton, known as the Côte d'Azur, the *"Fruits de Mer"* (seafood) reign supreme. I don't believe there is any spot in the world that has such a variety of magnificent gastronomic creations built around fish and shellfish.

Langouste is the most plentiful and popular of the shellfish, and most restaurants serve it grilled. But there is one restaurant on the Côte d'Azur that specializes in my favorite lobster dish, *Homard* (or *Langouste*) *à l'Américaine*. It is the Bijou Plage at Juan-les Pines, about 5 miles east of Cannes. The way it is done on the Côte d'Azur differs from the recipe that appears in my first cookbook, *With a Jug of Wine*, and I'd be hard put to decide which method I like best.

LANGOUSTE À L'AMÉRICAINE

1 *live lobster*	¼ *tsp. dried tarragon*
2 *tbsp. olive oil*	1 *bay leaf*
2 *tbsp. butter*	1 *oz. brandy*
1 *small onion*	*Dry white wine*
1 *small carrot*	1 *tbsp. butter*
1 *clove garlic*	1 *tbsp. flour*
2 *tomatoes*	1 *tsp. lemon juice*
1 *tbsp. fresh parsley*	2 *tbsp. heavy cream*

Split a live lobster in half lengthwise. Remove and discard the sac and intestinal tube, but reserve the coral. Separate the tail from the body, cut the body in two, and cut through the tail where the separations are marked. If your crustacean is a lobster, remove and break the claws.

In a large skillet heat 2 tablespoons each olive oil and butter. When hot add lobster pieces and sauté lightly until shells are red, turning lobster so that the flesh will actually come in contact with the fat. This should take about 10 minutes. Then remove lobster pieces to a separate plate.

To fat remaining in skillet add 1 small onion and 1 small carrot, both finely chopped, 1 clove garlic, finely minced and crushed, 2 tomatoes, peeled, seeded, and chopped, 1 tablespoon fresh parsley, chopped, ¼ teaspoon dried tarragon, and 1 bay leaf, crumbled. Let all simmer for 5 minutes, then return lobster pieces to skillet. Pour over all 1 ounce warmed brandy and set alight. When flame dies down add to contents of skillet enough dry white wine to cover lobster pieces, and salt and pepper to taste. Cover skillet and let contents simmer for ½ hour.

Remove lobster pieces to a serving dish. To the sauce in the skillet blend in lobster coral creamed with 1 tablespoon each butter and flour. Correct seasoning if necessary, and add 1 teaspoon lemon juice and 2 tablespoons heavy cream. Heat through, then strain sauce over lobster pieces. Serve with flaky boiled rice.

Along the Côte d'Azur of France, from Nice to Menton, there are three roads. The Basse Corniche runs along the Mediterranean Coast practically at sea level. The Moyen Corniche is higher, with a succession of amazing views, and the Grande Corniche is the highest, running on ledges and cornices cut out of the rock on Alpine slopes. This is the road built by Napoleon on the site of the ancient Aurelian Way.

On the Moyen Corniche, about midway between Nice and Menton is the quaint village of Eze, built like an eagle's eyrie on a needle of rock, looking down on the sea 1,300 feet below. The streets are so narrow and twisting that automobiles cannot enter the village. But you can park your car at the entrance to the village, and visit the fabulous exotic gardens, the ancient church, and the breath-taking panoramic views.

There is a charming restaurant, La Chèvre d'Or, located on a picturesque site dominating the sea. When we stopped there we had one of their langouste specialties, which was magnificent.

LANGOUSTE PROVENÇALE

2 *cloves garlic*	2 *tbsp. butter*
2 *tbsp. olive oil*	2 *onions*
¼ *lb. butter*	½ *cup sliced mushrooms*
Freshly ground pepper	2 *tsp. lemon juice*
4 *bay leaves*	4 *small ripe tomatoes*
3 *pinches dried tarragon*	1 *tbsp. chopped parsley*
2 *live langoustes (or lobsters)*	2 *oz. cognac*

French bread with garlic butter

In a heavy skillet put 2 crushed cloves garlic, 2 tablespoons of the best olive oil, ¼ pound butter, a sprinkling of freshly ground pepper, 4 bay leaves, and 3 pinches dried tarragon. Cook briskly for 5 minutes, then discard the garlic.

Split 2 live langoustes (or lobsters), remove the sac from back of head, and, if lobster, crack the claws well. Put the split sides down in the hot seasoned fat and cook briskly for 12 minutes. Then remove lobsters, and extract the meat. If there are claws, extract the meat from them and cut into about 1-inch dice, and cut remaining meat the same way. Discard shells.

Into the pan juices add 2 more tablespoons butter, 2 medium-sized onions (minced) ½ cup sliced fresh mushrooms, 2 teaspoons lemon juice, the pulp of 4 small ripe tomatoes put through a sieve to remove skin and seeds, and 1 tablespoon chopped parsley. Stir and sauté gently until thick and rich. Discard bay leaves and add lobster meat. Heat 2 ounces cognac, set it alight, and pour over contents of skillet. Mix all gently, and when flames die out serve the lobster with long, thin, slabs of French bread which have been spread with garlic butter (or a commercial garlic spread) on one side, then grilled on the buttered side.

On our way from Dijon to the Côte d'Azur, we of course stopped at the incredible city of Avignon, which is dominated by the 14th century Palace of the Popes. For some seventy years the Holy See was located here on the banks of the Rhone River, and during that time two palaces were built. The size and height of the palaces were amazing, and we spent hours touring what we could of them.

We had a delicious meal at the Lucullus, a two-star restaurant on the Rue de la République, not too far from the Palace of the Popes. We had a langouste specialty which was wonderful—a sort of Lobster Thermidor.

LANGOUSTE À LA CRÈME

2 1½-lb. langoustes	1 tsp. grated onion
4 tbsp. olive oil	Dash celery salt
⅓ cup sliced mushrooms	3 tbsp. flour
Dash paprika	1 cup light cream
¼ tsp. dry mustard	½ cup dry sherry
1 tbsp. chopped parsley	3 oz. Roquefort cheese
Salt and pepper	

Split 2 1½-pound live langoustes, removing the sac at the back of the head.

Put 4 tablespoons olive oil in a large skillet, heat it, and then put the langoustes in, split side down. Cover and cook slowly for about 10 to 12 minutes. Remove langoustes from skillet, remove meat from the bodies, reserving the shells, which should be kept warm.

To the oil the langoustes were cooked in (adding a little more if necessary) add ⅓ cup sliced fresh mushrooms, and sauté until browned (about 6 minutes). Then add dash paprika, ¼ teaspoon dry mustard, 1 tablespoon chopped parsley, 1 teaspoon grated onion, and a dash celery salt. Mix well, then add 3 tablespoons flour, and blend well. Next gradually add 1 cup light cream and ½ cup dry sherry, and cook until mixture is thickened, stirring constantly. Then add the meat from the langouste, diced, to the sauce, and season to taste with salt and pepper.

Fill the shells with langouste mixture. Sprinkle over top of each filled shell crumbled Roquefort cheese (you'll need about 3 ounces). Bake in a 450-degree oven for 10 minutes, then serve, garnished with parsley.

In Normandy, the inevitable Calvados, cream, and butter all contribute to make a luscious lobster dish.

LOBSTER NORMANDY

3 *1½-lb. lobsters*	3 *small carrots*
3 *tbsp. butter*	1 *bay leaf*
4 *oz. Calvados (or applejack)*	1½ *tsp. dried tarragon*
1 *cup dry white wine*	2 *tbsp. chopped parsley*
3 *tomatoes*	2 *tbsp. heavy cream*
2 *onions*	1 *tbsp. butter*

Split three 1½-pound lobsters, clean, and put them in a heavy skillet in which 3 tablespoons butter have been heated. Cook until lobsters turn red, then pour over them 4 ounces Calvados or applejack, and light it. When flames die out add 1 cup dry white wine, 3 chopped tomatoes, 2 chopped onions, 3 small carrots, diced, 1 bay leaf, 1½ teaspoons dried tarragon, and 2 tablespoons chopped fresh parsley. Simmer for about 20 minutes, then remove lobsters. While sauce is reducing extract the claw meat (if an eastern lobster) and add it to the body shell. When sauce has reached a good consistency strain it (rubbing solids through) and add 2 tablespoons heavy cream and 1 tablespoon butter (combined with coral, if any), check seasoning, then divide sauce among and over the 6 lobster halves. Put halves under broiler until tops begin to color, then serve to 6.

They have a most unusual way of serving lobster at Au Vert Bocage, a charming restaurant in Paris. It is brought to the table in a veritable *vert bocage,* a green thicket of shrubbery which in this case is lettuce and watercress. You have no idea of the eye appeal—and the taste appeal!

LOBSTER MEAT AU VERT BOCAGE

1 *lb. uncooked lobster meat*	3 *tbsp. dry sherry*
Flour	*Tabasco sauce*
2 *eggs*	2 *whole cloves*
½ *lb. butter*	1 *bay leaf*
1 *pint heavy cream*	*Pinch ground mace*
½ *cup chili sauce*	*Salt*
1 *tbsp. brandy*	*Lettuce*
	Watercress

Cut 1 pound uncooked lobster meat into ½ inch dice, dip in flour, then in 2 eggs, lightly beaten, and sauté in ½ pound butter until pieces are golden brown. Reserve and keep hot.

In the top of a double boiler combine 1 pint heavy cream, ½ cup chili sauce, the lobster coral (if meat comes from live lobsters), 1 tablespoon brandy, 3 tablespoons dry sherry, dash of Tabasco sauce, 2 whole cloves, 1 bay leaf, pinch ground mace, and salt to taste. Cook over hot water in bottom of double boiler for about 5 minutes, stirring constantly until mixture is smooth. It should have the consistency of heavy cream.

To serve, make a bed of crisp lettuce on bottom of an oblong casserole. Lay sautéed lobster pieces on lettuce bed, and decorate each end of casserole with watercress, which has been tucked underneath the lettuce to give the effect of growing watercress. Spoon hot sauce over lobster meat and serve *immediately*.

In the chapter on soups I detailed the delectable *Bisque de Homard* of Jules Petit, *chef de cuisine* at Drouant's, one of the finest seafood restaurants in Paris. Here is his recipe for lobster. It is very simple, yet utterly delicious. It calls for lobster, but langouste can be used.

LOBSTER DROUANT

1 *live lobster (or langouste)*	1 *cup Béchamel sauce*
Salt and pepper	1 *tsp. dry mustard*
Butter	*Few grains cayenne pepper*
Grated Parmesan cheese	

Split a live lobster in half lengthwise and remove the sac and intestinal tract, which are discarded. Season with salt and pepper, dot each half with butter and broil under a not too hot flame for about 15 minutes. Then remove meat from lobster and claws, and cut into slices. Reserve shells.

Make 1 cup Béchamel sauce (or use 1 cup rich cream sauce) and blend into it 1 teaspoon dry mustard and few grains cayenne pepper. Spread a thin layer of sauce in bottom of the 2 half shells of lobster. Fill shells with sliced lobster meat, cover with sauce, sprinkle with grated Parmesan cheese, and brown in a 400-degree oven until cheese is melted.

The langouste, or spiny lobster, is the one most frequently found in Italy. The Italians seem to prefer their langoustes put live into boiling salted water, and when cooked, served with butter or oil and lemon.

One night in Naples we went across the street from our hotel to the minute rocky island in the Bay of Naples on which the Castel dell' Ovo is located. The island is connected to the shore by a short pier, and fronting on the tiny harbor of Santa Lucia are three or four famous restaurants, with outdoor dining pavilions. We had dinner at one of them, Ciro's, and I had a very delicious lobster dish called *Aragosta alla Florio*. The head waiter spoke excellent English, and obtained the recipe for me.

ARAGOSTA ALLA FLORIO
(Lobster with Marsala)

2 *large boiled langoustes*	*Dash paprika*
(*or lobsters*)	⅛ *tsp. dry mustard*
¼ *lb. sliced mushrooms*	½ *tsp. salt*
3 *tbsp. butter*	1 *tbsp. chopped parsley*
3 *tbsp. flour*	¼ *cup Florio Marsala wine*
1½ *cups milk*	¼ *cup grated Parmesan cheese*

Sauté ¼ pound sliced fresh mushrooms in 3 tablespoons butter until tender (about 7 minutes), then remove from skillet. Blend 3 tablespoons flour into butter, then slowly add 1½ cups milk and cook until thickened, stirring constantly. Remove meat from 2 large boiled langoustes or lobsters and cut up (save the tail shells). Mix lobster meat, diced, mushrooms, dash paprika, ⅛ teaspoon dry mustard, ½ teaspoon salt, and 1 tablespoon chopped parsley, and stir into sauce. Slowly add ¼ cup Florio dry Marsala wine and blend well. Spoon mixture into lobster shells, sprinkle with ¼ cup grated Parmesan cheese, and bake in 400-degree oven until cheese begins to brown. Serves 4.

Opinions differ as to the quality of oysters in Europe, but not in England. There are two varieties that are marvelous—Colchesters and Whitstables. The two Mr. Bentleys, who run one of London's best seafood restaurants, are not only restaurateurs, they are also oyster farmers, and sell their produce all over England. The best, of course, are kept for their oyster bar, which is visited regularly by connoisseurs.

France has three principal varieties of oysters—Portugaises, Marennes, and Bellons. These latter are the only ones that come close to the American oyster. There are a great many little bistros that make a specialty of selling oysters to passers by; the oysters are stacked in wicker baskets on the sidewalks.

Strangely enough, in most parts of France (except Normandy) the idea of cooking oysters seems to be considered preposterous. An unusual feature of some restaurants is that you can be served a plate of assorted oysters on the half shell, and this is a very popular hors d'oeuvre.

We only had oysters once in Italy, and really they were not technically oysters at all, but *Datteri*. They are shaped like a date stone, and are very delicious. They were served to us at the Biblioteca Valle in Rome. They were on the half shell, covered with a piquant bit of sauce, and placed under the broiler. They should not be missed by a Rome visitor.

I only picked up three worthwhile oyster recipes in Europe, one in France, one in England, and one in Ireland. They are all excellent.

OYSTERS PERNOD

24 *oysters in shells*	½ *onion*
Garlic	4 *slices bacon*
Pernod	2 *tsp. butter*
½ *green pepper*	1 *tsp. Roquefort cheese*
1 *tsp. Worcestershire sauce*	

Remove 24 oysters from their shells, lightly rub the deep side of each half shell with a cut clove garlic, deposit a drop of Pernod in each shell, and then replace the oysters.

Chop half a seeded green pepper and half an onion very fine. Take 4 slices bacon, cut each slice into thirds, then halve each third lengthwise (making 24 pieces). In a saucepan melt about 2 teaspoons butter with a teaspoon Roquefort cheese, and then add 1 teaspoon Worcestershire sauce.

Place a piece of bacon over each oyster in its half shell, sprinkle the onion and green pepper mixture over the bacon-topped oysters, and dribble a bit of the butter-cheese mixture over each oyster. Place oysters in half shells on salt-filled baking sheet and place under broiler for about 10 minutes, or until bacon crisps. Serve immediately to 4.

This recipe from England has a most unusual combination of flavors.

BAKED OYSTERS WITH WALNUT BUTTER PASTE

24 *oysters in shells*	½ *tsp. dried chervil*
½ *cup sweet butter*	3 *tsp. brandy*
½ *cup finely ground walnuts*	*Pinch cayenne pepper*
1 *clove garlic*	*Grated Parmesan cheese*

Cream together ½ cup sweet butter, ½ cup finely ground walnuts, 1 clove garlic, finely minced, ½ teaspoon dried chervil, 3 teaspoons brandy, and a pinch cayenne pepper. This should all be blended into a smooth paste.

Set 24 oysters in their half shells on a baking sheet filled with hot rock salt. Cover each oyster with about 2 teaspoons of the butter-walnut paste. Sprinkle oysters with grated Parmesan cheese and bake in a 450-degree oven for about 5 minutes, or until lightly browned. Serve immediately to 4.

Where else but in Ireland would you find a dish called Oysters Emerald? And where else in Ireland would you find almost anything prepared any better than in the kitchens of the Shannon Free Airport? I wandered into the kitchens two or three times and talked to Chef André Fernon, and it's amazing what can be turned out there. But back to Oysters Emerald from the Emerald Isle.

OYSTERS EMERALD

6 *oysters*	1 *tsp. chopped chives*
¼ *pint Mornay sauce*	1 *tbsp. mixed chopped parsley,*
2 *oz. freshly cooked spinach*	*dill, and chervil*
Dry white wine	1½ *oz. grated Parmesan cheese*

Mix the Mornay sauce and the spinach. Remove oysters from shells and gently poach them in a little wine until edges begin to curl. Mix the chives, parsley, dill and chervil (if you have the fresh dill and chervil, use it; if not use ¼ teaspoon each dried dill and chervil, and make up balance of tablespoon with chopped fresh parsley) through the cheese sauce–spinach mixture. Put a little of the sauce in each shell. Place oysters back in shells and put a little of sauce over them. Sprinkle the oysters with grated cheese, and place under broiler until sauce on top becomes lightly brown. Serve with lemon wedges.

Dublin Bay prawns are famous wherever Irishmen gather, and they are indeed the most succulent of morsels. The second outstanding dinner we had at the Gresham Hotel in Dublin featured Prawns Provençale with a lobster sauce, and the blended flavors were exquisite.

PRAWNS PROVENÇALE
Lobster Sauce

1 *cup fish stock*	1 *tbsp. flour*
1 *cup cream*	2 *tbsp. lobster coral*
1 *tbsp. butter*	½ *cup Cognac*
3 *tbsp. butter*	6 *large tomatoes*
1 *medium onion*	2 *tbsp. chives*
6 *large mushrooms*	2 *tbsp. butter*
1 *small clove garlic*	48 *shelled cooked prawns*
1 *cup of the lobster sauce*	4 *tbsp. butter*
1 *cup cream*	*Cooked rice*

Make the lobster sauce first. In a saucepan place 1 cup each fish stock and cream. Bring to a boil, and then add 1 tablespoon each flour and butter creamed together. Whisk all until smooth and creamy, and then add 2 tablespons lobster coral and ½ cup Cognac. Blend well, and keep warm.

In a large pot or saucepan put 3 tablespoons butter, 1 medium-sized onion finely chopped, 6 large fresh mushrooms, sliced, and a small clove garlic, crushed. Cook until onions and mushrooms are tender. Then add 1 cup of the lobster sauce, which has been passed through a fine sieve, 1 cup cream, 6 large tomatoes, peeled, seeded, and sliced finely, 2 tablespoons finely chopped chives, and 2 tablespoons butter. Whisk lightly to blend, and keep hot.

Preheat 4 dozen shelled, deveined, cooked prawns in 4 tablespoons butter, and then arrange them on a bed of flaky cooked rice. Cover all with the sauce, and serve very hot to 4.

One of the most fabulous meals I have ever had in my life was served in the Bali Restaurant at the beach resort of Scheveningen, near The Hague. The Bali is a large, rambling structure with a number of dining rooms, and they specialize in Javanese food.

Our luncheon was their famous *Rijsttafel,* or rice table. First you help yourself to lovely, flaky rice. Added to this is a little bit of soup, called *Sajor.* Next you serve yourself from the different dishes offered and arrange the food around your plate. Then you take a spoonful of rice every time and take some of this or that with it; in this way you can best become acquainted with the different tastes.

I counted over forty different dishes on the huge serving table beside our luncheon table—meats, vegetables, poultry, little omelets, boiled eggs in a special sauce, peanut cakes, peanut sauces, peanuts, fried coconut, and so on and so on and so on. One of the dishes was called Monkey Hair, but it was only infinitesimal slivers of dried meat.

Everything was absolutely delicious, and we ate and ate and ate until we could eat no more. It was an unforgettable experience.

Another day when we were touring Scheveningen we stopped at a little restaurant for a bite of lunch, and we had a simple yet most piquant shrimp dish. In Dutch it was called merely shrimps over rice.

SHRIMPS OVER RICE

12 oz. bottle stale beer	½ bay leaf
¼ cup chopped onions	1½ lbs. raw srimp, shelled
1 tsp. salt	2 tbsp. butter
Sprig parsley	2 tbsp. flour
2 slices lemon	8 oz. can tomato sauce
½ tsp. sugar	

Empty a 12-ounce can or bottle of stale beer in a saucepan and add ¼ cup chopped onion, 1 teaspoon salt, sprig parsley, 2 slices lemon and ½ bay leaf. Bring to a boil, then add 1½ pounds raw shrimp, shelled and cleaned. Simmer for 5 minutes, remove shrimp, strain the liquid and reserve it.

Melt 2 tablespoons butter in a separate pan, blend in 2 tablespoons flour, then gradually add an 8-ounce can tomato sauce, ½ teaspoon sugar, the cooked shrimp, and strained liquid. Bring to a boil, stirring constantly. Serve over cooked rice to 4.

French-fried, or deep-fried shrimps have been a culinary favorite for a long time. The Japanese excel in this method of cooking shrimp, and the Chinese are not far behind. But I don't believe anyone can improve on the Deep Fried Prawns Thomand that I had at the restaurant at the Shannon Free Airport. "It's the beer in the batter that does the trick," I was told.

DEEP FRIED PRAWNS THOMAND

2 lbs. prawns	1 tbsp. melted butter
Salted water	Salt and pepper
12 slices lean bacon	1 tsp. dry mustard
2 eggs, separated	6 oz. sieved flour
1 12-oz. bottle beer	Kettle hot fat

Cook the prawns in boiling salted water. Lift off tails, shell and devein. Roll each prawn in half a slice of raw lean bacon, and secure with a toothpick.

Make the batter as follows: First separate the eggs, then beat the yolks with the beer and melted butter. Add the salt and pepper to taste, and the mustard, and pour all on to the flour. Mix well to effect a nice consistency. Finally whip the whites of eggs until stiff, and fold them into the batter.

Dredge the prepared prawns with flour, shake them well, and dip them one at a time into the batter, and then into the pot or kettle of fat heated to deep frying temperature. Cook for 5 minutes, then drain on paper toweling. Serve with any piquant sauce, or a chilled mayonnaise to which sliced gherkins have been added.

I have always been very fond of scallops. My favorite recipe, *Coquille Saint Jacques,* is in my first cookbook, *With a Jug of Wine.* But in Paris I had luncheon with Georges Normand, one of the heads of the French Tourist Bureau, at Pierre's, across the street from Drouant's. Pierre's is a cut above a bistro. It is tremendously popular for luncheon among men whose offices are in the neighborhood of the Opera. Georges suggested fried scallops, saying that at Pierre's they were very simply prepared, but very delicious. And indeed they were.

FRIED SCALLOPS PIERRE

20 *small bay scallops*	*Pinch dried marjoram*
4 *tbsp. butter*	1 *tbsp. chopped parsley*
2 *tsp. shallots (or little green*	¼ *cup dry white wine*
onions)	*Salt*
Freshly ground pepper	

For 2 persons thoroughly wash 20 small bay scallops. Put them in a medium-sized heavy skillet, along with 4 tablespoons butter, 2 teaspoons finely chopped shallots (or little green onions), a pinch dried marjoram, 1 tablespoon finely chopped parsley, ¼ cup dry white wine, and salt and freshly ground pepper to taste. Cover skillet and cook gently for about 20 minutes, or until liquid is reduced to an almost syrupy consistency. Watch carefully toward end of cooking, for the sauce must not be too liquid, nor completely reduced. With the scallops serve a delicate dry white wine, and crusty French rolls.

The northern tip of Wales, bordering on the Irish Sea, is magnificent country. We were on our way early in the morning from Chester, and reveled in the beauty of the landscape and the sea. Suddenly we came upon a fantastic place, a white castle out of fairyland, stretching, with its eighteen battlemented towers, along a wooded hillside, 200 feet above the sea. And its name is as fantastic as its character—Gwrych Castle.

We spent a couple of hours going through the castle and grounds, and then we went on to Colwyn Bay, where we stopped for luncheon. The dish was a scallop pie, and it was very delicious, served hot from the kitchen.

SCALLOP PIE

Pastry dough
¼ cup grated Swiss cheese
1 cup ripe olives
1½ cups milk
1 onion
1 lb. scallops
Few sprigs parsley
½ tsp. salt
½ cup water

2 tbsp. chopped green pepper
½ cup chopped celery
2 tbsp. butter
3 eggs
2 tbsp. flour
1 tsp. salt
¼ tsp. dried thyme
½ cup grated Swiss cheese
2 tsp. Worcestershire sauce

First make a pastry dough to fill a 9-inch pie plate, adding ¼ cup grated Swiss cheese during mixing of dough. Cut 1 cup ripe olives into wedges, and combine 1½ cups milk with 1 finely minced onion. Drain 1 pound scallops, cut into bite-size pieces, set aside.

In a saucepan add a few sprigs parsley and ½ teaspoon salt to ½ cup water. When hot, simmer scallops about 5 minutes, then drain. Sauté 2 tablespoons chopped green pepper and ½ cup chopped celery in 2 tablespoons butter about 5 minutes. Beat 3 eggs with 2 tablespoons flour and 1 teaspoon salt until smooth. Then stir in onion-seasoned milk, ¼ teaspoon dried thyme, ½ cup grated Swiss cheese, 2 teaspoons Worcestershire sauce, the scallops, olives, and sautéed vegetables. Mix well, then pour into unbaked pie shell. Bake in a 375-degree oven 40 to 45 minutes, or until knife inserted in center comes out clean. This serves 6 to 7.

Shortly before Mrs. Wood and I left Paris Georges Normand of the French Tourist Bureau, took us to lunch at his very swank club on the Avenue de l'Opéra, le Cercle Républicain. Our first course was *Moules à la Marinière,* and I have never eaten better. This is the simple way they are done.

MOULES À LA MARINIÈRE

3½ *pints mussels in shells*	*Pinch dried thyme*
1 *medium-sized onion*	⅓ *bay leaf*
1 *shallot (or little green onion)*	*Pinch finely ground pepper*
5–6 *parsley sprigs*	8 *tbsp. dry white wine*
1½ *oz. butter*	

To "open" the mussels put 3½ pints (thoroughly washed and scrubbed) in a saucepan, add the medium-sized onion and shallot (or little green onion) both finely chopped, 5 to 6 parsley sprigs, a pinch dried thyme, ⅓ bay leaf, a pinch finely ground pepper, and 8 tablespoons dry white wine. Cover the pan tightly and put on a brisk fire. At the end of 2 minutes shake the pan well. Do this two or three times during the cooking, which should take only about 6 minutes in all. The mussels should then be cooked and their shells wide open. Add 1½ ounces butter, and serve them as they are, with their juices.

6 ⚡ MEAT

During our nearly two years of traveling about Europe we never had beef that could compare in any way with the beef of England and Scotland. There are differences of opinion as to the relative merits of English beef and Scotch beef, but I must confess I could not detect any great difference. The roasts and steaks are superb in texture and flavor, and usually they are cooked to perfection. The only complaint I had about the roast beef is that it was sliced too thin for me. I like a slice of roast beef at least a quarter of an inch thick; unless I directed otherwise it was sliced about an eighth of an inch thick.

In France the province of Normandy furnishes excellent beef, due largely to the lush grass upon which the cattle feed. Burgundy, however, is probably the best beef country in France, and the best quality of beef comes from the Charolais steers. More and more you will find "Charolais Beef" on the menus of the better French restaurants.

In Italy the finest beef comes from Tuscany. Nowhere else in Italy is the beef so full of flavor and so tender.

Switzerland and Germany, however, are not noted for their beef roasts and steaks. Veal predominates in Switzerland, as it does in Italy, and pork is the outstanding meat of Germany.

Some years ago I reviewed Madame Prunier's book, *Prunier's,* in the book section of the *Chicago Tribune.* It was a fascinating story of the establishment of the original Prunier's in Paris, of Madame Prunier's father, of the establishment of Prunier's in London, and it was filled with scores of unusual anecdotes about the great and famous who patronized both places.

Shortly after we had established ourselves at the Park Lane Hotel in London I went to the restaurant to pay my respects to Madame Prunier. In five minutes we had established an *entente cordiale,* and spent an hour talking about food, wine, restaurants, and similar things dear to both of our hearts. Before I left she insisted that Mrs. Wood and I have dinner at Prunier's, and asked me to include two or three gourmet friends. So a few nights later Mrs. Wood and I, Stanton Delaplane, his wife Susan, and his daughter Chris took a cab to Prunier's, and were seated at a beautifully appointed table in the smart and sophisticated red dining room.

Madame Prunier was a most gracious hostess and mistress of ceremonies, and selected a menu that was a gastronomic masterpiece. I had my favorite hors d'oeuvre, *Escargot de Bourgogne,* and Mrs. Wood had those tender and savory British oysters, Whitstables. The entree was *Tournedos Boston,* a specialty of Prunier's, and it was accompanied by cold asparagus with a vinaigrette sauce. The dessert was Crêpes Prunier's. A Batard Montrachet was served with the first course, a 1953 Château Petrus, with the tournedos, and Krug Champagne with the crêpes. Coffee and brandy followed.

The entree and dessert can easily be duplicated in any American home. The dessert will be detailed in the chapter on desserts, and here is the recipe for *Tournedos Boston* to serve 2.

TOURNEDOS BOSTON

12 *oysters in shells*	4 *tbsp. Hollandaise sauce*
Oyster liquor	2 *5-oz. tournedos of beef*
Juice ½ lemon	3 *oz. butter*
1 *tsp. butter*	*Salt*
1 *tbsp. Béchamel sauce*	*Freshly ground pepper*

Remove 12 oysters from their shells and put them in a saucepan with their own liquor, the juice of ½ lemon, and 1 teaspoon butter. Heat and poach oysters for a few minutes, or until edges begin to curl. Remove oysters, drain, and keep warm. Strain and reduce the liquid to about ¾ cup, or add a little hot salted water, if necessary, to make ¾ cup. Add 1 tablespoon Béchamel sauce and 4 tablespoons Hollandaise sauce.

Place two 5-ounce tournedos of beef (the heart of a filet

mignon) in a shallow pan in which 3 ounces butter have been melted. When butter is hot add the tournedos, and sauté about 3 minutes on one side. Sprinkle with salt and freshly ground pepper, turn, and sauté on other side for 3 minutes, repeating salt and pepper.

Place tournedos on hot plates and garnish each with 6 oysters. Then thickly coat each oyster-topped tournedos with the sauce. This serves 2.

This recipe for a delicious tournedos dish came from Chef Olanio, of Pan American Airways. This line is noted for the fine food it serves on its overseas flights, and many of the French specialties are masterpieces.

TOURNEDOS HELOISE

4 *tournedos of beef, each*	¾ *lb. fresh mushrooms*
1-*inch thick*	*Lemon juice*
4 *oz. butter*	2 *oz. butter*
8 *artichoke bottoms*	½ *cup heavy cream*
Butter	1 *tsp. meat glaze*
4 *slices Pâté de Foie Gras*	½ *tsp. flour*
1 *canned truffle*	3 *tbsp. water*
¼ *cup Madeira wine*	

In a heavy skillet heat 4 ounces butter, then sauté the tournedos about 3 to 4 minutes on each side. Around the edge of a round heated platter place the artichoke bottoms, which have been heated in butter, and place the sautéed tournedos on top. On each tournedos place a slice of pâté de foie gras, and top with a slice of truffle. Fill the center of platter with the sliced mushrooms which have been sprinkled with lemon juice, sautéed in butter for 6 to 7 minutes, and then heated with ½ cup heavy cream.

To the skillet in which tournedos were sautéed add 1 teaspoon meat glaze, ½ teaspoon flour, 3 tablespoons water, and ¼ cup Madeira wine. Blend this well until smooth, and simmer over low heat for 2 or 3 minutes. Then strain, and pour the Madeira wine sauce over tournedos. This serves 4.

Even though your wallet is stuffed with French bank notes of large denominations, and your Dun & Bradstreet rating is A-1, don't sell the Parisian bistros short. This may be heresy, but we had more fun, and practically as good eating, in the bistros as we did in the expensive restaurants and hotels.

I don't believe there is anything comparable in America to the Paris bistro. They are usually small, unpretentious restaurants, often run by a couple (Monsieur or Madame does the cooking, and the other presides at the bar). There may be one or two waiters or waitresses to serve you. The food and wine, often regional, are always wonderful, and the prices are very reasonable. Tables and banquettes run along the wall, or walls, and there is a delightful intimacy about the rooms. Likely as not, you'll soon find yourself in sprightly conversation with your neighbors, even though their English is limited and your French is halting.

We found Chez Pauline, which was close to our hotel, to be a charming and cozy little bistro, serving superb Burgundian food. Our main dish was one of the specialties of the house, *Steak au Poivre,* flambéed with Armagnac. This is how it is done.

STEAK AU POIVRE
  (Peppered Steak)

2 *filets of beef, each weighing*	2 *oz. butter*
about 5 ounces	1 *tbsp. olive oil*
Salt	2 *oz. Cognac*
Coarsely ground peppercorns	1 *tbsp. heavy cream*

Have ready 2 filets, or tournedos, of beef, each weighing about 5 ounces. Salt them lightly and press plenty of coarsely ground black peppercorns into both sides of the filets.

Heat 2 ounces butter and 1 tablespoon olive oil in a shallow skillet. When very hot put in the filets and sear them on both sides. Then lower flame and cook about 4 minutes per side. They should be rather rare. Remove filets to a hot platter and keep warm.

Warm 2 ounces Armagnac (or Cognac), set it alight, and pour into skillet with its juices. Lift pan from fire and rotate until flame dies out. Return pan to low heat, slowly stir in 1 tablespoon heavy cream, blend well, and pour sauce over filets.

I have had steak with a tomato and garlic sauce (called *Bistecca alla Pizzaiola,* twice. Once was in Naples using a rump steak, and once at the Continental Hotel in Milan using an entrecôte. In southern Italy where the meat may be a little tough, the steak is cooked first, then the sauce is added, the pan covered, and the whole cooked until the steak is tender.

The following is the recipe for an entrecôte (or rib steak) from the very fine Continental Hotel in Milan, Italy.

BISTECCA ALLA PIZZAIOLA
(Steak with Tomato and Garlic Sauce)

1½ lb. *fine rib steak*	*Salt and pepper*
1 *tbsp. olive oil*	3–4 *cloves garlic*
1½ *lbs. ripe tomatoes*	¼ *tsp. dried oregano*

Using a fine rib steak, cook it *a pointe* (brown on outside and pink in the center). In a separate saucepan put a small amount of olive oil (about 1 tablespoon) and when hot add 1½ pounds ripe tomatoes, peeled and chopped, salt and pepper to taste, 3 or 4 sliced cloves garlic, and ¼ teaspoon dried oregano. Cook until all is thoroughly heated (the tomatoes must not be allowed to become pulpy). Then spread this sauce thickly over the steak, and serve at once to 2.

To me, *Boeuf à la Bourguignonne* is one of the greatest dishes in the world. It is really a very simple dish, being merely good beef stewed in Burgundy wine, with late starters added of onions and mushrooms. But the very long cooking brings out an intermingling of flavors in the finished dish that I think is unsurpassed. I make the dish very frequently for guests, and the recipe, which came from Dijon, France, is in my first cookbook, *With a Jug of Wine.* But on my recent trip to Dijon, I made a delightful discovery with respect to the preparation of the dish.

On December 1st, 1962, in Dijon, I was inducted into the Burgundian *Ordre des Grands Ducs d'Occident,* and made an *Officier de Charles Temeraire.* This is a very old order, made up of those who are devoted to the promotion and to the drinking of Burgundy wine.

The induction ceremonies and banquet were held in the cellars of a 13th century monastery. The huge vaulted room was profusely decorated, the great pillars with Christmas evergreen, and on the tables were very large candelabras holding red candles. There were trumpeteers, instrumentalists, wonderful singers, and folk dancers, all in native Burgundian costumes. There were a great number of distinguished guests—the ambassadors to France from Norway and Turkey, generals, state officials, and regional dignitaries.

During dinner I sat next to an old Burgundian who spoke excellent English. Naturally we dwelt on the subject of food, and he was particularly interested to learn that I wrote on food. I told him that my favorite dish was *Boeuf à la Bourguignonne,* and he beamed! Then he told me of a very delightful variation on the original recipe, which he said he preferred to the standard recipe. I made notes, and here is the recipe for *Boeuf à la Bourguignonne* with a marvelous touch.

BOEUF À LA BOURGUIGNONNE
(Burgundy Beef)

2 *lbs. lean beef in 1 piece*	*Generous pinch salt*
2 *slices bacon*	*Generous pinch pepper*
Cognac	*Generous pinch dried thyme*
2 *tbsp. bacon drippings*	*Generous pinch dried marjoram*
10 *small or 5 medium-sized onions*	½ *cup beef bouillon*
	1 *cup Burgundy*
1½ *tbsp. flour*	½ *lb. fresh mushrooms*

Get a piece of very lean, tender beef weighing about 2 pounds. Cut the bacon into small bits (about ½ inch square). Make little slits in the beef all over, and insert the bits of bacon in the slits.

Then let the beef soak in Cognac for at least 6 hours before cooking (prepare the beef about 9 A.M. if you are going to serve the dish around 7 P.M.).

Peel and slice the onions and fry them in the bacon drippings until brown, using a heavy skillet. Then remove to a separate dish. Cut the lean beef into about 1-inch cubes, and sauté them in the same drippings, adding a little more fat if necessary. When the cubes of beef are browned on all sides, sprinkle over them 1½ tablespoons of flour, and a generous pinch each of salt, pepper, thyme, and marjoram. Then add ½ cup of beef bouillon and 1 cup of Burgundy wine. Stir the mixture well for a moment, then let it simmer as slowly as possible for 3¼ hours. The mixture, during this cooking, should just barely bubble occasionally. If necessary, put a mat under the skillet. The liquid may cook away some, so add a little more bouillon and wine (in the proportion of 1 part of stock to two parts of wine) as necessary to keep the beef barely covered.

After the mixture has cooked the 3¼ hours, return the brown onions to the skillet, add ½ pound of sliced fresh mushrooms (you can add ¾ pound or a pound if you like mushrooms). Stir everything together well, and then let it cook for ¾ of an hour or even an hour longer. Again, it may be necessary to add a little more stock and wine. The sauce should be thick and dark brown. With this main dish serve crusty French bread, a tossed green salad, and your imported Burgundy, and follow it with a light dessert.

Ragoût is the French word for stew. But the French consider a ragoût such a delectable culinary masterpiece that their adjective for "relishing," "savory," "inviting," or "tempting" is *ragoûtant,* and the verb *ragoûter* means "to restore the appetite."

A fine ragoût is not difficult to prepare, and it is easy on the pocketbook and the chef. The less expensive (and more flavorsome) cuts of meat are called for; a ragoût requires no attention while cooking save for an occasional stirring. There are two "musts" however. Never use old or tired vegetables, and never allow a stew to boil.

Ragoût of Beef Dubonnet is very French, and uses the tangy, zestful apéritif wine, Dubonnet. We had the following dish at Pierre's restaurant, a most pleasant bistro just a short way from our hotel at the foot of the Avenue de l'Opera.

RAGOÛT OF BEEF, DUBONNET

2 lbs. round steak	2 whole cloves
Seasoned flour	½ tsp. salt
⅓ stick butter	½ tsp. freshly ground pepper
2 onions	½ cup Dubonnet
2 bay leaves	½ cup sour cream
½ cup chopped fresh parsley	

Cut 2 pounds round steak into 1-inch cubes, and shake them in a bag of seasoned flour until well dredged.

In a heavy skillet heat ⅓ stick butter, and add the cubes of beef. When cubes are well browned on all sides add to the skillet 2 thinly sliced onions, 2 crumbled bay leaves, 2 whole cloves, ½ teaspoon each salt and freshly ground pepper, and last ½ cup Dubonnet. Cover skillet and simmer gently until meat is tender, about 1 hour. If more liquid is required, add more Dubonnet as necessary. Just before serving add ½ cup each of sour cream and parsley, freshly chopped. Heat, and serve over flaky rice, or Bulghour. This serves 4.

Originally, the word "carbonades" meant meat grilled over hot coals, but, in this case at least, it is now used to mean slow stewing. *Carbonades Flamandes* was created by Flemish chefs, who combined the finesse of French cookery with the heartiness of German, or Dutch, cuisine, to produce a unique flavor blend all their own. The German influence is, of course, the use of beer. It is an inexpensive dish, and very easy to prepare, yet one that produces wonderful flavor dividends.

This is the way the Belgian housewife prepares it.

CARBONADES FLAMANDES
(Belgian Beef Stew)

2½ lbs. boneless beef	1 12-oz. bottle beer
Seasoned flour	1 clove garlic
3 tbsp. lard (or shortening)	2 4-inch pieces celery
4 tbsp. butter	3 sprigs parsley
4 medium onions	1 bay leaf
3 tbsp. flour	¼ tsp. dried thyme

1 tbsp. tarragon vinegar

Get 2½ pounds of boneless beef, either chuck, flank or round, and have it cut in cubes about 1½ inches. Dredge the meat cubes in seasoned flour.

In a heavy skillet or Dutch oven put 3 tablespoons of lard, or shortening, and when hot, brown the meat cubes on all sides. While the meat cubes are browning, put 4 tablespoons of butter in another skillet, and when hot sauté 4 medium onions, which have been sliced. When they are lightly browned, transfer the onions to the Dutch oven or skillet containing the browned meat cubes. Pour off all but 3 tablespoons of the butter (if necessary) and blend into the butter in the skillet 3 tablespoons of flour to make a light brown roux. When the roux is smooth and free from lumps, pour in one 12-ounce bottle of beer (dark beer is preferable), stirring constantly, and bring to the boiling point. Then pour this beer sauce into the Dutch oven or skillet containing the meat and onions. Also add a clove of garlic impaled on a toothpick, and a faggot, or bouquet garni, of seasonings. To make the faggot, place 3 sprigs of parsley, a crumbled bay leaf, and ¼ teaspoon of dried thyme in the curve of a piece of celery about 4 inches long. Cover with another piece of celery the same size, and tie the two pieces together securely with white thread.

Cover the skillet or Dutch oven, and cook over a low heat for about 2 to 2½ hours, or until the meat is tender. It may be necessary to add more beer, as the meat should be covered with the liquid. Just before serving, gently stir in a scant tablespoon of tarragon vinegar, and remove faggot and garlic.

The Carbonade is served to 6 in a rather deep dish. Plain

boiled potatoes are a "must" with this dish, and crusty French bread (to mop up the delicious sauce). And, of course, cold beer is the indicated beverage.

A great many French dishes are "one-dish meals," where vegetables and often potatoes are included in the recipe. Such a dish is *Boeuf à la Mode*. But it is not confined to the kitchens of working-class families. Parisienne gourmets love the dish, and it can be found in many Paris restaurants. It is prepared to perfection at Allard's, on the rue St.-André-des-Arts, in the 6th Arrondissement, not far from the Gare Montparnasse. This is an adaptation of their recipe. It takes time and a little effort to prepare, but it's worth it.

BOEUF À LA MODE

4- to 5-*lb. piece rump beef*	*Pinch grated nutmeg*
18–20 *strips salt pork*	2 *calf's feet, split*
2 *oz. brandy*	1 *cup condensed beef bouillon*
Chopped fresh parsley	2 *cups dry red wine*
Chopped chives	½ *cup chopped celery leaves*
Dried thyme	1 *tsp. chopped parsley*
Dried tarragon	1 *tsp. dried thyme*
Salt	1 *tsp. dried basil*
Freshly ground pepper	2 *cloves garlic*
3 *tbsp. bacon drippings*	2 *whole cloves*
2 *cloves garlic*	12 *small carrots*
3 *onions*	12 *small white onions*
2 *oz. butter*	

Get a 4- to 5-pound piece of beef suitable for pot roasting, such as a rump, and from 18 to 20 strips of salt pork suitable for larding. Your butcher can prepare these for you.

Marinate the salt pork strips in about 2 ounces brandy for about 2 hours. Then remove them and roll them in a mixture of chopped fresh parsley, chopped chives, dried thyme and tarragon. Lard the beef well with the treated salt pork strips (this can be done by using a larding needle, or by making deep incisions in the beef with a sharp-pointed, narrow knife, and pushing the strips into the incisions with an ice pick). Then rub the outside of the meat all over with a mixture of salt, freshly ground pepper, and a pinch of ground nutmeg.

Melt 3 tablespoons bacon drippings in a heavy pot, a Dutch oven, or a deep, heavy skillet. When fat is hot add 2 crushed cloves garlic, let them brown, then remove them. Sear the meat on all sides, and when nicely brown, drain off most of the bacon fat. Then add 3 sliced onions and 2 split calf's feet which have first been brought to a boil in water, then drained. Cover the pot and simmer the beef and calf's feet and onions for about 10 minutes. Then add 2 ounces brandy (use the brandy the salt pork strips were marinated in) and simmer about 5 minutes more. Next add 1 cup condensed beef bouillon, 2 cups dry red wine, ½ cup chopped celery leaves, 1 teaspoon each chopped fresh parsley, dried thyme and basil, 2 cloves garlic, and 2 whole cloves. Bring contents of pot to boil, then lower flame, and let simmer slowly for 2½ hours, covered.

In the meantime parboil 12 small carrots and 12 whole small white onions in water, drain, and brown them in butter in a skillet. After meat has cooked the 2½ hours uncover, add carrots and onions, cover again, and let cook 2½ hours longer, or until meat is tender. Then remove calf's feet from the pot, take off their meat, and return the meat to the pot.

Remove the meat to a deep serving dish and surround it with the vegetables. Skim any grease from the top of the gravy, then pour the gravy over the meat and vegetables. Serve any excess gravy in a gravy boat.

In serving, slice the meat against the grain, so that the larding will show as small white spots in the meat slices.

When my first cookbook, *With a Jug of Wine,* was published in London for Great Britain and the Commonwealths, one of my favorite recipes in the American edition, Beefsteak and Kidney Pie, was omitted. I was surprised, for this is a classic English dish. So, out of curiosity, I wrote my London publishers asking why it was not included in their edition.

Their reason was most interesting. "This particular recipe was omitted," they wrote, "partly because it contained wine, which would be against our traditional usage with which the recipe was associated. We are a nation of Steak and Kidney Pie eaters and we wouldn't like to get ourselves involved in an argument as technical as this might threaten to be."

Beefsteak and Kidney Pie is indeed one of the great and favorite dishes of England. But the variations on the main theme to be found on the menus of many fine English restaurants is amazing. For instance, Simpson's-in-the-Strand lists on its menu Steak, Kidney and Mushroom pie, and also Steak, Kidney, Mushroom and Oyster Pudding. The famous Ye Olde Cheshire Cheese has as its specialty Steak, Kidney, Mushroom and Game Pudding. Rules, on their menu, merely list Steak and Kidney Pie.

The following recipe is one that I got from England many years ago, and, as has been my custom with many dishes, I added wine to the recipe. Everyone who has ever tasted the dish has raved over it, and among my guests have been people who live in England.

BEEF, KIDNEY, AND MUSHROOM PIE

1 *lb. veal kidneys*	1 *bay leaf*
Salt	1 *tbsp. Worcestershire sauce*
Vinegar	*Freshly ground pepper*
2 *lbs. rump steak*	1 *cup condensed beef bouillon*
Flour	1 *cup dry red wine*
1 *clove garlic*	3 *tbsp. butter*
3 *tbsp. bacon drippings*	1 *cup sliced mushrooms*
1 *medium onion*	3 *oz. brandy*
2 *pinches dried thyme*	*Flaky pastry crust*
2 *pinches dried marjoram*	*Cream*

Soak 1 pound veal kidneys for 1 hour in cold salted water to which 2 tablespoons vinegar have been added. Then drain kidneys, clean, and trim away any gristle and tubes, and slice thin. Cut 2 pounds of ½ inch thick rump steak into 1 by 1½ inch pieces.

In a Dutch oven sauté 1 clove garlic, sliced, until brown in

3 tablespoons bacon drippings. Remove garlic and add cubed beef, which has been dredged with flour. Brown meat on all sides, then add 1 medium onion, chopped fine, 2 pinches each of dried thyme and marjoram, a crumbled bay leaf, 1 tablespoon Worcestershire sauce, and salt and freshly ground pepper to taste. Cook for about 5 minutes, then add 1 cup condensed beef bouillon and 1 cup dry red wine. Cover closely and simmer over a low flame for about 1½ hours, or until meat is nearly tender. Stir occasionally, and if necessary, add a little more bouillon and wine in equal parts.

Put 1 tablespoon butter in a saucepan and when it is bubbling add the sliced kidneys and cook for about 5 minutes, then add them to the simmering meat. Add about 2 more tablespoons butter to saucepan, and put in 1 cup sliced fresh mushrooms. Sauté these gently for about 7 to 8 minutes, then add them to the simmering meat and kidneys.

Now add 2 tablespoons flour to the butter in the saucepan, and when well blended, add this roux to simmering meat, kidneys and mushrooms, and stir until all is well blended. Next stir in 3 ounces brandy, remove from heat, and pour all into a buttered casserole or round baking dish, and set aside to cool.

Prepare a rich crust, using your favorite pie crust recipe, and chill dough in refrigerator. Then roll out pastry so that is about 1 inch larger in diameter than casserole. Press it down in a fluted edge around rim of casserole. Cut a few slits on top to allow steam to escape. Brush top of pastry crust with cream, and bake in a 450-degree oven for 15 minutes. Then reduce heat to about 300 degrees, and cook for about 15 to 20 minutes longer, or until pastry is a rich brown.

Cold ale, stout, or beer goes best with this dish.

A popular dish among middle-class British families is a sort of stew of beef, tripe, and vegetables, which is delicious.

I have never encountered Casserole of Steak and Tripe on the menus of London restaurants, nor on the menus of the better-class English hotel restaurants. But in the north of England, particularly when the weather is cold, the dish comes into its own, and you will occasionally come across it in restaurants or hotel dining rooms.

After leaving Dumfries, Scotland, we had a rather rough time on the ferry that crosses the Solway Firth. It was cold, and we stopped at the Crown and Mitre Hotel in Carlisle for a warming drink. On the luncheon menu I saw Casserole of Steak and Tripe, and I succumbed. The following is the recipe, but I have taken the liberty of adding a touch that I think usually improves stews— a bit of red wine.

CASSEROLE OF STEAK AND TRIPE

2 tbsp. bacon drippings	1½ lbs. fresh honeycomb tripe
¾ lb. lean beef	2 tsp. salt
2 cups chopped onion	½ tsp. cracked peppercorns
2 cups sliced carrots	Pinch dried thyme
1½ cups chopped celery	Pinch dried marjoram
½ cup sliced leeks	¼ tsp. grated lemon rind

1 cup dry red wine

In a heavy skillet heat 2 tablespoons bacon drippings, and when hot add ¾ pound lean beef (from chuck or round) cut in cubes about ½ inch in size. Brown the beef on all sides over a fairly hot flame.

In a large bowl mix together 2 cups each chopped onions and sliced carrots, 1½ cups chopped celery, and ½ cup sliced leeks. Place this vegetable mixture in an earthenware casserole. On top of vegetables put the browned cubes beef and 1½ pounds fresh honeycomb tripe, which has been washed in cold water and cut into strips about ½ inch by 2 inches.

Sprinkle over contents of casserole 2 teaspoons salt, ½ teaspoon cracked peppercorns, pinch each dried thyme and marjoram, and ¼ teaspoon grated lemon rind. Then pour over all 1 cup dry red wine. Cover the casserole tightly, and simmer on top of the stove for 1½ to 2 hours, or until tripe is tender. Serve very hot from the casserole to 4–6.

German cooking and German food are not for fragile and delicate appetites. Many of their dishes are definitely on the hearty side, with dumplings, thick soups, sausages, dark and heavy breads, rich cakes and tortes. But don't get me wrong— I love the food of Germany, and a great many of their dishes have wonderfully blended flavors. And their wines are light and delicate, with exquisite bouquets. From the Rhineland and Moselle regions come some of the very finest white wines in the world.

Germans are particularly fond of "sweet-sour" mixtures. To my mind one of the greatest of these is sauerbraten, or braised pickled beef.

In Cologne we were most fortunate in staying at the Dom Hotel, which is just across the street from one of the greatest cathedrals in Germany. Cologne is a lovely city on the Rhine, with beautiful parks, and a mixture of the old and new in architecture. Cologne also has some excellent restaurants, and one in particular was most unusual, Die Bastei. The restaurant is on two levels with the upper level entirely glass enclosed, and one gets a magnificent view of the Rhine and the city of Cologne. It is a luxury restaurant, with excellent dinner music, dancing, faultless service, and an extensive menu of wonderful German and Continental dishes. We had sauerbraten as our main course, and this is an adaptation of their recipe. It is not too difficult to prepare, but it does take a little time.

SAUERBRATEN

4-lb. piece rump or round of
   beef
2½ cups dry red wine
1½ cups tarragon vinegar
1 tsp. salt
1 tsp. black peppercorns
½ tsp. dried thyme
½ tsp. mace
⅛ tsp. sage
¼ tsp. allspice

1 tsp. dry mustard
3 bay leaves
12 whole cloves
2 large onions
1 large carrot
6 sprigs celery tops
3 tbsp. bacon drippings
2 tbsp. flour
5 gingersnaps
1 cup sour cream

2 tbsp. Madeira wine

Put a 4-pound rump of beef (in one piece) in a large enamel, earthenware, or stainless steel kettle. Mix together 2½ cups dry

red wine, 1½ cups tarragon vinegar, 1 teaspoon salt, 1 teaspoon
black peppercorns, ½ teaspoon each dried thyme and mace, ⅛
teaspoon dried sage, ¼ teaspoon allspice, 1 teaspoon dry mustard,
3 bay leaves, 12 whole cloves, 2 large onions, peeled and sliced,
1 large carrot, sliced, and 6 sprigs celery tops. Pour over meat.
Cover with doubled cheesecloth, and let meat marinate for 4
days at room temperature, turning meat twice each day in the
marinade.

On the day of cooking melt 3 tablespoons of bacon drippings in
a heavy skillet, put in the meat, taken from the marinade, and
brown it on all sides. Then put piece of meat in a heavy kettle, or
large Dutch oven.

Blend about 2 tablespoons flour with bacon drippings remaining in skillet, and then gradually pour in the marinade. Add 5
crushed gingersnaps, and cook until thickened. Add this sauce to
meat, and simmer slowly over a low flame until meat is tender,
about 3 hours. If necessary, add a little more red wine.

When meat is cooked and tender, remove to a hot platter and
slice. Into the gravy stir 1 cup commercial sour cream and 2
tablespoons dry Madeira wine. Heat and blend, then pour gravy
over meat and serve. With sauerbraten, potato pancakes are a
"must"!

Accounts differ as to when the most praiseworthy comestible,
oxtails, was first used as food in more or less modern form. One
story gives credit to the thrifty French Huguenot refugees in
England around 1685. They saw tanners discarding the tails
from their hides, and bought them for use in cooking.

But the more picturesque tale is that, during the reign of terror
following the French Revolution, a starving nobleman observed
that the Paris tanners discarded the ox tails before treating the
hides. He begged for a couple of tails, which were freely given him.
He took them home and made a soup with them. It proved to be
so delicious that soon hordes of hungry nobles were besieging the
tanneries for oxtails!

We had a delicious dish of oxtails in mustard sauce in a little
restaurant in Shepherd's Market, Mackensie's. Shepherd's Market

is a most interesting spot, about halfway between Piccadilly and Curzon Street. There are all sorts of curious shops, a few small restaurants, and the well-known Shepherd's Tavern. Mackensie's was a gem, however. It was small, quiet, and the food excellent, as this recipe will prove.

OXTAILS IN MUSTARD SAUCE

3 *lbs. oxtails*	1 *cup dry red wine*
2 *tbsp. butter*	2 *tbsp. tomato paste*
3 *medium onions, minced*	1 *tsp. seasoned salt*
1 *tbsp. dry mustard*	1 *tsp. salt*
1 *tbsp. arrowroot*	*Dash cayenne pepper*
1 *cup condensed beef bouillon*	½ *cup sour cream*

Chopped parsley

Brown 3 pounds oxtails cut in 1½ inch pieces in 2 tablespoons butter, then remove them from skillet. Stir into drippings 3 medium onions, minced, 1 tablespoon each dry mustard and arrowroot, and 1 cup condensed beef bouillon and dry red wine. Cook over low heat, stirring constantly, until thickened and smooth. Then mix in 2 tablespoons tomato paste, 1 teaspoon each seasoned salt and salt, and a dash cayenne pepper. Now return the browned oxtails to the sauce, cover, and cook for 3 hours, or until oxtails are tender. Just before serving stir in ½ cup commercial sour cream and sprinkle with parsley. Let heat, then serve with noodles or steamed rice. This serves 4 to 5.

After leaving Germany, we were frequently asked, "What section or cities did you like best in Germany?" And our reply was always the same—"That's an impossible question to answer, because we loved every part of Germany we visited." Actually, we visited twenty-seven German cities, traveling the length and breadth of the country. Each city had its own peculiar charm, and the countryside was gorgeous, with its autumn colorings. And the food and wine and beer were out of this world.

Berlin, of course, was an experience never to be forgotten. West

Berlin was almost as gay and fascinating as Paris; East Berlin was sepulchral. There are many excellent restaurants in West Berlin. One we particularly enjoyed was the Aben, out on the Kurfürstendamm, where General Lucius Clay loved to eat. There we had that terrific East Prussian dish, *Königsberger Klops.*

Königsberger Klops are really meatballs, but meatballs raised to an epicurean pinnacle. They are not fried or stewed, but boiled, then simmered in a sardine and caper sauce.

KÖNIGSBERGER KLOPS
(German Meatballs)

¾ lb. chuck beef, ground	1 tbsp. lemon juice
¾ lb. veal, ground	2 tsp. Worcestershire sauce
¼ lb. pork, ground	2 tbsp. chopped parsley
2 small hard rolls	¼ tsp. dried marjoram
½ cup light cream	5 cups beef bouillon
1 medium onion, chopped	1 cup dry white wine
6 tbsp. butter	4 tbsp. flour
4 anchovy filets	1 tsp. dry mustard
2 beaten eggs	2 small boneless sardines
1 tsp. salt	⅓ cup drained capers
¼ tsp. freshly ground pepper	1 tbsp. chopped parsley

Juice ½ lemon

Have ¾ pound each chuck beef and veal and ¼ pound pork ground twice. Also break up 2 small hard rolls and soak in ½ cup cream for about 10 minutes, then press the excess liquid from them. Also sauté 1 medium onion in 1 tablespoon butter until lightly browned.

Put the ground meats, the moistened hard rolls, the sautéed onions, and 4 anchovy filets through the food grinder, using the finest blade. Then add to this 2 lightly beaten eggs, 1 teaspoon salt, ¼ teaspoon freshly ground pepper, 1 tablespoon lemon juice, 2 teaspoons Worcestershire sauce, 2 tablespoons chopped parsley, and ¼ teaspoon dried marjoram. Mix everything thoroughly, and shape mixture into 12 balls.

Heat 5 cups condensed beef bouillon and 1 cup dry white wine in an iron kettle. When liquid is boiling, carefully drop the meat balls in, turn down the flame, and simmer slowly for 15 to 20 minutes, covered. Then remove meatballs from the stock, and keep them hot while the gravy is being made.

Mix 1 teaspoon dry mustard with 4 tablespoons flour, and cream that mixture together with 4 tablespons butter. When the roux is smooth, add enough of the hot stock the meatballs were boiled in to make a thin paste, free from lumps. Turn up the flame under the stock, then stir the roux into the stock, cook and stir until smooth and boiling.

Mash 2 small boneless sardines with 1 tablespoon butter, then stir into the gravy, blending well. Then add ½ cup drained capers, 1 tablespoon chopped parsley, and juice of half a lemon. When all is blended, add the meatballs to the gravy, and serve. Boiled parsley potatoes, or *spatzle* (small dumplings) go best with this dish.

We tried meatballs in three different countries—Holland, France, and Italy, and all were different, and delicious. This first is from Holland.

DUTCH MEATBALLS

1 *lb. ground beef*	2 *cups sliced mushrooms*
1 *tsp. salt*	1 *tsp. lemon juice*
Pinch cayenne pepper	1 *beef bouillon cube*
½ *tsp. ground cumin seed*	1 *tsp. salt*
¾ *tsp. ground coriander seed*	⅛ *tsp. pepper*
⅓ *cup fine breadcrumbs*	⅛ *tsp. garlic powder*
1 *tbsp. bacon drippings*	1 *tbsp. paprika*
2 *cups sliced onions*	1 *cup sour cream*

Combine 1 pound ground lean beef, 1 teaspoon salt, pinch cayenne pepper, ½ teaspoon ground cumin seed, ¾ teaspoon ground coriander seed, and ⅓ cup fine dry breadcrumbs. Mix well and shape into 1 inch balls.

Heat 1 tablespoon bacon or sausage drippings in a skillet, add meatballs, and brown on all sides. Then add 2 cups thinly sliced onions and sauté until limp. Add 2 cups (½ pound) sliced fresh mushrooms, 1 teaspoon lemon juice, and a beef bouillon cube, and cook until mushrooms are tender, about 7 minutes. Then stir in 1 teaspoon salt and ⅛ teaspoon each black pepper and garlic powder. Combine 1 tablespoon paprika with 1 cup sour cream, and add to contents of skillet. Heat only until hot, then garnish with chopped fresh parsley and serve at once. Serves 4 generously.

The second meatball dish we had in an unpretentious little restaurant in St.-Jean-Cap-Ferrat, facing out on the bay. Being a Provence recipe, of course it has olives in it.

MEATBALLS WITH OLIVES

1½ lbs. ground lean beef	¼ cup sifted flour
¾ cup finely chopped onion	1 cup sour cream
¼ cup fine cracker meal	1 10½-oz. can condensed consommé
1 clove garlic	3 tbsp. tomato paste
1½ tsp. salt	1 tsp. Worcestershire sauce
¼ tsp. pepper	¼ tsp. salt
2 oz. dry red wine	1½ cups pitted Italian black olives
2 tbsp. sausage drippings	

Combine 1½ pounds ground lean beef, ¾ cup finely chopped raw onion, ¼ cup fine cracker meal, 1 clove minced garlic, 1½ teaspoons salt, ¼ teaspoon pepper, and 2 ounces dry red wine. Mix well and shape into 1-inch balls. Heat about 2 tablespoons bacon or sausage drippings in a heavy skillet and brown the meatballs on all sides. After browning drain off any excess fat and set meatballs aside while making sauce.

Blend ¼ cup sifted flour into 1 cup commercial sour cream. Then combine this with a 10½-ounce can condensed consommé, 3 tablespoons tomato paste, 1 teaspoon Worcestershire sauce, and ¼ teaspoon salt. Mix well. Return meatballs to skillet, pour sauce over them, cover skillet, and cook 10 to 15 minutes. Just before serving add 1½ cups pitted black Italian olives which have been cut into medium-size pieces. Stir to blend, heat thoroughly, and serve to 5 to 6.

The Italians call meat balls *polpette,* and they can be made from either raw or cooked beef. They have a distinctive flavor, and are usually formed into little flat cakes and fried.

We had them for luncheon cooked in a sauce at the Hotel Vittoria in Brescia, on our way from Venice to Milan.

POLPETTE
(Italian Meatballs)

1 *lb. ground lean beef*	2 *tbsp. grated Parmesan cheese*
Grated rind 1 small lemon	*Salt and pepper*
2 *tsps. chopped parsley*	2 *oz. olive oil*
2 *cloves garlic*	2 *oz. flour*
½ *cup soft breadcrumbs*	1 *cup condensed consommé*
Milk	½ *cup dry white wine*
1 *egg*	½ *cup cream*

Combine 1 pound ground lean beef, the grated rind of a small lemon, 2 teaspoons chopped parsley, 2 cloves garlic, minced, ½ cup soft breadcrumbs which have been soaked in milk for about 15 minutes, then drained and squeezed dry with the hands, 1 egg, slightly beaten, 2 tablespoons grated Parmesan cheese, and salt and pepper to taste. Flour a breadboard—and your hands—and form the mixture into flattened little balls, about ¾ inch thick and 2 inches in diameter. With your finger make a little dent on the top of each ball or cake, which makes them lighter.

In a heavy skillet heat 2 ounces olive oil, and when hot, add the *polpette,* and let them cook about 2 minutes on each side. Then remove and drain them on paper toweling.

To the oil in the skillet add about 2 ounces flour, and blend well. Then add 1 cup condensed consommé, ½ cup each dry white wine and cream. Cook, stirring constantly, until mixture is thickened and smooth. Return the *polpette* to the sauce, cover, and let all heat through thoroughly. Serve to 4.

It is a rare occasion when we visit a night club or cabaret. As a rule the food is mediocre and expensive, the drinks ditto, and the entertainment not worth the cost of the evening. However, in Zürich, a number of people told us not to miss going to Kindli, which is a restaurant that was established in 1440. We were assured that we would have excellent Swiss food, and see a typical Swiss folklore show, with outstanding music and vocalists. So, we capitulated, and made a reservation for a Saturday night. It turned out to be one of the most enjoyable evenings we spent in Europe.

The raftered restaurant is quite large, and lighted by candles stuck in wine bottles on each table. We were greeted by Werner Schmid, one of the owners, and producer of the fabulous production *Rose Marie,* which ran for a month on an open air stage on the shore of Lake Zürich. We had excellent martinis, and while drinking them we talked to Herr Schmid, and Leona Irwin, the choreographer of *Rose Marie.* Incidentally, she used to be with the Muriel Abbot dancers at the Palmer House in Chicago.

The entertainment started at eight. There was a ten-piece orchestra and two vocalists. The music was wonderful, Swiss and German melodies; the pianist played Bach to perfection; and such delightful yodeling I have seldom heard. The featured vocalist was a gorgeous blonde with a fine voice, and very amusing in her comic songs. In a way she reminded me of Phyliss Diller.

The food was terrific. Our entree was another famous Swiss specialty, *Fondue Bourguignonne.* It was delicious, and really a conversation piece, because you cook the food yourself at your table.

FONDUE BOURGUIGNONNE
(Beef Cooked in Oil)

Hot oil	*Sweet-sour sauce*
Thick Bernaise sauce	*Catsup-mustard sauce*
Tartar sauce	*Cubes raw tenderloin of beef*

Cubes raw, lean bacon

The waiter first brought on a rather deep earthenware kettle filled with very hot oil, and set it on an alcohol burner between Mrs. Wood and me. Then he brought each of us a large plate, on which were a thick Bernaise sauce, tartar sauce, a sweet-sour sauce, and a catsup-mustard sauce. On the other half of the plate were several pieces of raw tenderloin of beef, each cut about ¾ inch square, and several cubes about the same size of raw, lean bacon. We were each given 2 long wooden skewers. The skewers serve as your cooking and eating ware.

You spear a piece of beef, put it in the kettle of oil, and let it cook for about a minute or less. Then take it out, dip it in one of the sauces, and into your mouth. In the meantime the other skewer, with a cube of bacon on it, is cooking, and when done, you do the same thing with it as you did with the beef.

The variety of sauces gives an exciting different flavor to the beef and bacon cubes, and it is really loads of fun to cook the food yourself. For more than two people you can have a pot of oil for each two, or a larger pot for four people. When you serve Fondue Bourguignonne, you'll never have a dull dinner party!

One of the most engaging qualities of lamb is its delicate yet almost neutral flavor. With few exceptions, it should never be smothered by very strong or pungent vegetables or seasonings. However there are pronounced flavors which definitely enhance lamb, and one of these is garlic. A few slivers of garlic inserted into a leg of lamb before roasting does wonders. Mint is an herb with a pronounced flavor that marries perfectly with the lamb flavor. Try a mint *gravy* sometime instead of a mint sauce.

To me, the most exotically beautiful restaurant I have ever been in in all my life is the Omar Khayyam at 50 Curzon Street in London. A mystic, Near Eastern atmosphere has been created in this restaurant, which occupies two floors. One room is done in the most exquisite blue imaginable, with indirect lighting. It is below the street level, and adjacent to it is a lounge that makes you think you are in a luxurious Turkish palace. Around three sides of the room deep cushions are piled, and the floor is covered with rare Persian rugs. There you can sip after dinner liqueurs and

Turkish coffee, and, if one is so inclined, smoke the *narguile* water pipes. In the dining room is a small orchestra playing Persian stringed instruments, and twice during the evening Turkish "belly dancers" perform their exotic dances, wearing little but strings of beads! Yet their dancing is beautiful, and is in no way cheap or crude.

The menus are gorgeous, illustrating in full, rich colors scenes from the *Rubaiyat* of Omar Khayyam. The food is marvelous, and the hors d'oeuvres are by far the best obtainable in London.

We lunched once at Omar Khayyam's, as the guests of the owners, Nicky and Sheila Tarayan, at a luncheon given for the Lebanese dancing troupe which later performed at Albert Hall. And we dined there twice, and each meal was an unforgettable gastronomic experience.

One of our entrees was an authentic *shashlik,* and I have never eaten better. The following recipe has been adapted to American kitchens.

SHASHLIK

2 *lb. boned leg of lamb*	¼ *tsp. ground cinnamon*
1 *tsp. salt*	1 *tbsp. Worcestershire sauce*
½ *tsp. freshly ground pepper*	3 *tbsp. olive oil*
2 *medium onions, chopped*	¼ *cup vinegar*
1 *clove garlic*	*Dry red wine*
1 *bay leaf*	*Bacon slices*
1 *tbsp. chopped parsley*	*Small ripe tomatoes*
¼ *tsp. ground cloves*	*Mushroom caps*

Brandy

Get a 2-pound boned leg of lamb, and cut into pieces about 1½ inches thick and 2 inches square. Cut off any excess fat, and cut the meat into slices about ¼ inch thick.

In an earthenware bowl mix together 1 teaspoon salt, ½ teaspoon freshly ground black pepper, 2 medium-sized onions, chopped, 1 clove garlic, finely chopped, a crumbled bay leaf, 1 tablespoon chopped parsley, ¼ teaspoon each ground cloves and ground cinnamon, 1 tablespoon Worcestershire sauce, 3 table-spoons olive oil, and ¼ cup vinegar. Into this put the lamb pieces, mix all gently, and cover with dry red wine. Cover the bowl and allow to marinate for at least 8 hours at room temperature.

When ready to cook the shashlik have ready bacon slices cut in thirds, thick slices small ripe tomatoes, and large mushroom caps.

Remove the lamb pieces from the marinade and dry with paper toweling. Then thread individual spits or skewers in the following manner: lamb piece, bacon piece, mushroom cap, tomato slice. Continue in this order until skewers are filled. At the end of the skewer place a cube of bread painted with olive oil to keep the contents of the skewers from falling off.

In the home place a wire rack in the broiler section of the stove so that the filled skewers will be as close to a hot broiler flame as possible. Underneath the rack place a pan to catch the drippings. Put the filled skewers on the rack, turning them as they cook, so so that they will be brown all over. The shashlik is ready to eat when the meat is well cooked and starts to blacken on the edges— about 10 minutes.

When shashlik is done remove skewers from the rack, sprinkle them with brandy, and set alight. As flames die out slip the contents of the skewers off onto a hot plate. Serve with a pilaf.

A neglected cut of lamb that can be delicious, and is quite inexpensive, is breast of lamb. It can be cut in serving pieces and either cooked on top of the range or baked; it can be broiled; or it can be stuffed and baked.

While we were living in St.-Jean-Cap-Ferrat I went into the butcher shop in Beaulieu one day, but I had no idea what to get for dinner. The owner of the shop (who incidentally was the brother of Madame Nicole, and spoke perfect English), suggested breast of lamb. I said I didn't know how to cook it. He laughed, and went over to his mother, who was acting as cashier that day (she alternated between her daughter's store and her son's store, as the mood struck her). A lengthy conversation in French ensued, then the son wrote out directions in English as his mother gave them to him in French. I took a breast of lamb back to the apartment, and the directions, and the necessary comestibles, and the resulting dish was marvelous.

ANCHOVY STUFFED BREAST OF LAMB

2-lb. breast of lamb	*⅓ cup chopped fresh parsley*
2 cups soft breadcrumbs	*1 egg*
1 2-oz. can flat anchovy filets	*Pepper*
1 medium onion	*Dry sherry*

Ask your meat dealer to prepare a 2-pound breast of lamb for stuffing (he'll make a pocket in it). For the stuffing combine 2 cups soft breadcrumbs, a 2-ounce can flat anchovy filets, drained and chopped, 1 medium-sized onion, chopped, ⅓ cup fresh parsley, chopped, 1 beaten egg, and pepper to taste. Moisten with a little dry sherry, and stuff the breast of lamb with the mixture. Fasten with skewers, and place on a rack in a shallow roasting pan. Bake in a 350-degree oven 2 to 2¼ hours, or until lamb is tender. If there is any accumulation of fat, pour it off. This serves 4.

One night we dined in the home of friends in Paris, and the entree was a wonderful leg of lamb, cooked in rather an unusual manner. Naturally, I asked for the recipe, and my hostess wrote it out for me. Then, a few months later, we had a note from Edith Drennan, of Chicago, and she mentioned a little trick she had discovered with a leg of lamb.

"The other night," she wrote, "I tried something on a leg of lamb. I dusted the whole surface of the leg with curry powder before roasting. The gravy had a delicate curry flavor, and the whole thing was delicious." She also said she made a few pockets here and there in the lamb, and filled them with dried rosemary.

The first time I had an opportunity to try the Parisienne recipe for a leg of lamb I decided to combine Edith Drennan's touch. The result was fabulous.

ROAST LEG OF LAMB

4–5 *lb. leg of lamb* •	6 *stalks celery*
3–4 *slivers garlic*	6 *small carrots*
Dried rosemary	2 *cloves garlic*
Salt and pepper	12 *tiny new potatoes*
Curry powder	*Salt and pepper*
12 *small white onions*	4 *tbsp. butter*
6 *leeks* (*white part*)	1 *cup water*

1 *cup rosé wine*

In a 4- to 5-pound leg of lamb insert 3 or 4 slivers garlic near to the bone. Also make about 4 gashes in the meat with a sharp knife, and push a bit of dried rosemary into each gash, or pocket. Salt and pepper the lamb, and dust the whole surface of the lamb lightly with curry powder.

In the bottom of a large roasting pan place 12 small white onions, peeled, white part of 6 small leeks, 6 stalks celery, 6 small carrots, 2 cloves garlic, and 12 tiny new potatoes, scraped. Salt and pepper the vegetables, dot with 4 tablespoons butter, and then lay a grill in the pan over the vegetables. Place the leg of lamb on the grill so that it doesn't touch the vegtables. Add to the vegetables 1 cup each water and rosé wine. Bring the liquid to a boil on top of the stove, then cover the roaster and place in a 325-degree oven. Allow about 20 to 25 minutes per pound of lamb for cooking time, but remember lamb is more succulent when it is slightly pink when carved. If necessary, add more rosé wine during the cooking period.

When the cooking time is completed take the roaster out of the oven, and let it stand for about 15 minutes. Serve the vegetables and the juices with the sliced lamb. If a thicker gravy is desired, add a flour and butter roux to the juices, stir until smooth, and strain. Serve in a gravy boat separately.

We found a delightful little Italian tavernetta on the via Aurora, about a block from the Hotel Majestic, the hotel where we stayed both times we were in Rome. It didn't have a high rating in the Michelin Guide for Italy, but it was a charming place, loaded with atmosphere, called the Piccolo Mondo. Just opposite the entrance was a table loaded with the most gorgeous and varied appetizers I have ever seen, not just little dabs, but large portions. Our dinner that night was a lamb dish that the owner recommended, and it was delicious. I can't seem to find the Italian name, so I'll just call it Lamb Casserole Italienne.

LAMB CASSEROLE ITALIENNE

2 *tbsp. olive oil*	1 *clove garlic*
1 *medium onion*	¼ *tsp. dried basil*
1 *lb. cubed cooked lamb*	¼ *tsp. dried oregano*
2 *cups elbow macaroni*	2 *tsp. salt*
Boiling salted water	1 *tsp. sugar*
2 *15½-oz. cans Italian*	⅛ *tsp. pepper*
tomatoes	8 *oz. mozzarella cheese*

Heat 2 tablespoons olive oil in a skillet, then add 1 medium onion, sliced, and 1 pound cubed cooked lamb. Cook until lamb pieces are browned on all sides. Drain off drippings, if necessary. Meanwhile cook 2 cups (8 ounces) elbow macaroni until *al dente.*

Combine 2 15½-ounce cans of Italian tomatoes, the cooked macaroni, 1 clove garlic, crushed, ¼ teaspoon each dried basil and oregano, 2 teaspoons salt, 1 teaspoon sugar, ⅛ teaspoon pepper, and lamb mixture. Turn into a 2-quart casserole, and top with 8 ounces mozzarella cheese, sliced. Bake in a 350-degree oven for 30 minutes. Then put under broiler (5 to 7 inches from heat) for 3 to 5 minutes, or until cheese is browned. This serves 4.

Contrary to general belief, only a very few of the world's immortal culinary masterpieces are creations of master chefs, prepared in the grand manner of *haute cuisine*. Nearly all of them are regional dishes that originated in peasant kitchens, calling for comestibles that are inexpensive and plentiful.

One of the most celebrated examples of the French *cuisine bourgeois* comes from the province of Languedoc, in southern

France. Its full name is *Le Cassoulet de Midi*. Basically, it is a dish of French white beans cooked in a pot with various kinds of pork and sausage. But, depending on the region, other items are added. The original dish, from Castelnaudary, used ham, pork rind, fresh pork, and spiced sausages. In Carcassonne mutton and sometimes partridges are added. In Toulouse, lamb and preserved goose also go into the pot.

The French white bean and preserved goose (*confit d'oie*) are rare in America. But in place of the French beans our navy beans, pinto beans, Italian white kidney beans, or "black-eyed Susans" can well be used. In place of the preserved goose, roast goose or roast duck may be used, although it is not essential.

A number of years ago I got the recipe for the original dish from Castelnaudary. On this trip I obtained the recipes for the Carcassonne and the Toulouse version. But at the excellent restaurant, Le Grand Comptoir, the proprietor gave me his recipe for a cassoulet which combines the three Languedoc versions. This is my adaptation.

CASSOULET
(Bean and Meat Stew)

2 *lbs. dried beans*	4 *quarts water*
½ *lb. fresh pork rind slices*	1 *lb. small link sausages*
¼ *lb. bacon* (*in* 1 *piece*)	4 *tbsp. lard*
1 *onion*	1 *medium onion, minced*
2 *cloves*	1 *lb. shoulder pork, boned*
1 *carrot*	1 *lb. boned breast of lamb*
6 *cloves garlic*	*Salt and pepper*
¼ *tsp. dried thyme*	½ *cup dry white wine*
6 *peppercorns*	*Roast duck meat* (*optional*)
1 *bay leaf*	*Roast goose meat* (*optional*)

Soak 2 pounds dried beans (of your choice) overnight in cold water. Drain beans and place in a pot or kettle together with ½ pound fresh pork rind slices tied in a bundle, ¼ pound bacon in 1 piece, 1 onion studded with 2 cloves, 1 carrot, 6 cloves garlic, minced, ¼ teaspoon dried thyme, 6 peppercorns, bruised, and a bay leaf. Cover contents completely with water (about 4 quarts) and bring to boil. Reduce flame and simmer very, very gently for about 1½ hours, or until beans are tender.

While beans are cooking lightly brown 1 pound small link sausages in a skillet. In another large skillet heat 4 tablespoons lard. Then add 1 medium onion, minced, and 1 pound each boned shoulder of pork and boned breast of lamb, both cut in ¾ inch cubes and seasoned with salt and pepper. Let cubes of meat brown on all sides, then pour in the skillet ½ cup dry white wine. Stir to loosen any meat particles. Let simmer for a couple of minutes, then add liquid in skillet to the beans, reserving cubes of meat.

When beans are cooked remove onion and carrot and discard them. Also remove from beans the pork rind and bacon, and cut bacon into ½ inch cubes.

On the bottom of a large earthenware casserole place the pork rind in a layer, then add ½ of the beans. On top of bean layer place browned cubes of meat, the bacon cubes, and the sausages, each one cut in half. If you have any roast duck or goose left over, add it to the other meats. Then pour in the remaining beans and their juices. Cover casserole and put in a 225-degree oven and let it cook at least 4 hours, or even longer, if you wish.

Serve to 6 or 8 from the casserole, giving a portion of each meat and a generous serving of beans to each guest. I like crusty French bread and a dry white wine with this dish.

"The empire of the pig is almost universal and his qualities less contested than any other. Without him, no bacon, and therefore no cooking. . . . Everything in a pig is good. What ingratitude has permitted his name to become a word of opprobrium?"

Thus did Grimod de la Reynière, an early 19th century attorney turned cookbook writer, eulogize the source of so many gastronomic delights in his *Almanach des gourmands*. And I agree with him, for practically every part of our porcine friend is downright good eating, from the feet on up.

Nowhere is there a greater example of this than in Germany.

German cuisine abounds in mouth-watering pork dishes. Nürnberg's taverns and grills offer a profusion of pork dishes; boiled pork, knuckles, snout, clavicle, heart, bacon, and even fried ears! Frankfurters are, of course, world famous. Westphalia is a "Homeland of Ham." The specialties of the Ruhr district are bacon and beans, and "Potthast," a delicious peppery pork dish.

We had a most savory pork chop dish in a little wayside inn on the "Romantic Road" from Würtzburg to Augsburg. I failed to put down the German name, but it consisted of pork chops, apples and beer.

PORK CHOPS WITH APPLES AND ONIONS IN BEER

1¼ lbs. center cut pork chops	¾ pint beer
2 tbsp. bacon drippings	Salt and pepper
1 medium onion	3 whole cloves
1 lb. tart apples	1 bay leaf
1 tbsp. flour	1 strip lemon rind

Trim the excess fat from 1¼ pounds of center cut pork chops, loin chops are the best.

Heat 2 tablespoons of bacon drippings in a heavy iron skillet, and fry in it 1 medium sized onion, sliced, until limp but not browned. Add to the onions 1 pound of tart apples, peeled, cored, and rather thickly sliced. Continue to fry slowly until apples are tender. Then push the apples and onions to one side of the skillet, and blend 1 tablespoon of flour into the fat. Then add ¾ pint beer, and stir well while coming to a boil.

Place the apples and onions in a lightly greased casserole. Place the pork chops on top of the apples and onions and salt and pepper them to taste. Add to the casserole 3 whole cloves, 1 bay leaf, and a strip of lemon rind. Pour over all the thickened beer gravy. Cook in a 300-degree oven for about 1½ hours, or until the pork chops are thoroughly cooked. Serve from the casserole, and of course the perfect accompaniment is tall glasses of chilled beer.

We first came in contact with the Mediterranean at St.-Raphaël. We had encountered a lot of cold and rain on our way down to the Côte d'Azur, and the sight of the blue sea and the sunny skies were welcome indeed. We stopped overnight at the Excelsior Hotel, and we had two exceptional delicacies there, the best croissants at breakfast that we had ever eaten, and for dinner *Côtes de Porc aux Cerises* (pork chops with a cherry sauce). This is the recipe adapted to American availabilities.

CÔTES DE PORC AUX CERISES
(Pork Chops, Cherry Sauce)

4 *pork loin chops*	¾ *cup chopped walnuts*
Salt and pepper	½ *tsp. nutmeg*
2 *tbsp. olive oil*	2 *tbsp. lemon juice*
1 *oz. kirsch*	2 *tsp. cornstarch*
1 *lb. can pitted dark sweet*	
cherries	

Sprinkle 4 loin pork chops cut 1 inch thick with salt and pepper. Heat 2 tablespoons olive oil in a skillet and cook chops until browned on all sides. Drain off drippings and flambé chops with 1 ounce warmed kirsch. Add drained syrup from a 1-pound can pitted dark sweet cherries (reserving cherries), ¾ cup chopped walnuts, and ½ teaspoon nutmeg. Cover skillet and cook over low heat 45 to 60 minutes, turning chops occasionally. Remove chops to heated serving platter. Gradually stir 2 tablespoons lemon juice into 2 teaspoons cornstarch, then slowly stir the corn-starch mixture into cherry syrup mixture. Add reserved cherries and cook over low heat, stirring constantly, until thickened and clear. Serve cherry sauce with the chops.

On our way from Bologna to Parma we stopped in Modena for luncheon at a most interesting restaurant on the Piazza Roma, almost across from the Ducal Palace. We had *Costa di Maiale* (pork chops) with Marsala, and they were out of this world to me, because I am particularly fond of foods cooked with Marsala.

COSTA DI MAIALE AL MARSALA
(Pork Chops, Marsala)

4 *pork chops*	2 *small cloves garlic*
½ *tsp. dried rosemary*	*Dry white wine*
1 *tsp. dried sage*	1 *tbsp. butter*
½ *tsp. salt*	*Hot water*
¼ *tsp. freshly ground*	½ *cup Florio Virgin Dry*
pepper	*Marsala*

Mix together ½ teaspoon dried rosemary (which has been well-rubbed between the palms), 1 teaspoon dried sage, ½ teaspoon salt, ¼ teaspoon freshly ground pepper, and 1 large or 2 small cloves garlic, finely minced. Moisten this mixture with just a few drops dry white wine to bind, then coat each side of 4 pork chops with the mixture, patting it in well.

Melt 1 tablespoon butter in a skillet and in it brown the chops on both sides. Then pour enough hot water in the skillet to almost cover the chops. Cover the skillet and cook gently over a low flame for 45 minutes to an hour. When the water has evaporated, and the chops are well browned, pour into the skillet ½ cup Florio Virgin Dry Marsala wine. Simmer about 3 to 4 minutes more, then serve to 4.

Burgundy's most famous product is its wines, and they are the best and greatest in the world. But Burgundy is almost equally famous for its superb food, as anyone who has traveled the length and breadth of the province will testify. Nowhere else in France can one get such beef as that which comes from Charolles; nowhere else in the world can one find such huge and luscious snails. Mustard is another splendid Burgundian comestible, and its Morvan ham is superb.

Dijon was the ancient capital of the Dukes of Burgundy. Their palace today houses a wonderful museum filled with paintings, sculpture, and objects of art. Some of the tombs on display are exquisite beyond words.

In former years there were two outstanding restaurants in Dijon—the Restaurant Trois Faisans, and the Restaurant Pré aux

Clercs. At one time I believe the Trois Faisans had three stars in the Michelin Guide. But today the two restaurants have merged into one, and are located on the semicircular place de la Libération. The cuisine of the new restaurant, called the Pré aux Clercs et Trois Faisans, maintains the reputation of the former two, with M. Colin as the chef de cuisine. We had *Jambon du Morvan rôti à la Crème* the night we dined there. This is the adaptation of the recipe M. Colin wrote out for me.

JAMBON DU MORVAN RÔTI À LA CRÊME
(Baked Ham with Cream)

4 *slices baked ham*	*Lemon juice*
1 *tbsp. sweet butter*	*Small lump butter*
½ *cup dry white wine*	1 *tbsp. butter*
½ *lb. mushroom caps*	¼ *cup mushroom liquid*
½ *cup boiling water*	*Flour*
Pinch salt	¾ *cup cream*

Heat 4 slices baked ham, each cut about ¼ inch thick, in 1 tablespoon sweet butter, turning slices to cook lightly on each side. Add ½ cup dry white wine, and when wine is reduced to ¼ cup, remove ham slices to serving dish and keep warm.

While ham is heating put ½ pound mushroom caps in a saucepan with ½ cup boiling water, a pinch salt, a little lemon juice, and a small lump of butter. Cover, and boil mushrooms for 3 minutes. Drain mushrooms (reserving liquid), chop them, and sauté in 1 tablespoon butter for about 5 minutes. Remove from fire and keep warm.

To the liquid in the skillet the ham slices were heated in add ¼ cup mushroom liquid, and stir in enough flour to make a light roux. Let cook, stirring constantly, until blended and smooth, then add ¾ cup cream. Blend well and let heat through. The cream sauce should have the consistency of thick cream. To serve, cover ham slices with the chopped mushrooms, then pour over all the sauce.

It has been said that there is no other meat that can match veal in delicacy of flavor. But you must know veal to get the utmost out of it in cooking.

Veal is, of course, the flesh of a young calf. It is at its succulent best when the calf has had no other food but its mother's milk supply—two and a half to 3 months old. At that time its flesh will be white. But after a calf has fed on grass its flesh will be pink, or even reddish, and not as tender.

Cuts, too, vary in tenderness. Some require longer cooking. The best cuts of veal are slices from the leg, and, after having been flattened with a cleaver or wooden mallet, are called scallops of veal. It is from these that the world-famous Wiener Schnitzel comes. Scallops, almost paper thin, are marinated about an hour in lemon juice. Then they are wiped, sprinkled with salt and pepper, pulled through beaten egg, coated with fine breadcrumbs, and sautéed in hot butter for 2 minutes on each side. This dish was one of the glories of old Vienna.

I have often been asked, "Are the veal dishes in Italy superior to those in France?" My reply has always been, "Is a silver dollar better than a dollar bill?"

I have been served superb veal dishes in both France and Italy. Trying to be impartial, I am detailing seven of the outstanding veal dishes I have had in each of both countries. If you wish, you can try the entire fourteen over a period of time. Then you can draw your own conclusion.

Florence is a city that defies description in anything less than a fat volume. Its churches, art galleries, palaces, open-air museums of sculpture, shops (particularly those on the Ponte Vecchio —the bridge across the River Arno housing scores of jewelry and silver shops), and its breathtakingly beautiful surrounding hills are treasures that it would take years to assimilate. And you will never forget that Michelangelo lived and worked in Florence.

We were fortunate in our choice of a headquarters, the Hotel Bristol Helvetia. It was kitty-corner across from the Strozzi Palace, which dates from the end of the 15th century, and is the finest private palace in Florence. We were within walking distance of most of the principal points of interest in the heart of Florence, and, what is always of importance to us, it was very close to the offices of the American Express and the Bank of America d'Italia. Incidentally, the proprietor of the hotel, Mr. Baumgartner, was a walking encyclopedia of good eating places in Florence.

The restaurants in Florence were absolutely wonderful, and each meal was a gastronomic delight.

Paoli's is one of the finest restaurants in Florence, and certainly the oldest. Guido Pini, the proprietor, told me that it dated back to the 15th century. It is quiet, and its rooms, with vaulted ceilings, are pleasant and restful and elegant. Our entree was an outstanding one, Scaloppine al Marsala with chicken livers.

SCALOPPINE AL MARSALA WITH CHICKEN LIVERS

4 *veal scallops*	3 *tbsp. Marsala wine*
Flour	¼ *lb. fresh peas*
Salt and pepper	1 *clove garlic*
2 *oz. butter*	1 *tbsp. chopped fresh parsley*
2 *chicken livers*	1 *tbsp. finely minced ham*

For 2 people use 4 veal scallops cut from the filet or leg, about ¼ inch thick, with a total weight of about 10 ounces. Flatten the slices with a wooden mallet, and flour them lightly. Season with salt and pepper to taste. In a heavy skillet heat 2 ounces butter and put in the scallops. Over a high heat lightly brown them on both sides. Then add 2 chicken livers cut in small pieces and cook about 3 minutes. Lower the heat and add 3 tablespoons Marsala wine, and then add ¼ pound peas which have been cooked with a clove garlic, a tablespoon each chopped fresh parsley and finely minced ham. Cover the skillet and let whole cook very gently for about 15 or 20 minutes. Serve veal scallops on hot plates with chicken livers and peas poured over them.

The fame of Alfredo's restaurant in Rome, where the walls are covered with autographed pictures of the great and near-great, and where delectable *fettuccine* is mixed with a golden fork and spoon is world wide. But what is confusing to the visitor in Rome is that there are *three* Alfredo's!

In the old days Alfredo, a master showman, had his restaurant on the Via della Scrofa. It was there that Douglas Fairbanks and Mary Pickford presented him with the gold fork and spoon. And it was there that he earned his title as the King of *Fettuccine*.

But came a time when Alfredo, no doubt worn out by his calisthenics with the fork and spoon, retired, and his restaurant was finally bought by an ex-waiter.

But, as with all great showmen, retirement palled on Alfredo. He missed the great crowds, the adulation, and the theatrics of his profession. So he came out of retirement and opened another restaurant on the Piazza Augusto Imperatore, which is indeed a show place.

We first went to Alfredo alla Scrofa. Autographed pictures still line the walls, but the interior is unpretentious (they still have those revolving fans suspended from the ceilings). It is quiet, the food is excellent, but we found the service not all that it should be. We had *fettuccine,* of course, and our main dish was a delicious *Saltimbocca alla Romana.* This is the way it is prepared.

SALTIMBOCCA ALLA ROMANA
(Scallops of Veal with Ham)

8 *small veal cutlets*	*Freshly ground pepper*
8 *slices boiled ham*	*Grated Parmesan cheese*
Dried sage	2½ *oz. butter*
	1 *cup Florio Marsala wine*

Have your butcher cut 8 smallish cutlets from the leg of veal. At home place the cutlets between sheets of wax paper and flatten them with a wooden mallet until they are about a scant ¼ inch thick. They should measure about 3 inches square. Get enough boiled ham to make 8 slices the same size as the veal cutlets (use Prosciutto ham if you can get it).

The Italians place a leaf of fresh sage on each veal-ham slice. Use this if you have it. If not, sprinkle a little dried sage over each veal-ham slice. Also sprinkle over each veal-ham slice about

½ teaspoon grated Parmesan cheese. Dust lightly with freshly ground pepper, and then roll them up, fastening each with a toothpick.

In a skillet melt 2½–3 ounces butter, and when it is hot put in the rolls and gently sauté them until they are browned all over, about 10 minutes or so. Then pour over them about 1 cup Florio Marsala wine. Let it bubble for a minute, then cover the skillet and gently simmer the contents until meat is quite tender, and the sauce reduced, about 10 to 15 minutes. Remove rolls to a hot platter, remove the toothpicks, and pour the sauce over. This serves 4.

A great favorite of the Milanese is *Ossi Buchi,* a sort of a stew utilizing the foreleg of young Lombardy calves. It is not a dish that is featured on the menus of fine restaurants and hotels, although it was wonderfully made for us at the very swank Villa d'Este, and at what I consider the finest restaurant in Milan, Giannino's. It is a really lusty and savory peasant dish, and can easily be made in any American kitchen.

OSSI BUCHI
(Veal Shanks)

2 *lbs. calves' shinbones*	*Pinch dried rosemary*
Flour	*Pinch dried oregano*
1 *oz. butter*	½ *cup dry white wine*
1 *oz. olive oil*	¾ *lb. fresh tomatoes*
Salt and pepper	½ *cup consommé*
1 *small carrot*	2 *tbsp. chopped fresh parsley*
1 *onion*	*Grated rind small lemon*
1 *stalk celery*	1 *clove garlic*

Get about 2 pounds of the meaty part of the foreleg shinbone of a young calf (not more than 3 months old, if possible), and have them sawed into 2 inch lengths.

In a heavy, rather deep skillet heat 1 ounce each butter and olive oil. In this place the pieces of the veal shinbone, that have been floured, with the bones horizontal. While they are cooking turn them frequently so that they brown all over. When golden brown arrange them in the skillet so that the pieces are upright (with bones vertical) in order that the marrow in the bones does not fall out as they further cook. Salt and pepper them to taste, and add 1 small carrot, 1 onion, and 1 stalk celery, all chopped, and a pinch each dried rosemary and dried oregano. Cover skillet and simmer for 10 minutes. Then add ½ cup dry white wine, ¾ pound fresh tomatoes, coarsely chopped, and ½ cup consommé. Again cover and simmer gently for 1½ to 2 hours (adding equal portions of wine and consommé from time to time if necessary), or until meat is tender.

Prepare a mixture of 2 tablespoons chopped fresh parsley, the grated rind of a smallish lemon, and 1 clove garlic, chopped. The Milanese call this mixture *gremolata,* and it is an essential part of *Ossi Buchi* in Milan. It is sprinkled on the top of the dish just before serving to 4. Traditionally, a *Risotto alla Milanese* accompanies this dish.

During more than three months traveling in Italy, Mrs. Wood and I stopped at three hotels that I do not believe can be surpassed anywhere in the world from the combined points of view of comfort, charm of environment, service and courtesy, and superb food. Two of the hotels were in large cities—the Grand Hotel Continental in Milan and the Royal Hotel in Naples—and the third was the world-famous resort hotel—the Villa d'Este in Cernobbio, on Lake Como.

The Continental is more or less in the heart of Milan, and within walking distance of the tremendous cathedral and La Scala Opera House, to say nothing of the American Express and the Bank of America. Two of the managing directors are Costantino and Luigi Gallia, both men of great charm who speak perfect English, and who treat their guests as friends rather than clients. The rooms are exceedingly comfortable, with every convenience. And the food is delicious beyond words. We ate most of our dinners in the lovely dining rooms of the Continental while in Milan.

One hot night at the Continental we had a magnificent dinner of cold minestrone and cold roast veal with tuna fish sauce, accompanied by a chilled bottle of Soave Bolla white wine.

VITELLO TONNATO
(Cold Veal, Tuna Fish Sauce)

2-lb. leg veal, boned   Mayonnaise
Anchovy filets   Canned tuna fish
                    Veal stock

Roast a boned leg of veal weighing about 2 pounds (having pierced the meat here and there with a sharp knife, and into the slits place bits of anchovy filets). Let veal cool, and after having removed fat, add a little water to juices in pan to make a stock.

For the sauce make a tuna fish mayonnaise. To a good mayonnaise (bought or home made) add mashed or pounded canned tuna fish with some of the oil. Incorporate this purée gradually into mayonnaise (5 ounces mayonnaise and 2 ounces tuna fish). Thin this to the consistency of thick cream with veal stock. Pour sauce over cold veal, sliced thinly, refrigerate overnight, and serve next day.

Nowhere in Italy is the cooking so famous, so lusty, and so toothsome as it is in Bologna. While the city has many fascinating treasures, you always look forward to the end of the day when you can eat Bolognese food (I'll have more to tell you about Bologna in another chapter).

A typical Bolognese method of treating veal is exemplified in their famous *Costolette alla Bolognese*—veal cutlets. You'll see this item on menus all over Europe and America, but it will be but a weak imitation of the original, which we had in Bologna.

COSTOLETTE ALLA BOLOGNESE
(Bolognese Veal Cutlets)

4 veal cutlets   1 oz. Marsala wine
2 eggs   4 slices lean ham
Fine breadcrumbs   ¼ lb. mozzarella cheese
6 oz. butter   2 tbsp. grated Parmesan cheese

Get 4 cutlets cut from the boned leg of veal, about ¼ inch thick (each weighing about 6 ounces) and season with salt and pepper. Beat 2 eggs lightly and dip cutlets first in egg and then in fine breadcrumbs (about 1 cup). Heat 6 ounces butter and 1 ounce Marsala wine in a skillet, and brown cutlets on both sides. Then arrange cutlets on a broiler pan. Cover each cutlet with a thin slice lean ham (prosciutto, if obtainable) cut to fit size of cutlet. On top of ham put thin slices mozzarella cheese (about ¼ pound needed). Sprinkle over topped cutlets about 2 tablespoons grated Parmesan cheese. Over all pour butter from skillet. Broil (about 4 inches from source of flame) until cheese is soft and slightly brown. Serves 4.

Thin slices of veal, covered with various mixtures, then rolled up and secured and cooked in a skillet, are very popular in Italy. They are called *braciolette, bocconcini,* and the very tiny ones, threaded on skewers, are called *Quagliette di Vitello* (Little Veal Quails). At Sabatini's, one of Florence's finest restaurants, we had *Bracioline alla Fiorentina,* stuffed veal rolls cooked in Marsala, and, to my mind, they were the best of all.

BRACIOLINE ALLA FIORENTINA
(Stuffed Veal Rolls)

12 *thin slices veal*	2 *tbsp. minced fresh parsley*
Salt and pepper	*Pinch nutmeg*
½ *cup finely minced ham*	2 *tbsp. butter*
¾ *cup ricotta cheese*	2 *tbsp. olive oil*
1 *clove garlic*	2 *oz. dry white wine*
2 *mushrooms*	4 *oz. Florio Marsala wine*

Have ready 12 thin slices veal cut from the leg, each measuring about 3½ inches square. Lightly season them with salt and pepper.

Combine ½ cup finely minced ham, ¾ cup ricotta cheese (or firm cottage cheese), 1 clove garlic, finely minced, 2 mushrooms, which have been sautéed in butter for 5 minutes, minced, 2 tablespoons minced fresh parsley, and a pinch nutmeg. Blend all well and spread the mixture evenly on the 12 slices veal. Then roll the slices up, and secure them with toothpicks, or tie with thread.

In a heavy skillet heat 2 tablespoons each butter and very fine olive oil. Put in the veal rolls, and slowly brown them all over. Then add 2 ounces dry white wine and 4 ounces Marsala wine to the pan, and let the whole thing simmer until the sauce begins to turn syrupy. Serve immediately to 4.

The large, ripe tomatoes grown in the south of Italy are wonderfully flavorsome. In one of the restaurants in the miniature port of Borgo Marinaro, in Naples, we had a lovely veal dish with a tomato sauce.

VITELLO ALLA NAPOLETANA
(Neopolitan Veal)

1½ lbs. veal steak	1 clove garlic
Flour	1 tsp. Worcestershire sauce
1 tbsp. butter	1 8-oz. can tomato paste
1 tbsp. olive oil	½ cup dry white wine
1½ tsp. salt	12 thin onion slices
⅛ tsp. black pepper	½ pt. sour cream

Remove any bones from 1½ pounds veal steak, or cutlets, ¼ inch thick (enough lean meat for 5 to 6 servings). Cut the meat into 5 or 6 serving pieces and pound some flour into both sides of the meat. Heat 1 tablespoon each of butter and olive oil in a large skillet or Dutch oven. Add the meat and brown slowly on both sides. If necessary, add more olive oil.

After the meat browns sprinkle it with 1½ teaspoons salt and ⅛ teaspoon black pepper. Add 1 clove garlic, minced, 1 teaspoon Worcestershire sauce, one 8-ounce can tomato paste, and ½ cup dry white wine. Place 12 thin onion slices over the meat, then cover and simmer for 25 minutes, or until meat and onions are tender. Add more dry white wine if the mixture begins to cook dry, or if a thinner gravy is desired.

Just before serving, spread sour cream over each one of the

meat pieces in the skillet (you'll need about ½ pint). Cover, turn heat down very low, and heat for 5 minutes. To serve, spread cooked rice or noodles over a hot platter, top with the veal slices, and spoon sauce over all. This serves 5 to 6.

Blanquette de Veau is the classic standby of the French cuisine Bourgeoise, a superb veal stew. I don't recall seeing it on any of the menus of the more or less expensive restaurants in Paris, but it is a specialty of at least four excellent Parisian bistros. I suppose it reaches its heighth of deliciousness in farmhouse kitchens, but I'll settle for what we had one night at one of our favorite bistros, Chez Pauline.

BLANQUETTE DE VEAU
(Veal Ragoût with White Sauce)

2 *lbs. lean veal*	12 *small white onions*
1 *quart water*	½ *lb. mushrooms*
1 *tsp. salt*	2 *tbsp. butter*
1 *large onion*	*Salt and pepper*
2 *whole cloves*	2 *tbsp. butter*
2 *small carrots*	2 *tbsp. flour*
Pinch dried thyme	2 *cups strained veal broth*
Celery leaves	½ *cup dry white wine*
1 *clove garlic*	2 *oz. dry vermouth*
1 *tbsp. chopped parsley*	2 *egg yolks*
1 *bay leaf*	1 *cup cream*
5 *whole peppercorns*	1 *tsp. lemon juice*
3 *tbsp. butter*	1 *tbsp. chopped fresh parsley*

Get 2 pounds lean veal, and cut the meat into cubes about 1 to 1½ inches. Bring 1 quart of water to boil in a deep saucepan after adding a teaspoon salt. Add the cubes of veal slowly, so the water continues to boil. Then add 1 large peeled onion cut in half, and each half stuck with a whole clove, 2 small carrots, sliced, a pinch dried thyme, a handful of celery leaves, a minced clove garlic, 1 tablespoon chopped parsley, a bay leaf, and 5 whole peppercorns. Cover the saucepan, turn down the flame, and simmer until veal is tender, about 1½ hours.

While veal is cooking melt 3 tablespoons butter in a heavy saucepan and add 12 small, peeled white onions. Cook until lightly browned, then lower flame and steam until they are tender, about 30 minutes. Also sauté ½ pound mushrooms, sliced, in 2 tablespoons butter until tender, about 6 minutes, and season with salt and pepper to taste.

When veal is tender remove pieces to a serving casserole, and add to veal pieces the small onions and mushrooms, and keep all warm. Then strain the broth, discarding the solids.

In a deep saucepan or skillet melt 2 tablespoons butter and blend in 2 tablespoons flour. Do not, however, let the flour brown. When roux is well blended slowly add 2 cups of the strained broth, ½ cup dry white wine, and 2 ounces dry (French) vermouth. Stir constantly while liquid is being added until smooth and slightly thickened. Bring just to the boiling point, then lower flame to a simmer. Add to the sauce 2 beaten egg yolks mixed with 1 cup cream, stirring constantly. Cook very gently (do not allow to boil) until sauce is smooth and thickened. Correct seasoning, if necessary, and add 1 teaspoon lemon juice.

To the sauce add the veal cubes, small onions, and mushrooms, reheat gently, and return all to the warm serving casserole. Sprinkle over all a generous tablespoon chopped fresh parsley, and serve. With this dish serve fluffy cooked rice, buttered peas, and, of course, a chilled dry white wine. Serves 5.

Another delectable veal stew we had in a Paris bistro was made with red wine.

VEAL STEW WITH RED WINE

1½ lbs. lean veal	1 tbsp. chopped fresh parsley
2 tbsp. butter	1 bay leaf
3 slices lean bacon, diced	1 tbsp. tomato purée
2 oz. brandy	Salt and pepper
2 cups dry red wine	1 tbsp. butter
2 cloves garlic	1 tbsp. flour

Cut 1½ pounds lean veal into 1 inch cubes, and brown them in 2 tablespoons butter, along with 3 slices lean bacon, diced. Then warm 2 ounces brandy in a ladle, set it alight, and pour brandy over veal cubes. When flames die out add 2 cups dry red wine, 2 whole cloves garlic, 1 tablespoon chopped fresh parsley, a bay leaf, 1 tablespoon tomato purée, and salt and pepper to taste.

Cover skillet and simmer the whole slowly for 1½ to 2 hours. Then uncover, and stir in a roux made from 1 tablespoon each butter and flour. Blend well until smooth, then cook about ½ hour longer. Serve with a dry red wine to 4.

The two most famous cheeses in the world are the Emmentaler of Switzerland, more popularly known as Swiss cheese, and the Roquefort cheese of France.

There is only one place in the world where the true Roquefort cheese is made, and that is in the little Gascon town of Roquefort-sur-Soulson, near the border of the Languedoc Province. There is still preserved in a French museum the original text of a law passed by the Parliament of Toulouse on August 31, 1666, which confirms the right granted by Charles VI and Francis I of France that the name "Roquefort Cheese" could only be applied to cheese cured in the natural coves of the Rocks of Combalon, which form the backdrop for the village.

There is almost no department of gastronomy in which Roquefort cheese doesn't fit in, always with profit to the final dish. This veal stew, a Gascony favorite, is an example.

RAGOÛT OF VEAL WITH ROQUEFORT CHEESE

1½ lbs. boneless veal	4 medium potatoes
Seasoned flour	2 medium onions
1 tbsp. butter	4 medium carrots
1 tbsp. olive oil	¼ cup chopped fresh parsley
1½ tsp. salt	¼ cup Roquefort cheese,
¼ tsp. pepper	crumbled
1½ quarts hot water	½ cup dry white wine

Get 1½ pounds boneless veal and cut in 1½ inch cubes. Shake the cubes in a bag containing seasoned flour until they are well coated. Heat 1 tablespoon each of butter and olive oil in a heavy skillet over a medium flame, then add the floured veal cubes and brown well on all sides. Then add 1½ teaspoons salt, ¼ teaspoon pepper, and 1½ quarts hot water. Cover, and cook over a low flame about 1 hour, or until veal is almost tender. Then add 4 medium-sized potatoes, pared and sliced, 2 medium sized onions, sliced, 4 medium-sized carrots, cubed, and ¼ cup chopped parsley. Cover and cook ½ hour, or until vegetables are tender. Remove meat and vegetables to a hot platter, and add ¼ cup crumbled Roquefort cheese and ½ cup dry white wine to liquid in skillet, and cook over a low flame until cheese is melted. Serve the cheese sauce over the meat and vegetables to 6.

Most gourmets agree that there is no other meat that can match veal in delicacy of flavor, provided, of course, that the flesh comes from very young calves which have never eaten grass. But older veal can be made into delicious stews, such as one we had in a little restaurant, La Crémaillère, in Montélimar. Montélimar, by the way, is the home of the famous nougat, and almost every store, be it a laundry, a tobacco store, a drug store, or "you name it" store, displays and sells the marvelous candy. But back to the veal stew with white wine.

VEAL STEW WITH WHITE WINE AND PAPRIKA

2 *lbs. veal*	1 *4-oz. can mushroom stems*
3 *tbsp. butter*	*and pieces (with liquid)*
¼ *cup flour*	1 *onion*
¾ *cup hot water*	1 *tsp. paprika*
¾ *cup dry white wine*	*Salt and pepper*
2 *tbsp. chopped parsley*	1 *cup sour cream*

Get 2 pounds of veal cut from the leg, and with the flat side of a cleaver or a wooden mallet pound it to not over ¼ inch in thickness. Then cut the veal into strips about 2 inches wide and 4 inches long.

Heat 3 tablespoons butter in a large, heavy skillet. Add the veal slices and brown them slowly on both sides. Then stir in ¼ cup of flour, and when blended, add ¾ cup each of hot water and dry white wine. Cook, stirring constantly, until the mixture is thickened and smooth. Then add a 4-ounce can of mushroom stems and pieces, including the liquid, 2 tablespoons chopped parsley, 1 thinly sliced onion, 1 teaspoon paprika, and salt and pepper to taste.

Cover the skillet tightly, and simmer gently, for 45 minutes to an hour, or until veal is tender, stirring frequently. Just before serving, stir in 1 cup commercial sour cream, heat, and serve with buttered noodles to 5 or 6.

With our apartment in St.-Jean-Cap-Ferrat as a base, we used to make little forays into the country along and behind the coast. We fell in love with Mediterranean Provence, and found the cooking marvelous. Frequently, we'd have some dish, and then some time later we'd cook it at the apartment to see how close we could come to the original. The average was pretty good! This is a veal dish we liked, which I call:

OLIVE VEAL WITH SHERRY GRAVY

1 lb. veal shoulder, sliced	¼ cup olive oil
¼ cup flour	1 cup condensed consommé
⅛ tsp. pepper	1 tsp. lemon juice
¼ tsp. celery salt	2 tbsp. above seasoned flour
1 egg, beaten	¼ cup chopped pimento-
1 tbsp. cold water	stuffed green olives
⅔ cup fine breadcrumbs	3 oz. dry sherry

Get 1 pound of veal shoulder, sliced. Combine ¼ cup flour, ⅛ teaspoon pepper, and ¼ teaspoon celery salt. Dredge the veal with this mixture, reserving 2 tablespoons of the seasoned flour for later use.

Combine 1 slightly beaten egg with 1 tablespoon cold water. Mix well, then dip veal into it, and then coat veal with about ⅔ cup fine breadcrumbs. Put ¼ cup olive oil in skillet and when hot brown the coated veal until golden brown on both sides. Add 1 cup condensed consommé and 1 teaspoon of lemon juice, and cook, covered, over a reduced flame for 30 minutes, or until meat is tender. Remove veal to hot platter and keep warm.

Add a little of the gravy to the reserved seasoned flour, blend well, and add this roux to the gravy. Cook over a low flame, stirring constantly, until thickened. Add ¼ cup chopped pimento-stuffed green olives and 3 ounces dry sherry. Heat to serving temperature, and serve gravy with the veal.

In many parts of France the birth of a calf is an exciting event, and the animal is almost as carefully tended and reared as a human infant. After the calves have gone to market, the first veal is eagerly bargained for by city restaurateurs.

The best veal chops are the loin chops, with or without a slice of kidney attached, and the rib chops. But because veal is a bland meat, even the chops need a flavor enhancement of wine and herbs and other seasonings. Typical is this delicious veal chop recipe from the Perigord province of France.

CÔTES DES VEAU
(Veal Chops)

4 *loin or rib veal chops*	8 *medium-sized mushrooms*
1 *oz. butter*	2 *cloves garlic*
1 *oz. olive oil*	1 *cup dry white wine*
Salt and pepper	*Flour and butter roux (optional)*

Heat 1 ounce each butter and fine olive oil in a heavy skillet. In this brown slowly 4 loin or rib chops, cut about ¾ inch thick, on both sides until tender (about 35 minutes). Salt and pepper them to taste, then remove to a heated platter and keep hot.

In the same skillet sauté 8 medium sized mushrooms, sliced, for about 5 minutes. Salt and pepper them lightly, then add 2 cloves garlic, minced, and 1 cup dry white wine. Bring the liquid to a boil, then turn down the flame quickly and simmer very gently for 5 minutes. Pour the mushrooms and juices over the chops and serve at once. If you prefer a slightly thickened gravy, stir a flour and butter roux into the mushrooms and juices and blend well.

From the Dijon region comes this recipe for *Côtelettes de Veau, Sauce Moutarde,* which are veal chops with a delightfully piquant mustard sauce.

CÔTELETTES DE VEAU, SAUCE MOUTARDE
(Veal Chops with Mustard Sauce)

4 *loin or rib veal chops*	3 *oz. dry sherry*
1 *oz. butter*	2 *tsp. Dijon mustard*
1 *oz. olive oil*	4 *oz. cream*
Salt and pepper	*Pinch salt*
1 *oz. butter*	*Small pinch freshly ground*
1 *small onion, minced*	*pepper*
1 *tsp. flour*	½ *tsp. Worcestershire sauce*

Heat 1 ounce each butter and fine olive oil in a heavy skillet. In this brown slowly 4 loin or rib veal chops (I prefer the loin chops with the kidney attached) cut ¾ inch thick, on both sides until tender (about 35 minutes). Salt and pepper them to taste, then remove to a heated platter and keep hot.

The sauce is very simple to prepare, and can be made in advance or while the chops are cooking. In a saucepan heat 1 ounce butter and add 1 small onion, minced. As the onion begins to brown add 1 teaspoon flour and blend in well. Then add 3 ounces dry sherry, 2 teaspoons Dijon mustard, 4 ounces cream, a tiny pinch salt, and a sprinkling freshly ground black pepper, and ½ teaspoon Worcestershire sauce. Stir and blend everything well, then add the sauce to the skillet and fat the chops were cooked in. Heat, stirring well, then pour over the chops and serve.

I told about *Mai Wein* in the chapter on fish, and gave a German recipe for making your own *Mai Wein.* It is a delightful beverage, and it combines beautifully with veal. A superb veal dish is this *Kalbesragout Mit Mai Wein.*

KALBESRAGOUT MIT MAI WEIN
(Veal Stew with May Wine)

1½ *lbs. lean veal*	1 *cup seedless white grapes*
Seasoned flour	12 *whole tiny white onions*
2 *tbsp. butter*	2 *young carrots*
1 *medium onion*	*Cooked rice*
1½ *cups May wine*	*Cooked peas*

Flour and butter roux (*optional*)

Cut 1½ pounds lean veal into ¾ inch cubes, and shake them in a bag of seasoned flour. Place 2 tablespoons butter in a Dutch oven, and when hot add 1 medium onion, sliced. Sauté until golden brown (about 5 minutes). Then add floured veal cubes and brown on all sides. Next add 1 cup May wine, bring just to a simmer, then cover and simmer 1 hour. Uncover, add 1 cup white seedless grapes, 12 whole tiny peeled white onions, 2 young carrots, cubed, and ½ cup May wine. Recover, and simmer another half hour.

On a hot serving platter arrange a circle of cooked rice (about 3 cups), and inside a border of 1 package frozen peas, cooked according to directions on package. Ladle veal stew into the center, and serve immediately. If you prefer a thicker gravy, drain off liquid from stew, thicken with a flour and butter roux, and return to stew. Serves 4 to 6.

A number of years ago (at least a dozen) I had a wonderful veal dish in the Swiss Chalet of the Bismark Hotel in Chicago. It was called *G'schnetzlets,* and it was so delicious that I persuaded Theodore Meyer, the executive chef of the Bismark, to give me the recipe. Later, I included it in my second book, *More Recipes With a Jug of Wine.*

On the evening of August 8th, 1963, Mrs. Wood and I had dinner at the lovely old Veltliner Keller restaurant in Zürich. I have detailed our hors d'oeuvre in a previous chapter. But what was our main dish? *G'schnetzlets!*

How do the two recipes compare? Well, they are both tops for my money. However, I must confess that the dish at the Veltliner Keller was a little more elaborate and flavorsome, and I prefer it.

G'SCHNETZLETS
(Minced Veal à la Swiss)

1 *lb. veal tenderloin*	1 *cup fresh mushrooms,*
Flour	*chopped*
Salt and pepper	1 *cup chicken broth*
Paprika	1 *cup dry white wine*
2 *oz. butter*	½ *cup cream*
1 *onion, chopped*	1 *tbsp. chopped fresh parsley*

Get 1 pound choice veal tenderloin. With a razor-sharp knife cut the veal into long, thin slices, about like a strip of bacon. Gather them up and dice them, so that each little morsel is about 1 inch square and ¼ inch thick. Sprinkle them generously with flour, salt and pepper, and paprika.

Melt 2 ounces butter in a heavy skillet, and when hot add the veal, and fry over a hot fire very quickly—about 2 to 3 minutes (it should not be overcooked). Remove veal pieces from skillet and add 1 chopped onion, turn down heat, and fry until limp.

Meanwhile stew 1 cup chopped fresh mushrooms in 1 cup chicken broth for about the same length of time it takes to cook the veal. Then put the cooked veal and onions into the mushroom-chicken broth mixture, and stir a few times.

Pour 1 cup dry white wine into the skillet the veal and onions were cooked in, and bring it to a boil. Then stir in veal-mushroom-broth-onion mixture. Blend everything well, then add ½ cup cream and 1 tablespoon chopped fresh parsley. Cook over a low heat, stirring constantly, for about 10 minutes, then serve.

To my mind the most delightful and certainly most attractive hotel in Zürich is the Carlton Elite. While it is located in the heart of the city, with entrances both on the main street, the Bahnhofstrasse, and on Nuscheler Strasse, it is exceedingly quiet and peaceful, and most modern.

We dined in two of their restaurants. One is an outdoor terrace, and the other is the La Locanda Ticinese, an exotically colorful Swiss-Italian tavern, opening off both the lobby and the outdoor dining terrace.

We celebrated Mrs. Wood's birthday in the Locanda Ticinese, and our meal was marvelous. The dinner entree was one of the most unusual and delicious veal dishes we had ever tasted, and I'm not excepting either France or Italy. It was called *Escalope of Veal Conca d'Oro*. In starting to detail it I discovered that some of the proportions were too vague, so I can't give the exact recipe. But this is the sketchy recipe.

On scallops of veal are put first a slice of chilled seasoned butter, made with butter, mustard, Worcestershire sauce, lemon juice, meat extract, salt, parsley, tarragon, sage, basil, garlic, shallot, and paprika. On top of the seasoned butter is a paste of ham, made by putting ham through a sieve, and mixing it with whipped cream, cognac and oregano. On top of this is a slice of raw ham cut the same size as the escalope of veal. The prepared escalops are fried in butter, and covered with chopped cooked zucchini, green peppers, and tomatoes.

One of the most refreshing changes from run-of-the-mill meat, poultry and seafood dishes are kidneys. Most frequently cooked with wine and/or brandy, they have a taste-teasing difference that is highly satisfying.

Although European connoisseurs consider kidneys to be one of the greatest delicacies, a great many Americans shun them, either because they have a prejudice against variety meats, or because they have eaten them improperly prepared and cooked.

Kidneys of quadrupeds are all edible. The most frequently used come from beef, pork, sheep or calves. The latter two have the most agreeable and delicate flavor.

In preparing veal and lamb kidneys before cooking, they should be cut in half lengthwise and the core and tubes removed. This is done with a sharp-pointed knife, or better still, with a curved pair of scissors, such as manicure or surgical scissors with curved blades. After cores and tubes have been removed the kidneys should be soaked in cold, salted water for an hour or so. After that, unless they are to be broiled, they are usually sliced.

Britons have a far greater appreciation of kidneys than do Americans. Broiled kidneys with bacon is a favorite British breakfast dish, and many of the best restaurants in London list it as a dinner entree as well. On two occasions I have had wonderful kidney dishes in fashionable and exclusive Mayfair restaurants. One was *Rognons Sauté aux Chipolatas* (kidneys sautéed with

small, spicy sausages) served at the Coq d'Or Restaurant, one of
London's finest and most beautiful French restaurants. Meuniny,
the chef de cuisine, wrote out the recipe for me.

ROGNONS SAUTÉ AUX CHIPOLATAS
(Kidneys Sautéed with Sausages)

6 *lamb kidneys*	4 *oz. dry white wine*
1 *oz. butter*	2 *oz. condensed consommé*
4 *chipolata sausages*	2 *oz. butter*
1 *shallot (or little green onion)*	*Salt and pepper*
Chopped parsley	

Clean 6 lamb kidneys and cut each into quarters. Sauté them in
1 ounce butter until they begin to brown slightly, about 5 minutes.
In a separate pan grill 4 chipolata sausages until nicely browned.
Place the sautéed kidneys and sausages in an earthenware casserole, or on a silver dish, and keep hot.

In the same pan the kidneys were sautéed in put a fairly good-
sized shallot, finely chopped (or little green onions, bulbs and
tops, finely chopped). When thoroughly heated but not browned
add about 4 ounces dry white wine and 2 ounces condensed consommé. Bring to a boil and reduce the liquid by half. Then add 2
ounces butter sliced in bits, swirling the sauce with a wire whisk
while adding the butter. Correct seasoning with salt and freshly
ground pepper to taste.

To serve, pour the sauce over the kidneys, top them with the
chipolatas, and sprinkle with chopped parsley. This serves 2.

We had a memorable kidney dish at the Hotel Continental in
Milan. Like everything else we had in the dining room, it was
superb, and this was a specialty of the chef.

ROGNONE TRIFOLATO AL COGNAC
(Kidneys Flambéed with Cognac)

½ *lb. veal kidneys*	3 *tbsp. Cognac*
3 *tbsp. butter*	2 *oz. cream*
1 *tsp. chopped parsley*	1 *tsp. French mustard*
Salt and pepper	

Prepare ½ pound veal kidneys for cooking, and cut them in thin slices. In a heavy skillet brown about 1½ tablespoons butter and put in the sliced kidneys. Let them cook a few minutes at full fire, then remove skillet from fire and drain off watery liquid. Then put about 1½ tablespoons more butter in skillet with sliced kidneys and let the whole brown lightly. Add salt and pepper to taste, a teaspoon finely chopped parsley, and 3 tablespoons of burning brandy. When flame dies out stir in about 2 ounces fresh cream and a teaspoon French mustard. Let all heat up, stirring little, then serve very hot to 2.

In Dijon we had kidneys cooked in Burgundy wine, and like all Burgundian dishes they were delectable.

ROGNONS BOURGUIGNON
(Kidneys in Burgundy)

6 *lamb kidneys*	2 *tbsp. flour*
Salt and pepper	1 *cup Burgundy wine*
Flour	½ *cup sliced fresh mushrooms*
7 *tbsp. butter*	1 *small green pepper*
1 *tbsp. chopped shallot* (*or*	*Paprika*
little green onion)	*Few grains cayenne pepper*
Salt	3 *tbsp. dry sherry*

After the standard initial preparation cut 6 lamb kidneys in slices about ¼ inch thick. Season with salt and pepper and dredge lightly with flour. Sauté in about 2 tablespoons butter until all sides are browned.

In another saucepan melt 4 tablespoons butter and add 1 tablespoon finely chopped shallot (or little green onion, bulbs and tops). Cook 5 minutes without letting butter or shallots brown. Then add 2 tablespoons flour and stir until well blended. Now gradually add 1 cup Burgundy wine and stir constantly until boiling point is reached. Pour this sauce into pan with kidneys, add ½ cup sliced fresh mushrooms which have been cooked in a tablespoon butter for 5 minutes, and 1 small green pepper which has been thinly sliced and cooked in boiling water for 8 minutes.

Season with salt, paprika, and a few grains cayenne pepper. Just before serving add 1 tablespoon butter and 3 tablespoons dry sherry.

Sweetbreads, or *Ris de Veau* as they are called in France, are one of the most delicate and delicious of dishes when they are properly prepared and cooked. In France, and in Italy, where veal is the most popular meat, you will usually find calves' sweetbreads cooked to perfection. Of course, sweetbreads are in the bland category, so cunningly devised sauces are very necessary to them. We had them a number of times on the Continent, and always the verdict was—"What a heavenly dish!"

In Paris there are two or three bistros and a lovely restaurant that specialize in *Ris de Veau,* that I know of. Au Vert Bocage and Au Bocage Fleuri prepare them in the Normandy fashion, with Calvados. Au Caveau Montpensier, a bistro near the Théâtre Français, serves them braised, and I would be hard pressed to choose between the two methods. However, you can judge for yourself by trying both. The following is the braised version.

A word about the initial preparation. Soak the sweetbreads in icy water for 1 hour. Then drain, and put them in simmering water, salted, to which the juice of a lemon has been added, for about 15 minutes. Cool in cold water, then trim away the tubes and membranes, being careful not to break the tissues. They are now ready to cook.

RIS DE VEAU, BRAISE
(Braised Sweetbreads)

1 *pair sweetbreads (1 lb.)*	*Pinch dried thyme*
2 *tbsp. butter*	*Pinch minced parsley*
1 *onion*	*Salt and pepper*
1 *carrot*	1 *cup condensed consommé*
¼ *cup chopped celery hearts*	½ *cup dry white wine*
2 *tbsp. chopped mushrooms*	1 *tsp. arrowroot*
1 *bay leaf*	*Dry white wine*

3 *tbsp. cream*

In an ovenproof casserole heat 2 tablespoons butter, then add 1 onion, sliced, 1 carrot, sliced, ¼ cup chopped celery hearts, 2 tablespoons chopped mushrooms, 1 bay leaf, and a pinch each dried thyme and parsley. Cook until vegetables are soft, then put in the casserole 1 pair prepared sweetbreads (about 1 pound), which have been seasoned with salt and pepper to taste, 1 cup condensed consommé, and ½ cup dry white wine. Cover the casserole and put in a 350-degree oven for about 45 minutes, basting occasionally.

When sweetbreads are done remove them from the casserole and keep warm. Strain the sauce through a fine sieve. If it is too thin add 1 teaspoon arrowroot dissolved in a little white wine. Bring to a boil, and when sauce begins to thicken, remove from fire and add 3 tablespoons cream. Mix well, pour sauce over sweetbreads, and serve at once to 2.

This is the Normandy version.

RIS DE VEAU, NORMANDE
(Sweetbreads, Normandy Style)

3 *pairs sweetbreads*	¼ *tsp. crushed peppercorns*
⅓ *cup butter*	*Salt and pepper*
2 *tbsp. chopped onion*	½ *lb. mushrooms*
¼ *tsp. dried rosemary*	3 *oz. Calvados (or applejack)*
¼ *tsp. dried basil*	1 *cup heavy cream*
	2 *egg yolks*

In a heavy skillet melt ⅓ cup butter and add 2 tablespoons finely chopped onions, ¼ teaspoon each dried rosemary, basil, and crushed peppercorns. Put 3 pairs prepared sweetbreads, which have been seasoned with salt and pepper to taste, in the skillet and sauté for 10–12 minutes. Then add ½ pound mushrooms, coarsely sliced, and continue to cook for another 10 minutes, or until sweetbreads are done.

Remove sweetbreads to a hot platter and keep warm. To the skillet add 3 ounces Calvados (or applejack) and 1 cup heavy cream to which 2 egg yolks have been added. Cook very gently (be very careful that the mixture doesn't boil) until sauce is thickened. Then pour sauce over sweetbreads and serve at once to 6.

The Italians certainly have a way with variety meats. Throughout Italy we have encountered liver, tripe, and kidneys made into dishes fit for the most exacting gourmet.

On our first night in Florence, Mr. Baumgartner, of the Hotel Bristol Helvetia, suggested a small cafe within walking distance of the hotel. "The Ristorante al Campidoglia," he said, "is not pretentious, nor is it frequented by tourists. But it is a haunt of Florentine gourmets, and for you I recommend it highly."

It was a rather plain but cheerful and comfortable place. Our apéritifs were Negroni. The first course was fettucini and peas in a tomato sauce. The entree was *Trippa alla Campidoglio,* and the dessert was little wild strawberries. The wine was an excellent Chianti, and we finished up with cafe expresso and Strega. And the check was a delightful finale—$7.20 for the two of us!

I have always thought that *Tripe à la Mode de Caen* could not be excelled, but I've changed my opinion. I like that of the Campidoglio much better. Here is how it is prepared.

TRIPPA ALLA CAMPIDOGLIO
(Tripe Florentine)

1 *lb. fresh honeycomb tripe*	1 *oz. bacon, diced*
Water	¼ *tsp. dried basil*
1½ *oz. butter*	*Salt and pepper*
1 *onion*	1 *lb. fresh tomatoes*
1 *clove garlic*	*Pinch sugar*
1 *stalk celery*	½ *tsp. dried marjoram*
1 *small carrot*	2 *oz. Florio Marsala*
Grated Parmesan cheese	

In a heavy skillet put 1½ ounces butter. When hot add 1 onion, 1 clove garlic, 1 stalk celery, and 1 small carrot, all chopped, 1 ounce bacon cut in dice, ¼ teaspoon dried basil, and salt and pepper to taste. Fry until the vegetables are limp, then add 1 pound fresh tomatoes, peeled and chopped, a pinch sugar, and ½ teaspoon dried marjoram. Simmer the whole until tomatoes are completely cooked—turned almost to a purée. Then pour in 2 ounces Marsala wine, blend, and add the tripe, cut into slices. Simmer the whole slowly for about an hour, or until the tripe is *al dente* (like pasta), slightly resistant to the bite. Remember that tripe must not be overcooked.

In serving, divide the finished dish among 4 hot plates, and sprinkle over each portion a generous layer of grated Parmesan cheese.

You can always stir up an argument among French gourmets as to whether the best *Tripe à la Mode de Caen* is made and served in Le Rabelais, the leading restaurant in the medieval city of Caen, in the Normandy province of France, or in Pharamond's, the 130 year old bistro in Les Halles, the great market place in Paris.

Certainly Pharamond's is more famous in the gastronomic world than Le Rabelais. Both rate one star (a good restaurant for its class from the point of view of cuisine), but Le Rabelais is given four crossed knives and forks (a top restaurant from the point of view of comfort and decor), while Pharamond's gets only one crossed knife and fork (a plain but good restaurant).

The decor of Pharamond's hasn't changed since 1900. It is unpretentious; you sit at banquettes placed along both walls of the restaurant, and the tables are covered with red checkered tablecloths. But you don't go to Pharamond's for decor, you go to have *Soupe a l'oignon* or *Tripe à la Mode de Caen* (from 7 A.M. on). This latter dish is so popular that it is said that hundreds of pounds of tripe come out of the kitchen every day!

The tripe is served in a sort of earthenware soup dish which is placed before you over a small pewter container containing glowing charcoal, thus keeping the tripe bubbling hot while you eat it. The tripe is cut in pieces about 2 inches square, and the sauce, or gravy, is only slightly thickened.

Pharamond's do not give out their recipes, but the following recipe comes from a cuisinier of Caen who is noted for her tripe. I think the flavor of her dish equals, if not surpasses that of

Pharamond's. It is thicker, and the tripe is cut in strips, which makes for easier eating.

TRIPE À LA MODE DE CAEN

3 *lb. fresh honeycomb tripe*	*Generous pinch dried marjoram*
4 *slices fat salt pork*	*Generous pinch mace*
2 *sliced carrots*	2 *large bay leaves*
2 *sliced onions*	8 *small peppercorns*
2 *chopped tomatoes*	2 *whole cloves*
2 *leeks*	1 *tsp. salt*
2 *stalks celery*	*Cayenne pepper*
1 *large green pepper*	1 *cup condensed beef bouillon*
1 *clove garlic*	1 *cup dry white wine*
2 *calves feet (meat and bones)*	6 *shallots (or little green*
1 *tbsp. minced parsley*	*onions)*
Generous pinch dried thyme	1 *cup Calvados (or applejack)*

Wash 3 pounds fresh honeycomb tripe in 2 or 3 changes cold water, drain, and cut in strips ¾ inch wide and about 2½ inches long. Line the bottom of an earthenware casserole (or a Dutch oven) with 4 slices fat salt pork. Add 2 sliced carrots and 2 sliced onions, 2 chopped tomatoes, 2 leeks, 2 stalks celery, 1 large green pepper rather finely minced, and a clove garlic, also minced. Over this vegetable layer arrange the strips of tripe, and add 2 calf's feet (meat and bones) cut up.

Season whole with 1 tablespoon minced parsley, a generous pinch each dried thyme, marjoram, and mace, 2 large bay leaves, 8 small peppercorns, slightly bruised, 2 whole cloves, 1 teaspoon salt, and a slight sprinkling of cayenne pepper. Cover whole with equal parts beef bouillon and dry white wine (probably a cup of each will be sufficient). Put cover on pot or casserole, seal edges with a flour and water paste, and bake in the slowest possible oven overnight, or for at least 12 hours.

When you break the seal and remove the cover, your nostrils will be assailed by the most heavenly odor you have ever experienced. But a final step remains. Add 6 finely minced shallots (or little green onions), and a cup of Calvados (or applejack). Heat thoroughly again, and then serve bubbling hot, with plenty of crusty French bread.

Calf's liver is a favorite all over Italy. In Venice we had *Fegato alla Veneziana,* which is liver and onions. It is a very delicious, yet simple, dish.

FEGATO ALLA VENEZIANA
(Calf's Liver Venetian Style)

Calf's liver	*Olive oil*
Onions	*Salt and pepper*
Minced parsley	

Onions are sliced very thin and gently cooked in olive oil in a covered skillet (just enough oil to cover bottom), until they are soft and golden yellow, about 30 to 40 minutes. Then the very best quality calf's liver is cut into the thinnest possible slices, added to the onions, and cooked only about a minute on each side. They are salted and peppered to taste, and minced parsley is sprinkled over all.

The quantities of liver and onions will, of course, vary depending upon the number of people served. I think about ½ pound liver will serve 2, and, depending upon how well you like onions, the amounts can vary from one half the amount of calf's liver to twice the amount (that would come to from ¼ pound to 1 pound).

Another extremely delicious liver dish was calf's liver cooked in Marsala wine.

FEGATO AL MARSALA
(Liver with Marsala Wine)

Thin slices tender calf's liver	*Lemon juice*
Flour	*Butter*
Salt and pepper	*Florio Marsala wine*
Chicken bouillon	

Dust very thin slices tender calf's liver lightly with seasoned flour and a bit of lemon juice. Cover the bottom of a heavy skillet with melted butter and put in the liver slices. Brown them quickly on both sides, then add an ounce of Florio Marsala wine for each two slices of liver, and a little chicken bouillon. Stir the sauce, and when it thickens serve the liver with a little sauce spooned over each slice.

In Belvoir Park, on the shore of Lake Zürich, in Switzerland, is one of the most remarkable establishments I have ever encountered. In a splendid mansion, once the home of a famous Swiss statesman, is a beautifully appointed restaurant, with a charming outdoor restaurant in the gardens adjoining the house. The food and service offered the public equals that of some of France's three-star restaurants, and are in every way perfection. But what makes the place extraordinary is that this magnificent home houses an ultra-modern training school for the catering industry, and hotel operations.

The younger students serve their apprenticeship as cooks and waiters. Most of the older students have several years of practical experience behind them, and wish to perfect their professional knowledge. The instructors are, of course highly skilled in their various fields, and the principal, Walter Hammer, is a master chef.

Mrs. Wood and I dined at the Belvoir Park Restaurant three times, and each time the food was perfectly prepared and cooked, and the service faultless. I spent one entire day at the school, attending classes, and watching the food being prepared. Following are two delicious dishes, among several, that I saw being made.

FOIE DE VEAU, SAUTÉ
(Calf's Liver Sauté)

1 slice tender calf's liver	2 tbsp. butter
1 tbsp. finely chopped onion	1 tbsp. Madeira wine
2 oz. Madeira sauce	

For one serving mince a slice of fine calf's liver cut about ½ inch thick, and weighing a little over 5 ounces. Cut it in half lengthwise, and with a razor-sharp knife cut each half in very thin slices. Also have ready a scant tablespoon finely chopped onion. In a small heavy saucepan or skillet put 2 tablespoons butter over fairly high heat. When butter is sizzling put in the minced onion and cook for a few seconds. Then add the minced liver, and cook for 1 minute only, stirring contents of pan with a fork. Then remove liver and onions to a hot plate. Into the skillet pour 1 tablespoon Madeira wine, then immediately add about 2 ounces Madeira sauce. Let this bubble up and pour sauce over minced liver and onions and serve immediately.

The second was *Brochette Belvoir*. The preparation of this dish takes time, but no ingenuity. You will need some tenderloin of veal, tenderloin of beef, calf's liver, cooked sweetbreads, slices bacon, and little pork sausages.

BROCHETTE BELVOIR

Veal	*Little pork sausages*
Beef	*Salt and pepper*
Liver	*Paprika*
Cooked sweetbreads	*Peanut oil*
Bacon	*Browned butter*

Cut pieces of veal, beef, liver, and cooked sweetbreads into pieces roughly about 2½ inches long, ¾ inch wide, and ¼ inch thick. Cut bacon into pieces 2½ inches long and ¾ inch wide. The little pork sausages should be 2½ inches long.

On a wooden skewer thread the ingredients in the following order: sausage, bacon, beef, bacon, sweetbread, bacon, liver, bacon, veal, bacon. Repeat the process, and top it off with sausage following the veal and bacon pieces. Cut off ends of skewer so that about ½ inch remains on each end. Sprinkle meat on skewer with salt and pepper to taste, and paprika.

In a large skillet pour enough peanut oil to just cover bottom, and heat oil. Place meat filled skewer in skillet and cook for about 2½ minutes. Then turn and cook another 2½ minutes, basting the cooked side with the oil. Remove meat to a hot plate, withdraw skewer, and pour a little browned butter over meat and serve immediately.

7 ⁂ GAME

The halloo of the hunter resounds through the history of mankind with a great cacophony of baying hounds, swooping hawks, whooshing arrows, exploding gunpowder, and buckshot.

In England, life, literature, and the larder revolved around the hunt. Even the sittings of Parliament were regulated by the hunting seasons. Today, the opening of the grouse season is almost a national holiday.

On the Continent the hunting of game was one of the most important phases of life, especially among the ruling monarchs and the landed nobility. Many of the great castles in Europe started out as hunting lodges, even the fabulous Fontainebleau. Even among the peasants wild game was the principal, and often the only hearty part, of the daily meal. Wild boar, deer, kid, hares, ducks, pheasants, and partridges were an important source of life-giving food.

Today these same animals and birds are found on the menus of hundreds of restaurants throughout Europe, not only in the little auberges and bistros and inns, but in the top flight eating places. As I look back on our nearly two years of travel, it seems to me that Germany offered the greatest variety of game.

In Ireland I don't remember of having encountered any domestic ducks. I suppose the reason is that there is so much marshland around the seacoast, particularly in the south of Ireland, that wild ducks are usually plentiful.

We had some delicious duck dishes in Ireland (they really know how to cook ducks, these Irish!). An outstanding one was devised by André Fernon, chef de cuisine at the Shannon Free Airport. It was served to us in the beautiful airport restaurant as the entree of a magnificent dinner. It's called, naturally, Duck à la Shannon.

DUCK À LA SHANNON

2 2½-lb. ducks	1 *large onion, chopped*
1 *quart beef bouillon*	1 *clove garlic*
1 *tbsp. chopped parsley*	3 *tbsp. sugar*
1 *tsp. dried thyme*	2 *oz. vinegar*
1 *bay leaf*	*Flour and butter roux*
1 *large carrot, chopped*	4 *oz. Irish whisky*

In a 300-degree oven roast two 2½ pound ducks for about 50 minutes to an hour, or until they are tender and nicely browned. Then cut them into serving portions (breasts and legs) and keep warm in the oven. Put the remaining carcasses into a pot and add 1 quart beef bouillon, 1 tablespoon chopped parsley, 1 teaspoon dried thyme, a bay leaf, a large carrot, chopped, a large onion, chopped, and a minced clove garlic. Let all this cook for an hour and a half.

In a large, shallow saucepan brown 3 tablespoons sugar until it caramelizes, then add 2 ounces vinegar. When well mixed add this to the sauce. Again mix well, then strain the sauce through a fine sieve into a saucepan, and add enough flour and butter roux to bring it to the consistency of thick cream. When smooth and well blended, strain again.

Place the portions of duck in a large saucepan and pour over them the strained sauce. Add 4 ounces Irish whisky, heat over a low fire for about 20 minutes, then serve.

Another of Chef Fernon's duck creations is called stuffed duckling Rineanna. This is named after the township in which the Shannon Free Airport is situated, where ducks abound.

STUFFED DUCKLING RINEANNA

1 *4–5-lb. duckling*	*Salt and pepper*
Brandy	1 *tsp. chopped parsley*
Flour	*Pinch nutmeg*
4 *cored apples*	¼ *tsp. fennel seeds*
2 *oz. butter*	*White breadcrumbs*
4 *large apples, quartered*	2 *tsp. chopped fresh mint*
4 *oz. cider*	*Arrowroot*
4 *oz. applejack*	*Water*

Melt 2 ounces butter in a saucepan and add 4 large peeled and quartered apples. When they are cooked, but not mushy, add 2 ounces each cider and applejack. Cook another 10 minutes, then season with salt and pepper to taste, a teaspoon chopped parsley, a pinch grated nutmeg, and ¼ teaspoon dried fennel. Mix well, then add enough white breadcrumbs to absorb the liquid so as to give a moist, stiff stuffing.

Rub a 4–5 pound duckling inside and out with brandy, then stuff with the prepared stuffing. Truss duckling, dredge with flour, place in a roasting tray, and roast in a 350-degree oven for 40 to 45 minutes. About 25 minutes before duck is done put 4 cored apples into oven.

When duck is tender and nicely browned remove from oven and keep warm. Strain off the pan liquor into a saucepan, add 2 ounces each cider and applejack, and reduce liquid to half its volume, taking care to skim off all grease. Then add 2 teaspoons chopped fresh mint, and thicken to a good sauce consistency with arrowroot dissolved in a little cold water.

Remove the twine and skewers from the duckling, and place it on a hot platter. Place baked apples around it. Just before serving pour the sauce over the duckling. This recipe should serve 4 people.

It seems to be part of the American credo that British cooks and cooking are dull, unimaginative, and stolid. I have heard many people say that one cannot get a really fine meal in England, not even, with a few exceptions, in London. But our experiences have been quite to the contrary.

On this trip abroad Mrs. Wood and I had our first taste of food prepared by British chefs on board the *Queen Elizabeth*. The head chef was Joseph MacDonald, a Scotsman, and his staff were British. Every meal we had, from luncheon the first day out to dinner the last night out, was superbly prepared and cooked.

No matter how many times one has crossed the Atlantic on a great liner, such as the *Queen Elizabeth* or the *Queen Mary* of the Cunard Lines, eating is always a unique pleasure. The great dining salons are the equal of the finest restaurants in New York, London and Paris from the point of view of decor and atmosphere. Except for the first and last nights out, everyone dresses for dinner, which subtly contributes to the feeling of a special occasion. The service is faultless. The menus provide a variety of superb dishes that few restaurants can equal. And if you have a desire for some special dish, you have only to notify your captain, and it will be served to you the next noon or evening. The wine list contains some of the finest wines, and best vintages obtainable, and at ridiculously low prices.

Among the notable entrees we reveled in on the *Queen Elizabeth* were Tournedos Rossini, sliced breasts of duckling with a cherry-Madeira sauce, and chicken stuffed pancakes with a Mornay sauce. Three exquisite desserts were Crêpes Montaigne (thin pancakes filled with a custard flavored with almond butter cream and Kirsch), Soufflé Clementine, and blueberry cheesecake.

The breasts of duckling with cherries was an unexpected treat. This is Chef MacDonald's recipe.

BREASTS OF DUCKLING WITH CHERRY AND MADEIRA SAUCE

1 *4–5 lb. duckling*	*Arrowroot*
2 *oz. Madeira wine*	*½ lb. canned pitted cherries*
	Butter

Braise the duckling in butter in a deep pan for 20 minutes only. Then remove the filets of the breasts lengthwise, and cut each into 10 thin slices and keep warm.

To the braising liquid, with the fat removed, add 2 ounces Madeira wine, and thicken the liquid with arrowroot to the consistency of a thin cream sauce. Strain this through a fine sieve, and add ½ pound drained canned pitted cherries. Let the sauce heat through. Place the cherries around the duck slices, coat thinly with the sauce, and serve the balance of the sauce separately.

There are many duck connoisseurs who eschew fancy duck preparations, and want their duck just plain roasted, whether it be wild duck, or that famous English bird, Aylesbury Duck. However, many of these plain roast duck fanciers do enjoy as basting agent a flavorsome wine or spirit, and I picked up two recipes in England that really were delicious. The first uses rum.

ROAST DUCK WITH RUM

1 *5-lb. duckling*	1 *clove garlic*
Brandy	¼ *lb. soft butter*
1 *orange*	¼ *cup Jamaica rum*
1 *onion*	*Salt*
¼ *tsp. powdered ginger*	

Wipe the cavity of a 5-pound duckling with a cloth soaked in brandy, then in the cavity place an orange (which has been pierced all around with a fork) and an onion, similarily pierced. Truss, and rub the outside of the bird with a bruised clove of garlic, and then with ¼ pound of soft butter. Roast in 400-degree oven for 15 minutes, then reduce the heat to 350 degrees, and continue to roast for 20 minutes to the pound in all. During the last half hour of cooking remove the fat and add ¼ cup of Jamaica rum, and baste. Salt before serving and sprinkle with ¼ teaspoon powdered ginger.

The second recipe uses a not too expensive yet sound Burgundy wine, with a wild duck.

WILD DUCK BURGUNDY

1 *dressed wild duck*	*Slices apple*
Brandy	*Slices celery*
Salt and pepper	½ *clove garlic*
Slices onion	*Soy sauce*
Slices orange	*Olive oil*
½ *to 1 cup Burgundy wine*	

Rub a dressed duck inside and out with a cloth soaked with brandy, then sprinkle the inside with salt and freshly ground pepper. Stuff the duck with slices of onion, orange, apple, celery, and a half clove garlic. Sew up vent and truss duck, and rub its breast with a mixture of soy sauce and olive oil. Place duck in an uncovered roaster or baking pan in a 400-degree oven. Roast 30 to 45 minutes, depending upon degree of doneness desired, basting often with Burgundy wine, using ½ to 1 cup. When duck is done, remove stuffing and discard, and serve to 2.

For some reason the flavor of oranges, both juice and peel, mates ideally with duck. One of the outstanding duck recipes is for *Duck à la Jus d'Orange,* which comes from a 15th century Italian cookbook, now in the Vatican library in Rome. But Caneton à la Bigarade runs a very close second, and is a masterpiece of French cuisine.

This recipe comes from Air France, which is unsurpassed for its superb French cuisine.

CANETON À LA BIGARADE
(Duck with Orange Sauce)

1 4-lb. duckling	Rind 1 orange
Brandy	Rind ½ lemon
Salt	Boiling water
Freshly ground pepper	¼ cup orange curaçao
1½ oz. butter	3 lumps sugar
Duck giblets	1 tbsp. water
1 onion	2 tbsp. vinegar
1 carrot	Juice 1 orange
¼ tsp. dried thyme	Juice ½ lemon
1 bay leaf	1 tbsp. arrowroot
Dry white wine	Orange sections
½ cup dry white wine	Watercress

Wipe about a 4-pound duckling inside and out with a cloth dampened with brandy. Truss it and rub with salt and freshly ground pepper. Heat 1½ ounces butter in a deep pot or roaster. Add the coarsely chopped duck giblets, 1 onion and 1 carrot, both diced, ¼ teaspoon dried thyme, and a crumbled bay leaf. On top of vegetables and giblets place duck. Put, uncovered, in a 400-degree oven and cook about 1 hour, basting from time to time with dry white wine. When duck is done remove it and keep warm.

Drain vegetable and giblet mixture in a large sieve and reserve liquid. Return vegetable and giblet mixture to the cooking pot or roaster, and heat on top of stove. Add reserved liquid and ½ cup dry white wine, and simmer gently until reduced by ⅓. Then strain into a saucepan, discarding solids, boil sauce gently, and remove top fat.

Remove thin rind from 1 orange and ½ lemon, and cut rinds into Julienne strips. Blanch strips in boiling water for 20 seconds, drain, and add to strips ¼ cup orange curaçao.

In the meantime heat 3 lumps sugar with 1 tablespoon water. When it has caramelized stir in 2 tablespoons vinegar. Then add juice 1 orange and ½ lemon, and blend in 1 tablespoon arrowroot previously dissolved in a little water.

After top fat has been removed from sauce bring to a light boil and add the sugar-juice mixture. Check seasoning and strain sauce over citrus strips and curaçao. Mix well and keep warm.

To serve carve and slice duckling onto hot platter and ladle a little sauce over. Garnish with orange sections and watercress. Serve balance of sauce in a sauceboat.

We stopped in York, England, particularly to see the cathedral. This is one of the notable cathedrals in England, built in 995, and is considered the finest of Norman construction in England. I have never seen a church so huge, so massive, and so powerful.

We stopped at the Chase Hotel, one of the most attractive hotels we encountered in England. We had a huge, luxurious room, and the dining room and the cocktail lounge were lovely.

I was particularly struck by the friendliness of the place. In the cocktail lounge I ordered two dry martinis. A very charming bar maid confessed that she wasn't sure she could make one that would satisfy an American, and asked me if I would mind making my own at the bar. She put everything before me, and watched with a great deal of interest (as did some of the customers at the bar) while I made the drinks.

The dining room was one of the few that we encountered in rural England that had dinner music. The service was excellent, and the food wonderful. Our entree was Duckling Grand Marnier.

DUCKLING GRAND MARNIER

1 *5-lb. duckling*	*Freshly ground pepper*
Brandy	*¼ lb. butter*
Salt	*Peel of 2 oranges*
	1½ oz. Grand Marnier

Rub a duckling weighing about 5 pounds inside and out with a cloth soaked in brandy. Sprinkle the cavity with salt and freshly ground pepper, and roast in a 400-degree oven 10 to 15 minutes per pound.

While duck is roasting prepare a special mixture of ¼ pound butter, salt and freshly ground pepper to taste, and the finely chopped peels of 2 oranges, devoid of any white part.

After the duckling is roasted, spread the orange peel and butter mixture on a copper or earthenware cooking platter and, over a low flame, melt the mixture together with 1½ ounces Grand Marnier. Place roasted duckling on the platter and baste for 10 minutes over the flame. Then sprinkle some Grand Marnier over duckling and flambé it.

Carve the duckling in the usual way, and serve very hot with the gravy. Wild rice should accompany this, and a Burgundy wine.

One of the most fascinating towns we stopped at on our way from Dijon to the Côte d'Azur was Orange, in Provence. Once upon a time it was a splendid Roman city, but today only two monuments of its former splendor remain. The first you see as you drive into town—a magnificent triumphal arch, which is well preserved. The second is the remains of a colossal Roman theatre, with walls one hundred and twenty-five feet high still standing, and the stage and seats still discernable. The next day we spent two hours poking about the ruins, and gaping at the spectacle.

Orange has an excellent restaurant, Le Provençal, which rates three crossed knives and forks and a star. It is a gay little place, with a Provençal decor. There was a banquet going on in the main dining room, but the smaller one to the right was more intimate and enjoyable. We had a magnificent *Terrine Maison à la gelée* to start with, and then the famous specialty of the house, *Canard aux Olives,* washed down with a lively Châteauneuf du Pape. This is the recipe for the duck that was given me by the proprietress.

CANARD AUX OLIVES
(Duck with Olives)

1 3½-lb. duck	1 cup dry white wine
Salt and pepper	1 bay leaf
2 tbsp. olive oil	Pinch dried thyme
2 tbsp. butter	Flour and butter roux
1 oz. brandy	2 tbsp. tomato purée
1 cup condensed consommé	1 cup pitted small Italian
	green olives

Cut a tender young duck, weighing about 3½ pounds, into 4 serving pieces, and salt and pepper them to taste. In a skillet heat 2 tablespoons each olive oil and butter, add the duck, and cook gently until pieces are golden brown on all sides. This takes about 40 minutes. Then pour over them 1 ounce warmed brandy which has been set alight. Cover the skillet and cook gently until duck is tender, about 30 minutes more. Remove duck pieces to a heated dish and keep warm.

To the juices in the skillet add 1 cup each condensed consommé and dry white wine, a bay leaf, and a pinch dried thyme. Let the liquid reduce until you have about 1½ cups remaining. Then thicken with a flour and butter roux, stirring until smooth, then add 2 tablespoons tomato purée. Add the duck pieces to the sauce, along with about 1 cup pitted small Italian green olives. Simmer until olives are well warmed, then serve over triangles of French bread sautéed in butter. This serves about 4.

One night in Paris we dined at Lasserre's with the Scudder Mersmans. To my mind, Lasserre's is the most beautiful restaurant in Paris, a magnificent dining place. It is a three star restaurant, so you know that the service and the food are among the finest in France. I had as an entree their roast pheasant, and it was one of the most delicious pheasant dishes I have ever tasted. I asked for the recipe, and it was promised me, but I never got it, so I cannot detail it here. But when you are in Paris don't miss Lasserre's, and the roast pheasant.

This recipe for roast pheasant from Normandy is very delicious, and if my taste memory serves me right, it was somewhat similar to the roast pheasant that we had at Lasserre's.

ROAST PHEASANT, NORMANDY STYLE

3 *tender young pheasants*	1 *clove garlic*
Brandy	½ *cup Calvados (or applejack)*
6 *slices bacon*	2 *cups chicken broth*
4 *tbsp. butter*	1 *tsp. salt*
8 *shallots (or little green*	½ *tsp. freshly ground pepper*
onions)	1 *pint cream*

½ *cup prepared horseradish*

Wipe 3 tender young pheasants, which have been plucked and drawn, inside and out with a cloth soaked with brandy. Then cover the breasts of each pheasant with slices of bacon (2 slices per bird) and tie the pheasants up so they will not lose shape. In a heavy iron skillet melt 4 tablespoons butter to which has been added 8 thinly sliced shallots (or little green onions) and a minced garlic clove. Brown the pheasants in the hot butter on all sides, then place them in a roaster and pour the contents of the skillet over them. Warm ½ cup applejack, light it, and pour it over the birds. When the flame dies out add 2 cups chicken broth, 1 teaspoon salt and ½ teaspoon freshly ground pepper. Put the roaster in a 375-degree oven and roast, uncovered, for 30 minutes, basting frequently. Then add 1 pint cream and ½ cup prepared horseradish to the sauce, and continue roasting for 15 minutes, continuing to baste frequently. Serve the birds on a heated platter with the sauce around them, accompanied by wild rice, currant jelly, and a fine burgundy. This will serve 4.

About six miles south of Avignon, in Provence, is the little village of Noves. It has a population of only around three thousand, yet here is located one of the great three-star restaurants of France, La Petite Auberge.

La Petite Auberge is an elegant little hotel and restaurant, with only eighteen rooms, layed out in an ancient estate. It is quiet and secluded, with lovely views of the countryside.

One of the famed specialties of La Petite Auberge is *Caneton en papillote aux herbes,* and this is the chef's recipe.

CANETON EN PAPILLOTE AUX HERBES
(Duck with Herbs Cooked in a Paper Bag)

1 *3½-lb. duck, quartered*	*½ tsp. dried thyme*
Duck liver	*½ tsp. dried chervil*
2 *shallots (or little green*	6 *sprigs fresh parsley*
onions)	1 *tsp. strong mustard*
6 *cloves garlic*	2 *cups dry white wine*
5 *oz. butter*	

Grind the liver, shallots, garlic, or mince them very fine, then add the thyme, chervil, parsley, mustard, wine, and 4 ounces melted butter, plus 1 ounce of butter softened with a spoon.

Sauté the duck pieces lightly in butter and then place them in a greased brown paper bag or a greased aluminum foil bag, spooning the sauce over all parts of the duck before closing the bag tightly. Then bake in a 350-degree oven for 40 minutes. This serves 4.

While we were staying at the Park Lane Hotel in London the chef, M. Viguers, loaned me one of his treasured possessions for a few days, *A Cook's Guide, and Housekeeper's & Butler's Assistant,* by Charles Francatelli, who had been the chef de cuisine at the old London Reform Club, and also chief cook to Queen Victoria.

The cookbook was published in London in 1888, and sold over 64,000 copies. There are nearly 1,100 recipes in the book, and include such things as "Royal Posset for a Cold" (groats, French wine, honey, and essence of cloves), "Cure for Chapped hands" (olive oil, spermaceti, virgin wax, camphor, and honey), "A Wash to Prevent the Hair from Falling out," "A Cure for Warts," and "A Cure for Chilblains."

The chapter on American drinks is priceless. Here is a recipe for a Cock-Tail: "Put 3 lumps of sugar in a tumbler with a dessert-spoonful of essence of Jamaica ginger and a wineglass of brandy; fill up with hot water."

The recipe for a mint julep is equally amazing. "The thin rind of half an orange, its whole juice free from pips, a sprig of green mint, a spoonful of sugar; fill up the tumbler with shaves of ice; add a glass of gin and a glass of sherry." This should make the entire population of Kentucky shudder for a full hour!

This is the recipe for a nightcap: "Half a pint of strong ale, a wineglass of brandy, a few drops of essence of cloves, 4 lumps of sugar, make hot, drink slowly—and make haste to bed." Mr. Francatelli neglected to add, "Sweet dreams."

But there are many sound and delectable recipes in the book, in spite of its Victorian aura. I was fascinated by the following pheasant recipe.

ROAST PHEASANT FRANCATELLI

1 *tender young pheasant*	*Pinch dried thyme*
½ *lb. chicken livers*	*Pinch nutmeg*
2 *oz. fatty ham*	*Pinch salt*
2 *shallots (or little green*	*Pinch pepper*
onions)	*Breadcrumbs*
1 *cup dry red wine*	

PÉRIGUEUX SAUCE

4 *truffles (or medium-sized*	¼ *small clove garlic*
mushrooms)	6 *filets of anchovies*
½ *pint brown sauce*	2 *oz. butter*
4 *oz. Madeira wine*	*Pinch cayenne pepper*
Pinch nutmeg	

Get ½ pound fat livers (chicken) and fry them with 2 ounces fat ham, 2 shallots (or little green onions) chopped, a pinch each dried thyme, nutmeg, pepper and salt. When nearly done pound all together in a mortar (I would finely chop them rather than make a paste), and add some breadcrumbs. Fill the inside of the pheasant with the stuffing, truss it and roast it (I would say put the stuffed pheasant in a 350-degree oven, and roast 30 minutes per pound of

bird), basting frequently (I would use about 1 cup dry red wine).
Serve with a Périgueux sauce.

Francatelli's recipe for a Périgueux sauce is: Chop 4 truffles
very fine (if you can't get truffles use 4 medium-size mushrooms)
and put them in a small saucepan with ½ pint brown sauce, 4
ounces Madeira wine, and as much garlic as will rest on the
point of a knife (I would say a quarter clove garlic, minced
finely). Boil for 10 minutes, then add a pat of anchovy butter
(made by mashing 6 anchovies and mixing with 2 ounces butter,
and seasoning with a pinch each cayenne pepper and nutmeg).
Blend well, and serve hot.

In the famous wine growing region of the Rhenish Hesse and
the Rhinegau, which slopes from the Taunus Mountains west-
ward to the Rhine, wild fowl is superb. A particular specialty is
pheasant roasted wrapped in bacon. Whether the garnishing sauce
should be flavored with a dash of cream or wine may become a
point of passionate controversy among gourmets.

We had a particularly succulent pheasant dish in Mainz, in
which the bird was sautéed, then covered with an intriguing sauce.

SAUTÉED PHEASANT IN WINE SAUCE

2 young pheasants	Pinch dried thyme
Salt	Pinch caraway seeds
Freshly ground pepper	½ cup dry white wine
6 oz. butter	1 cup cream
1 oz. gin	1½ cups sour cream
1 medium onion	Salt and pepper
4 large mushrooms	Dash Worcestershire sauce
2 bay leaves	Juice ½ lemon

Disjoint 2 young pheasants which have been plucked, cleaned and
skinned, and season to taste with salt and freshly ground pepper.
Place in a large heavy skillet containing 6 ounces hot butter, and
sauté slowly over low fire, turning frequently, until golden brown
on all sides. Then remove from skillet and place in a warm oven
while the sauce is prepared.

To juices in skillet add 1 ounce aquavit or gin, and stir from bottom of skillet to loosen all particles. Then add 1 medium-sized onion, cut julienne, 4 large mushrooms, also cut julienne, 2 bay leaves, and a pinch each dried thyme and caraway seeds. Let this simmer about 5 minutes over low flame, then add ½ cup dry white wine. Continue to simmer until onions and mushrooms are tender, then add 1 cup cream. Blend and simmer again for about 20 minutes. Remove from fire and add 1½ cups commercial sour cream, salt and pepper to taste, a dash Worcestershire sauce, and juice ½ lemon. Blend everything well, then put the pheasant pieces in the sauce. Return to fire, and let simmer very, very gently for about 20 more minutes. Serve pheasant pieces with sauce poured over them to 4.

The *Guide Michelin* is the traveler's bible in France, indispensable to anyone who doesn't know the country. It lists hotels and restaurants in thousands of towns, and rates them according to accommodations, comfort, service, prices and food.

Restaurants have two symbols in front of their listing; crossed knives and forks to indicate their class, and stars to indicate the quality of their cuisine. Five crossed knives and forks indicate a luxury restaurant, four a top class restaurant, and so on down to one, which indicates a plain but good restaurant. But the most important symbol is the star. Three stars indicate one of the best tables in France, and well worth the journey; two indicate excellent cuisine, worth a detour; and one indicates a good restaurant for its class. However, the absence of a star does not mean that a restaurant is not good.

In all of France there are only eleven restaurants that rate three stars. Five of these are in Paris, and six in the Provinces. Needless to say, these restaurants are expensive, but worth it. While we were in Paris we ate at three of the three star restaurants— Lasserre's, Tour d'Argent, and Maxim's. And frankly judging by the prices in the first class restaurants of New York, San Francisco, Chicago, and other metropolitan cities, the prices in the three star restaurants in Paris are far from exhorbitant. For instance, our dinner for two at the Tour d'Argent cost us $28.40, which included marvelous large martinis, two half bottles of wine, the famous Tour d'Argent duck, and after dinner liqueurs with our coffee, AND the tip!

Maxim's has been famous for many, many years. It is quietly luxurious, and its dignity belies its early 20th century reputation for unconventional gaiety. The service is deft and unobtrusive, and the food worthy of its three star designation.

One of Maxim's many specialties is *Cailles aux Raisins,* which I had. This is the recipe adapted for American housewives and amateur cooks.

CAILLES AUX RAISINS
(Quail with Grapes)

4 *dressed quail*	4 *large mushrooms*
Brandy	4 *tbsp. butter*
Salt and pepper	2 *tsp. dry vermouth*
4 *tsp. pâté de foie gras*	1 *oz. Cognac*
16 *white seedless grapes*	2 *cups white seedless grapes*

Thin bacon slices

Wipe 4 dressed and cleaned quail inside and out with a cloth soaked with brandy. Then lightly salt and pepper them, and in each cavity place 1 teaspoon pâté de foie gras, 3 or 4 white seedless grapes, and also divide equally among the cavities 4 large mushrooms, which have been finely chopped and sautéed in butter 4 or 5 minutes. Cover the breasts of the birds with thin slices bacon, then tie up the birds securely with strong thread.

In a skillet large enough to hold the 4 quail melt 3 tablespoons butter and add it to 2 teaspoons dry vermouth. Place quails in skillet and roast in a hot oven for about 10 minutes. Remove quails from oven and pour over them 1 ounce fine Cognac, which has been warmed and set alight. When flame dies out add 2 cups white seedless grapes, and baste everything well. Then cover skillet, return it to the oven, which has been reduced to about 300 degrees, and cook gently for about 5 minutes. Remove quail to plates, and pour the sauce and grapes over them. This is supposed to serve 4, but I was served 2 small quail with the sauce, and I picked the bones clean. Even the rather reserved waiter re-

marked in English, "You certainly know how to appreciate quail."
Mrs. Wood had *Poularde de Bresse* (chicken) in a casserole
with a Burgundy sauce, and she raved over it. We both had
Soufflé Grand Marnier, which was like eating a perfumed cloud.
Coffee and a Marc ended this heavenly meal.

For hundreds of years hare (or rabbit, as it is more popularly
known in America) has been considered a great delicacy in
Europe. While the peasants ate hare and relished it, it was also
a part of the *haute cuisine.* The great Escoffier, worshiped by
gourmets the world over, gives 17 recipes for hare in his book.
Master Chef Louis de Gouy, in his prized *Derrydale Game Cookbook,* gives 35 recipes for hare that he collected all over Europe.
In nearly all of the great restaurants of Paris Râblé (saddle) of
Hare, or *Civet de Lièvre* is featured on the menus. Lasserre's,
to my mind the finest restaurant in Paris, lists *Le Râblé de Lièvre
Grand Veneur* for two persons at 34 francs (which is roughly
$7.00). There is only one other item, woodcock flambéed, which
is more expensive.

Many of the bistros in Paris, which are noted for their superlative food, feature delectable rabbit dishes. Not only there, but
throughout France, the *Pâté de Lièvre* is superb, equaled to my
mind and taste, only by pâtés of mixed game, and venison.

I think the most delicious rabbit dish I had was in the dining
room of a tiny hotel (9 rooms!) in Senas. We had left Avignon
rather late and hadn't traveled a great distance before it began to
get dark. I could see that we would never make Aix-en-Provence
while it was light, and I will not drive on strange roads in strange
countries at night. There seemed to be no towns on the map, and
I was beginning to get desperate when we came upon this little
hotel by the side of the road, named Hotel du Luberon. It
looked fresh and clean, so in we went. We got a room AND bath,
the room very nicely furnished, and the bath most modern. After
we freshened up, and had a snort of bourbon in our room, we went
down to the dining room. It was small, but immaculate, with nice
napery, china and glassware. The waitress (who turned out to be
the daughter of Monsieur and Madame Roman, the owners) spoke
a little halting English, and she recommended *Civet de Lièvre*

Saint-Hubert. After dinner M. Roman came over to our table, and I gave him my card, and complimented him on the main dish. He was so pleased that he opened a chilled bottle of excellent champagne for us. He wrote out the recipe for me, and this is it.

CIVET DE LIÈVRE SAINT-HUBERT
(Rabbit Stew St. Hubert)

1 *4-lb. rabbit*	8 *peppercorns*
2 *onions*	*Pinch nutmeg*
2 *carrots*	*Dry red wine*
1 *large clove garlic*	2 *slices bacon*
½ *tsp. dried thyme*	4 *tbsp. olive oil*
2 *bay leaves*	2 *tbsp. flour*
3 *whole cloves*	2 *oz. warmed brandy*

Flour and butter roux (if necessary)

Cut a 4-pound rabbit in serving pieces. In a crock or deep bowl put in the rabbit pieces, 2 onions and 2 carrots, both sliced, a large clove garlic, chopped, ½ teaspoon dried thyme, 2 bay leaves, crushed, 3 whole cloves, 8 peppercorns, and a pinch nutmeg. Add enough dry red wine to cover contents of crock, and allow to stand at least 6 hours, turning rabbit pieces occasionally.

In a heavy earthenware stewpan put 2 slices bacon, cut in dice, and 4 tablespoons olive oil. When oil is very hot put in the drained rabbit pieces and vegetables from marinade. Cook until rabbit pieces are golden all over, then sprinkle in 2 tablespoons flour, and let it brown slightly. Then set 2 ounces warmed brandy alight and pour over contents of stewpan. Add strained marinade, and let cook for 1½ hours.

When rabbit is tender remove pieces to hot serving platter. If necessary thicken gravy with a flour and butter roux, heat, then strain gravy through fine sieve over rabbit pieces and serve.

Hare, or rabbit, can be cooked in almost every way chicken is cooked. I had three outstanding rabbit dishes in France. One was in Burgundy, and was patterned after *Boeuf à la Bourguignonne,* but the rabbit pieces were marinated first before cooking. Another was patterned after Chicken Marengo, and a third was cooked with orange juice. In Dijon we had a simple yet delectable hare dish in which the hare, disjointed, was fried in sweet butter until tender, then floured, and finally simmered in dry white wine. In one of the Paris bistros we encountered on the menu *Blanquette de Lièvre*, which was done in the manner of Blanquette de Veau. Here is the Burgundian dish.

CIVET DE LIÈVRE À LA BOURGUIGNONNE
(Hare Stewed in Burgundy)

1 4-lb. rabbit, disjointed	2 onions
2 sliced onions	1 clove garlic
2 sliced carrots	Seasoned flour
1 stalk celery	2 oz. brandy
1 bay leaf	1½ tbsp. flour
6 crushed peppercorns	Pinch dried marjoram
2 cups dry red wine	Pinch dried tarragon
3 tbsp. butter	½ lb. fresh mushrooms
¼ cup olive oil	4 tbsp. sour cream

Disjoint a rabbit (or have your butcher do it for you). Make a marinade with 2 thinly sliced onions, 2 carrots, sliced, a bay leaf, 1 stalk celery, chopped (including the leaves), 6 crushed peppercorns, and about 2 cups dry red wine (enough to cover pieces). Let the rabbit pieces marinate for at least 24 hours.

In a heavy skillet put 2 tablespoons butter and ¼ cup fine olive oil. When hot add 2 onions, chopped, and a minced clove garlic. Sauté the onions until they are lightly browned, then remove them from the skillet and reserve.

Drain the rabbit pieces, shake them in a bag containing seasoned flour, and put them in the skillet (adding a little more butter if necessary). Slowly sauté the pieces until they are golden brown on all sides. Then heat 2 ounces brandy, set alight, and sprinkle the burning brandy over rabbit pieces in the skillet.

When the flames have died out sprinkle the rabbit pieces with about 1½ tablespoons flour, and a pinch each of dried marjoram and dried tarragon. Then pour into the skillet the strained marinade. Cover the skillet and simmer the contents *very slowly* for about 1½ to 2 hours, or until rabbit is tender.

Uncover the skillet and add ½ pound fresh mushrooms, sliced, which have been sautéed in a tablespoon butter for about 7 minutes, and the reserved browned onions. Stir in about 4 tablespoons sour cream, simmer for about 10 to 15 minutes longer, and serve.

This is the recipe using orange juice, and it is an exciting dish.

CIVET DE LIÈVRE BIGARADE
(Hare Stewed in Orange Juice and Cointreau)

1 *3-lb. rabbit,*	½ *tsp. salt*
disjointed	1½ *tsp. cornstarch*
Brandy	¼ *cup Cointreau*
Seasoned flour	½ *cup dry white wine*
2 *tbsp. bacon drippings*	1 *medium green pepper*
1 *cup orange juice*	1 *cup drained mandarin*
¼ *cup fresh lime juice*	*oranges*

Rub a 3-pound dressed rabbit which has been cut in serving pieces with a cloth saturated with brandy. Place the pieces in a bag containing seasoned flour, shake well, and remove.

Heat 2 tablespoons bacon drippings in a skillet and put in the floured rabbit pieces. Brown them over a medium flame, turning until all sides are a golden brown. Then add to the skillet 1 cup orange juice, ¼ cup fresh lime juice, and ½ teaspoon salt. Cover, and simmer over a low flame for 40 minutes, or until rabbit is tender. Remove pieces to a hot platter, and keep warm while sauce is made.

Mix 1½ teaspoons cornstarch, ¼ cup Cointreau, and ½ cup dry white wine together, then add this mixture to juices in skillet, and blend the whole well. Then add 1 medium-sized green pepper, cut in thin strips, and 1 cup drained mandarin orange segments, cutting each segment in half. Cook over low flame about 5 minutes. Then pour sauce over rabbit pieces. Serves 4.

Much as I love Chicken Marengo, I believe I like Rabbitt Marengo even better.

CIVET DE LIÈVRE MARENGO
(Hare Marengo)

2 2½-lb. rabbits	2 tsp. minced parsley
Seasoned flour	4 tomatoes
¼ cup olive oil	1 cup dry white wine
4 small onions	1 tbsp. brandy
1½ cups sliced fresh	1 tbsp. tomato paste
mushrooms	1 tbsp. flour

Cut two 2½-pound rabbits, or a 5-pound rabbit, into serving pieces and shake in a bag containing seasoned flour. In a large skillet heat ¼ cup of finest olive oil, and sauté rabbit pieces until golden brown on all sides. Then remove rabbit pieces and keep warm.

In the same skillet put 4 small white onions, chopped, 1½ cups sliced fresh mushrooms, 2 teaspoons minced parsley, and, if necessary a little more olive oil. Cook this mixture until the mushrooms are tender (about 7 minutes), then add 4 peeled and sliced tomatoes, 1 cup dry white wine, 1 tablespoon brandy, 1 tablespoon tomato paste, and 1 tablespoon flour. Mix and blend these ingredients well, and allow to simmer over a medium flame for about 10 minutes. Then return the browned rabbit pieces to the skillet with the sauce, cover, and cook for about 30 minutes, or until the rabbit is completely tender. Serve in the sauce to 5 or 6.

To my mind, venison is the tops of all game food, and one of the most delicious of meats. Parenthetically, the name venison used to apply to the flesh of any sort of game or wild beast hunted for food, but it is now used to denote the flesh of deer. And, according to experts on the matter, the flesh of male deer, or buck, is superior to that of female deer, the doe.

Venison is sometimes inclined to be dry, and tough, but these two faults can easily be overcome. The dryness can be corrected by larding the meat before cooking, and the toughness can be dissipated by marinating the meat after it has been hung for the proper length of time.

I think it is generally accepted that the choicest cuts of a deer are the tenderloin, the chops and the haunch. The latter cut, of course, is best roasted.

I had a gastronomic field day in Germany, Holland, and Belgium with wild rabbit and venison. In Germany it is not illegal to sell venison (as it is in the United States) for the country seems to be overrun with deer. On all main roads throughout Germany, where they pass through or border on a forest, there are signs warning of possible deer crossings. I can't remember a restaurant or hotel that didn't list venison in one form or another—saddle, steaks, noisettes and ragoûts. Every dish I had was marvelous, for German cooks know how to age venison, and properly prepare it.

In Heidelberg we stopped at the famed Ritter Hotel. This architectural gem was built in 1592 and has been going strong ever since. It even survived the conflagration of 1693, which almost completely destroyed the city. But it seems that the general of the attacking forces liked the Ritter, and made it his headquarters, and so it was saved. The first floor, the dining rooms, the façade and the building itself are still just as they were originally, but the bedrooms and baths are all modern.

The first night we were there we had a magnificent venison ragoût for dinner. This is approximately how it is made.

HERB-SEASONED VENISON RAGOÛT

5 *lbs. venison*	2 *tsp. paprika*
1 *large onion*	1 *clove garlic*
2 *tbsp. little green onions*	1½ *cups diced carrots*
2 *large carrots*	1½ *cups diced celery*
5 *tbsp. butter*	1 *cup minced onions*
4 *whole cloves*	3 *cups condensed beef bouillon*
½ *tsp. dried thyme*	2 *large bay leaves*
½ *tsp. dried marjoram*	6 *green celery tops*
½ *tsp. dried tarragon*	6 *sprigs fresh parsley*
½ *tsp. dried basil*	*Pinch dried thyme*
½ *tsp. rosemary*	12 *peppercorns*
3 *cups dry red wine*	2 *tsp. salt*
Olive oil	½ *lb. fresh mushrooms*
Freshly ground pepper	¼ *cup butter*
¼ *cup bacon drippings*	¼ *cup flour*
1½ *cups sour cream*	

Cut 5 pounds of well hung and aged venison into 2 inch pieces. Fry 1 large onion, chopped, 2 tablespoons chopped little green onions, and 2 large carrots, chopped in 5 tablespoons butter. Add 4 whole cloves, ½ teaspoon each dried thyme, marjoram, tarragon, basil and rosemary, and 1 cup dry red wine. When vegetables are limp put everything through a coarse sieve, lightly rubbing solids through then discarding remainder. Brush venison with olive oil, dust with plenty of freshly ground pepper and salt, and pour marinade over venison and let it soak for about 8 hours.

To cook, melt ¼ cup bacon drippings in heavy frying pan. Take venison from marinade, drain it, then put it into the pan along with a crushed clove garlic. Sear meat until browned on all sides. Now arrange meat in a large casserole, and add 1½ cups each diced carrots and celery, 1 cup minced onions, 2 cups dry red wine, 3 cups condensed beef bouillon, 2 large bay leaves, about 6 green celery tops, about 6 sprigs fresh parsley, a very generous pinch dried thyme, 12 black peppercorns, gently crushed, and 2 teaspoons salt. Cover casserole and place in a 325-degree oven for 30 minutes. Then uncover and add ½ pound fresh mushrooms, sliced, and cook for about 30 minutes longer, or until meat is tender. (The cooking time will depend on how long the meat has been hung.)

Next, melt ¼ cup butter in a saucepan and stir in ¼ cup of flour. When mixture is well blended and free from lumps strain the liquid in which the venison has been cooked and pour it into the pan with the butter and flour slowly stirring all the time. When gravy has thickened and bubbled for about 3 minutes stir in 1½ cups sour cream and, if necessary correct for salt seasoning. Blend mixture well, adding 2 teaspoons paprika. Place venison and vegetables on a deep hot platter or serving dish, pour the sauce over, and serve immediately, garnished with fresh watercress. In most German restaurants a side dish of *Prieselbeeren* is served, but I also like currant jelly, which is easier to obtain in America.

On our trip through Germany our first stop was at Freiburg, the southwestern part of the country, about 40 miles north of Basel,

Switzerland. It is a charming city, with a mélange of modern and old world architecture. The medical college of the university is reputed to be one of the finest in the world. The Freiburg Münster Cathedral is magnificent, but it is surrounded by open air shops selling flowers, and scores of little booths selling sausages. The booths were operated by man and wife teams, and there were dozens of varieties of sausages cooking, onions frying, and in each booth were long rolls, and a pot of mustard. We hadn't had lunch and the sight of the sausages cooking, and the odor of the fried onions, made me ravenous.

We stopped at the very new and very modern Columbi Hotel, and our first dinner was in the *Weinstube* of the hotel, a charming room. The first item that caught my eye on the menu was *Rehrucken mit Rahmtunke und Rotkohl*. (Venison with a cream gravy and red cabbage.) Mrs. Wood, who is not overly fond of venison, had it with me, and she admitted that it was perfectly delicious.

I'd like to say, parenthetically, that when it comes to reading a German menu, I become lost in an impenetrable forest. And there are so many ways to list venison that I finally gave up trying to keep them sorted out. I don't know the names of half of the venison dishes I had, or which was which. So I'll just give them English names, and I hope German readers will forgive me!

VENISON RAGOÛT, COLOMBI

3 *lbs. shoulder of venison*	*Venison bones*
2 *cups dry red wine*	*Water*
1 *medium onion, sliced*	1 *onion, quartered*
1 *tsp. whole peppercorns*	1 *stalk celery*
1 *clove garlic*	1 *bay leaf*
1 *stalk celery*	1 *tsp. salt*
1 *carrot*	5–6 *tbsp. bacon drippings*
Pinch salt	4 *tbsp. flour*
⅓ *cup cream*	

In a pottery bowl place 3 pounds of venison shoulder meat cut in 1½ inch squares. Add 2 cups of dry red wine, 1 medium sized onion, sliced, 1 teaspoon whole black peppercorns, slightly crushed, 1 clove garlic, crushed, 1 stalk of celery, 1 sliced carrot, and a pinch of salt. Set the bowl and its contents in a cool place and let the meat marinate for about 3 days.

Cover the venison bones from which the meat was cut with water, add a quartered onion, stalk of celery, a bay leaf, and a teaspoon or so of salt. Simmer this for about 3 hours, then strain and store in the refrigerator until ready to use.

When ready to cook, place the marinated meat in a colander or large strainer, and drain thoroughly, saving the liquid marinade. In a heavy skillet melt 5 to 6 tablespoons of bacon drippings, and when hot, brown the venison pieces. When they are browned, transfer them to a pot or Dutch oven.

Pour off ⅓ of the fat the venison was browned in, and to the balance (about 3 to 4 tablespoons) add 4 tablespoons of flour. Let it bubble until the roux takes on a light brown color. Then add the strained marinade, and the strained venison broth, and bring to a boil. Then pour this over the meat, cover the pot, and simmer slowly until the meat is tender—1½ to 1¾ hours. Then add ⅓ cup of cream (which is at room temperature), let it come to a boil, and then serve.

Rothenberg is one of the cities along what the Germans call "The Romantic Way." It is a medieval town, and once a walled city. Some of the ancient walls and gates are still standing.

We stopped at one of the most charming hotels we had ever encountered, the Hotel Eisenhut. Our suite was like a French doll house, decorated and furnished in the most elegant style. The hotel is over five hundred years old, but it has been modernized to a degree that would put some of the newer swank American and European hotels to shame.

The food at the Eisenhut was perfectly wonderful, and the service was wonderfully perfect. One night for dinner we had a venison steak and I reveled in it.

VENISON STEAK

1 *venison steak, 1 inch thick*	4 *oz. Madeira wine*
Olive oil	1 *tsp. chopped chives*
Pinch ground ginger	1 *tsp. chopped parsley*
Butter	*Grated rind ½ lemon*
Salt and pepper	*Dash cayenne pepper*
2 *tbsp. butter*	2 *oz. currant jelly*

Rub a 1-inch thick venison steak with olive oil flavored with a pinch ground ginger, and let steak stand at room temperature for about an hour. Then, in a heavy skillet lightly greased with butter and sizzling hot, place the venison steak. Let it cook for about 3 minutes, sprinkle with salt and pepper to taste, and turn. Cook again for 3 minutes, season, and remove to hot platter.

To the skillet add 2 tablespoons butter, and when hot add 4 ounces Madeira wine, 1 teaspoon each chopped chives and chopped parsley, grated rind of ½ lemon, dash cayenne pepper, and 2 ounces currant jelly. Stir until well blended, replace steak in skillet, and simmer gently for 5 minutes. Serve very hot.

In the Mainzerhof Restaurant in Mainz I had another wonderful venison steak. If you should go to Mainz you should not fail to spend an evening in this beautiful restaurant, on the top floor of the Mainzerhof Hotel. The restaurant is surrounded with large glass windows, and the view of the city at night is like looking out on a fairyland.

VENISON STEAK

4 *small venison steaks*	½ *onion, finely chopped*
Salt	3 *mushrooms, sliced*
Freshly ground pepper	1 *tsp. flour*
Flour	⅓ *cup Rhine wine*
1½ *oz. butter*	1 *cup cream*
1½ *oz. olive oil*	½ *tsp. chopped chives*

Season 4 venison steaks with salt and freshly ground pepper, and dredge in flour. Heat ⅓ cup of shortening (half olive oil and half butter), and in this sauté the steaks over a low fire. When they are brown remove to a platter. In the shortening put ½ onion, finely chopped, and fry until they take on color. Then add 3 sliced mushrooms, and sauté for 1 minute. Then blend in 1 teaspoon flour, and let come to a bubble. Add ⅓ cup Rhine wine and 1 cup cream, and simmer for 5 minutes. Then place steaks and ½ teaspoon chopped chives in the sauce and heat, but do not boil. Serve at once.

This is one of three non-European recipes in this book. It is a recipe for venison chops which I devised myself, and everyone who has ever tasted them pronounce them the best they have ever had.

VENISON CHOPS M.W.

4 *loin venison chops, 1 inch*	*Freshly ground pepper*
thick	*Generous pinch ground ginger*
4 *tbsp. butter*	4 *oz. dry sherry*
Seasoned salt	2 *tbsp. currant jelly*

In a heavy iron skillet melt about 4 tablespoons butter. In the butter sprinkle seasoned salt and freshly ground pepper to taste and a generous pinch ground ginger. Mix well with a fork, and when butter is hot put in 4 venison loin chops about 1 inch thick. Cook for 4 minutes, then turn chops. Add to skillet 4 ounces dry sherry and 2 tablespoons currant jelly. Stir liquid until jelly is melted, and cook chops 5 minutes (from time they were turned). Pour gravy over chops on plates and serve to 2 or 4, depending on size of chops.

8 ❦ POULTRY

I guess wherever you go you'll always find chickens, which is a gastronomic blessing. You may find tough ones, old ones, and scrawny ones, but even these can be made palatable by a cunning cook. In our travels about Europe, we always enjoyed marvelous chicken dishes.

Experts have told me that the best chickens in Italy come from Tuscany, but we never had any cause for complaint in other provinces of Italy when it came to chicken. In Bologna and Florence they specialize in chicken breasts, which are unsurpassed.

In France, the finest chickens are raised in Bresse, which lies in the central part of Burgundy. Waverley Root, in his splendid book, *The Food of France,* tells how the Bresse chickens are matured on a heavy diet of corn. "After they have been killed," he writes, "they are bathed in milk and then powdered, so that they go to market a glistening white." Their flavor is most delicate, and when you see *Poulet de Bresse* on a menu, you know that you are getting the ultimate in chickens.

One of the notable entrees we had on the *Queen Elizabeth* going to Europe was a creation of Chef MacDonald called Chicken-Stuffed Crêpes, Mornay. It was light, yet exquisite in taste, and was accompanied by a lovely Montrachet.

CHICKEN-STUFFED CRÊPES, MORNAY SAUCE

CRÊPES

1 *cup sifted flour*	*Pinch salt*
1 *egg*	1 *cup milk*
	2 *tbsp. melted butter*

FILLING

3 tbsp. butter	Butter
2 tbsp. flour	¾ lb. diced cooked chicken
1 cup cream	Salt
1 tbsp. finely chopped shallots	Freshly ground pepper
(or little green onions)	½ cup dry sherry
½ cup chopped mushrooms	Few drops lemon juice

MORNAY SAUCE

1 cup Béchamel (or cream)	2 egg yolks, lightly beaten
sauce	3 tbsp. grated Parmesan cheese
3 tbsp. condensed consommé	1 tbsp. butter

Make the little thin crêpes first. Prepare a batter with 1 cup sifted flour, 1 egg, pinch salt, and 1 cup milk. The batter should have the consistency of cream. Add 2 tablespoons butter, melted. Make pancakes one by one, in a small buttered frying pan.

To make the filling melt 3 tablespoons butter in top of double boiler (the lower section half filled with boiling water). Blend 2 tablespoons flour with 1 cup cream until smooth, then add to melted butter. Stir constantly until mixture begins to thicken (about 3 minutes) then add 1 tablespoon finely chopped shallots (or little green onions) and ½ cup finely chopped mushrooms which have been sautéed in butter. Cook 3 minutes more, stirring constantly. Then add about ¾ pound diced cooked chicken, stir well, and heat through for 5 minutes. Season to taste with salt and freshly ground pepper, then add ½ cup dry sherry and few drops lemon juice. Turn heat well down and keep mixture hot over hot water in bottom of double boiler.

The third step is to make the Mornay sauce. To 1 cup hot Béchamel sauce (or cream sauce) add 3 tablespoons condensed consommé, 2 lightly beaten egg yolks, and 3 tablespoons grated Parmesan cheese. Blend well, then add 1 tablespoon butter, bit by bit, stirring it in with a whisk.

To serve, distribute the chicken mixture over the pancakes, roll them up, and place in a shallow fireproof baking dish, pour the Mornay sauce over, and put under the broiler until lightly browned. Serve at once.

In the chapter on fish I mentioned the special dinner devised by Guy Bracewell Smith, the owner-manager of the Park Lane Hotel, featuring fruits in every course. With the fish course, Filet of Sole Caprice, it was bananas. The main course was Chicken Breasts Hawaiian, and here is Chef Viguers' recipe for a delectable dish.

SUPRÊME DE VOLAILLE HAWAIIENNE
(Chicken Breasts with Pineapple)

4 *chicken breasts*	4 *oz. butter*
Salt	8 *slices pineapple* (*canned*)
Freshly ground pepper	*Powdered sugar*
Flour	2 *tsp. meat glaze*
Melted butter	4 *oz. dry sherry*
Fine breadcrumbs	4 *oz. butter*

Get 4 good sized chicken breasts and remove the skin. Slightly flatten them, season to taste with salt and freshly ground pepper, and dust with flour. (Because these were served after breaded filets of sole, they were not bread-crumbed, but normally, after being dusted with flour, the breasts are passed through melted butter, then coated with fine breadcrumbs.)

Melt 4 ounces butter in a skillet, then gently sauté the breasts on both sides until they are golden brown. When tender, remove from skillet and keep hot.

Dip 8 slices pineapple in powdered sugar and cook under broiler until they are nicely browned. Remove and keep warm.

To make the sauce, bring to a boil 2 teaspoons meat glaze with 4 ounces sherry. Then turn heat very low and add 4 ounces butter gradually. Blend, and heat thoroughly, but do not let boil.

To serve, place 2 glazed pineapple slices on each breast of chicken, and divide the sauce over each portion. This serves 4.

Mr. Stone, the suave and charming restaurant manager at the Park Lane hotel is an expert chef, and would occasionally prepare some very fine dish for us at our table. One night Mrs. Wood and I were dining with Guy Bracewell Smith and his lovely wife, Helene. Mr. Stone devised an exquisite chicken dish that he prepared at the table for us. He called it *Suprême de Volaille Hélène,* in honor of Mrs. Smith. This is his recipe.

SUPRÊME DE VOLAILLE HÉLÈNE
(Chicken Breasts Helene)

2 *whole chicken breasts*	*Salt*
2 *oz. butter*	*Freshly ground pepper*
½ *cup sliced button*	2 *oz. dry sherry*
mushrooms	2 *oz. cream*
¼ *tsp. dried tarragon*	¼ *tsp. paprika*
	Chopped parsley

Melt 2 ounces butter in a sauté pan over moderate heat. Add about ½ cup sliced button mushrooms and a scant ¼ teaspoon dried tarragon leaves. When mushrooms become hot make room in the center of the pan for 2 chicken breasts each split in half, seasoned with salt and freshly ground pepper. Cook slowly for approximately 15 minutes, turning once. When cooked push the chicken breasts and mushrooms to one side of pan, and increase the heat under the empty side. Pour in 2 ounces dry sherry, set alight, and when flame dies out add 2 ounces fresh cream and ¼ teaspoon paprika. Blend all well together, then sprinkle with chopped parsley. Place the chicken breasts on hot plates, and cover with sauce. This serves 2.

The Coq d'Or, on Stratton Street in Mayfair, is one of London's finest restaurants. Nowhere at similar establishments is luxury and formal service blended so happily with a touch of friendly welcome. And, of course, the food is superb. The second time we were there we had a magnificent dish of capon breasts and mushrooms with brandy.

SUPRÊME DE VOLAILLE
(Chicken Breasts)

6 *breasts of capons*	2 *tbsp. grated onion*
Salt	1 *lb. sliced fresh mushrooms*
Freshly ground pepper	1 *cup chicken bouillon*
½ *cup butter*	2 *oz. brandy*
1 *tsp. dried rosemary*	1 *oz. dry sherry*
	1 *cup sour cream*

Season 6 breasts of capons with salt and freshly ground pepper. In a skillet put ½ cup butter and 1 teaspoon dried rosemary. When butter is hot add the chicken breasts and sauté until golden brown on both sides. Remove breasts from skillet, and in the same butter sauté 2 tablespoons grated onion and 1 pound sliced fresh mushrooms for about 5 minutes. Return breasts to skillet, add 1 cup chicken bouillon and simmer, covered, for 45 minutes.

Remove capon breasts from skillet and keep hot. Add to the pan 2 ounces brandy and 1 ounce dry sherry, and simmer for 5 minutes. Remove skillet from fire and add 1 cup thick commercial sour cream, stirring it in well. Return skillet to heat and simmer very gently for about 2 minutes, stirring constantly. If the sauce is too thick add more chicken broth; if too thin, add more sour cream. Pour the sauce over the capon breasts and serve to 6.

Another very excellent restaurant is L'Ecu de France, on Jermyn Street, just off Piccadilly. It is very French, and very luxurious in its decor. It is always crowded, so Londoners must find it very good.

The night we were there the Maître D suggested an unusual dish, which I was rather surprised to see on the menu. It was Poussin Polonaise, which is, or was, a rather celebrated Polish dish. "Poussin" means a small, young chicken.

POUSSIN POLONAISE
(Chicken Polish Style)

1 3½-lb. chicken	1 lb.-13 ozs. can tomatoes
¼ cup fresh lemon juice	1 cup dry white wine
½ tsp. salt	2 tbsp. tomato paste
Pepper	3 whole cloves
¼ tsp. ground cinnamon	1 stick cinnamon
4 oz. butter	Salt and pepper

Have a 3½ pound chicken cut into serving pieces. Sprinkle pieces with ¼ cup fresh lemon juice, then sprinkle them with a mixture of ½ teaspoon salt, a little pepper, and ¼ teaspoon ground cinnamon. Chill for 20 minutes, then drain pieces. Melt 4 ounces butter in a heavy skillet over medium heat, add the chicken pieces, and brown them well on all sides. Then remove and keep warm.

Combine a 1-pound, 13-ounce can tomatoes, 1 cup dry white wine, 2 tablespoons tomato paste, 3 whole cloves, 1 stick cinnamon, and salt and pepper to taste. Mix well, then cook in the skillet over medium heat for about 15 minutes, stirring occasionally. Then add the browned chicken pieces to the sauce, cover, and cook over medium heat about 45 minutes, or until chicken is tender.

When we drove into the ancient Roman city of Vienne, on the banks of the Rhone river, late one afternoon, we had high hopes of having a fabulous dinner at what is said to be the finest dining place in France, the three-star Restaurant de la Pyramide. But we were a few days too early, and it had not yet opened. So, that evening we walked a short distance from our hotel to Le Bec Fin, where we had an extraordinarily fine meal in most pleasant surroundings.

Our entree was *Coquelet en Champagne,* and to my mind it surpassed any chicken dish I have ever eaten, and I do not except the *Poularde de Bresse en casserole Duchesse de Bourgogne* we had at Maxim's in Paris. Monsieur Baris, the *propriétaire,* wrote out the recipe for me.

COQUELET EN CHAMPAGNE
(Chicken in Champagne)

1 *tender frying chicken*	2–3 *finely chopped shallots (or*
Salt	*little green onions)*
Freshly ground pepper	4–5 *thin slices truffles*
3 *oz. butter*	*(optional)*
2 *oz. Armagnac (or brandy)*	½ *cup champagne*
1 *tbsp. chopped parsley*	¾ *cup heavy cream*

Cut a tender frying chicken into quarters and season to taste with salt and freshly ground pepper. Heat 3 ounces butter in a skillet and add the chicken quarters. Let them cook slowly, turning occasionally, until they are golden brown on all sides.

Heat 2 ounces Armagnac (or a fine brandy), light it, and pour over chicken pieces. Shake the skillet until the flames die out. Then add to the skillet 1 tablespoon chopped parsley, 2 or 3 finely chopped shallots (or little green onions), and (this is optional) 4 or 5 thin slices truffles. Next add ½ cup champagne. Blend everything well, then cover skillet and let contents cook slowly until chicken is tender, about 25 to 30 minutes.

Remove chicken quarters to a very hot platter. To the liquid in the skillet add ¾ cup heavy cream and blend it in well. Correct seasoning and let the sauce reduce a little. Then pour it over the chicken quarters and serve at once.

The French Riviera is part of Provence, so you will find all of the Provençale dishes served along the Côte d'Azur. When you get as far east as Nice, however, some Italian borrowings begin to creep into the cooking. But, if possible, this only enhances the lusty, colorful, and highly aromatic quality of Nicoise food.

In the neighboring town of Beaulieu-sur-Mer the proprietor of the grocery store where I shopped gave me her recipe for chicken which I shall call, in her honor, Chicken Nicole.

CHICKEN NICOLE

1 *large tender frying chicken*	*Small jar artichoke hearts*
2 *tbsp. butter*	4 *ripe tomatoes*
2 *tbsp. olive oil*	20 *pitted Italian black olives*
Salt	8 *tiny new potatoes*
Freshly ground pepper	1 *cup chicken bouillon*
2 *cloves garlic*	1 *cup rosé wine*
¼ *tsp. dried oregano*	*Flour and butter roux (if*
¼ *tsp. dried thyme*	*necessary)*

½ *tbsp. lemon juice*

Disjoint a large but tender frying chicken. In a large skillet heat 2 tablespoons each butter and olive oil, then add the chicken pieces, which have been seasoned with salt and freshly ground pepper. Cook them slowly until they are golden brown on all sides. Then add 2 cloves garlic, halved, ¼ teaspoon each dried oregano and dried thyme, and contents of a small jar of artichoke hearts, 4 ripe tomatoes, peeled, seeded, and cut in large pieces, 20 pitted Italian black olives, 8 tiny new scraped potatoes, 1 cup each condensed chicken bouillon and dry rosé wine, and ½ tablespoon lemon juice.

Cover the skillet and let the contents cook very slowly over a low flame for about 1 hour, or until chicken and potatoes are tender. The sauce should not be too thin, but if it is, add a little flour and butter roux, blending it in well. This recipe should serve 4.

Another chicken recipe from Provence is this one we had in a little bistro, La Bouillabaisse, on the rue Cléry, not far from the Bourse. This restaurant specializes in Provençale dishes, and while it is a typical bistro, the food is excellent, and it is not expensive.

POULARD PROVENÇALE
(Chicken Provençale)

1 3½-lb. chicken	3 oz. brandy
Lime juice	1 clove garlic
Salt	½ cup minced onion
Freshly ground pepper	4 ripe medium tomatoes
3 oz. butter	1 cup sour cream
½ cup grated Parmesan cheese	

Have a 3½-pound chicken cut up into serving pieces. Sprinkle the pieces with fresh lime juice, and season to taste with salt and freshly ground pepper.

In a heavy skillet melt 3 ounces butter and when it is hot put in your chicken pieces and brown them slowly on both sides. Then pour over them 3 ounces heated brandy and ignite. When the flames die out add 1 minced clove garlic and ½ cup minced onion to the skillet, and cook gently until onions are tender, but not brown. Add 4 medium ripe tomatoes, coarsely chopped, cover the skillet, and simmer for about 35 minutes, or until chicken is tender.

Remove chicken pieces to a warm serving dish and to the mixture in the skillet add 1 cup commercial sour cream and ½ cup grated Parmesan cheese. Heat over a very low flame, stirring constantly, until sauce is well blended and hot. Correct seasoning, if necessary, then pour the sauce over the chicken pieces and serve.

The following recipe was given to me by an American friend who has lived in Paris for many years. She is noted for the intriguing flavor accents that she imparts to her dishes. We had this dish one night in her apartment near the Champs Elysée.

CHICKEN ORANGE

1 3-lb. frying chicken	1 oz. dry white wine
¾ cup flour	1½ cups milk
2 tsp. grated orange rind	¼ cup orange juice
1 tsp. paprika	¼ cup Cointreau
1 tsp. salt	¼ tsp. powdered ginger
¼ tsp. pepper	Salt
Bacon drippings	Freshly ground pepper

Have a 3-pound frying chicken cut into serving pieces. In a paper bag combine ¾ cup flour, 2 teaspoons grated orange peel, 1 teaspoon paprika, 1 teaspoon salt, and ¼ teaspoon pepper. Shake the chicken pieces in this (not more than 2 pieces at a time), and then let the coating dry on them. Reserve the remaining seasoned flour mixture.

In a heavy skillet pour enough bacon drippings to cover the bottom of the skillet ¼ inch deep. When hot, brown the chicken pieces in it slowly, turning them to lightly brown on all sides, about 15 to 20 minutes. Then add an ounce of dry white wine, cover the skillet, and cook about 35 minutes, or until chicken is tender. If you like the chicken pieces crisp, uncover the skillet during the last 10 minutes of cooking. When done, remove chicken pieces and keep warm.

Pour off from the skillet all the fat except 2 tablespoons. Blend in 3 tablespoons of the seasoned flour that has been reserved and cook, stirring constantly, until bubbly. Then remove skillet from fire and stir in 1½ cups milk, ¼ cup orange juice, ¼ cup Cointreau or orange curaçao, and ¼ teaspoon powdered ginger. Blend everything well, and let simmer for about 5 minutes. Season to taste with salt and freshly ground pepper, and serve sauce with or over the chicken. This serves 4.

The classic chicken dish in Italy is Chicken alla Cacciatora, or Chicken Hunters' Style. The chicken is cut into serving pieces, and cooked with vegetables and mushrooms in either red or white wine. We had it three times in Italy, and in each case it was delicious beyond words. The first two times were in the hotels l'Hermitage and Savoia in Rome, and the third time was in the Hotel Royal in Naples.

The Royal Hotel is one of the finest hotels in Italy. Our ultramodern room had a balcony, and looked out over the entire Bay of Naples. Immediately in front of us, literally across the via Partenope, was the ancient Castel dell'Ovo, once occupied by the famous Roman general and epicure, Lucullus.

Signore Giuseppe Chimirri, Director of the Royal, was as interested in Mrs. Wood and me as though he were a godfather. He alerted his whole staff, and the service we received was fabulous. In the dining room particularly, our slightest desire was tantamount to a command. Every meal we had in the beautiful dining room was a masterpiece. When we left, he presented me with five recipes, one of which was for Chicken alla Cacciatora.

CHICKEN ALLA CACCIATORA ROYAL

2 2-lb. chickens	2 cups Italian tomatoes
Seasoned flour	1 tbsp. tomato paste
1½ oz. butter	Salt and pepper
2½ oz. fine olive oil	2 tbsp. chopped parsley
1 large clove garlic	Generous pinch dried rosemary
2 medium onions	Generous pinch dried oregano
2 slices canned pimento	1 cup dry white wine
2 cups sliced mushrooms	

Cut 2 tender chickens (about 2 pounds each) into serving pieces, and shake them in a bag with seasoned flour.

In a heavy skillet put 1½ ounces butter, 2½ ounces pure olive oil, and a large clove garlic, minced. When the fat is hot, add the chicken pieces along with 2 medium-sized onions, peeled and chopped. Sauté until the chicken pieces are a nice golden brown. Then add to the skillet 2 slices of canned pimento, chopped, 2 cups of canned Italian tomatoes, 1 tablespoon tomato paste, salt and pepper to taste, 2 tablespoons chopped parsley, a generous pinch each of dried rosemary and dried oregano, and 1 cup dry white wine. Cover and simmer gently for about 1 hour. Then add 2 cups thinly sliced mushrooms, and continue simmering, covered, for about 30 minutes longer, or until chicken pieces are tender. Serve as hot as possible. Personally, I like a Chianti with this dish, but a dry white wine can be served. String beans make a nice accompaniment, or spaghetti, or noodles, *al burro* (with butter).

One of the loveliest parts of Italy we visited was Umbria, located just about in the center of the peninsula. It is one of the few provinces that does not touch upon the seas, and its hills have an unsurpassed beauty, especially in the late spring. On our way from Rome to Florence we stopped for three days in Perugia, the capital, and we wished we had had the time to remain in and about Perugia for three weeks.

We spent one of our days in the nearby town of Assisi, an ancient town on the slopes of Mount Subasio, where we visited the Basilica of St. Francis, the buttressed church of Santa Clara, and the utterly amazing group of ultra modern buildings of the Pro Civitate Cristiana, an Apostolic lay association devoted to promoting the Christianization of contemorary society through a deep, wide knowledge of Christ.

Perugia is perhaps best known for its Italian University for foreigners; for Perugina chocolates, which are probably the best in the world; and as the home of Perugino, the great Italian painter who taught the young Raphael. There are dozens of buildings and churches that are intensely interesting.

We stopped at the lovely old Brufani Palace Hotel, which was the home of the Brufani family. The food there was out of this world, and the genial manager, Signor Nando Curti, gave me recipes for two dishes, *Risotto alla Montefalchese* and *Chicken Arrabbiato*.

CHICKEN ARRABBIATO

1 2-lb. frying chicken	Salt and pepper
1 large onion	4 oz. dry red wine
4 oz. olive oil	1 large tomato

Cut up a big onion and put it in water for about half an hour. Then dry it and put it in a skillet containing 4 ounces hot olive oil. When cooked, remove onion and reserve. In same skillet put a cleaned and cut up 2-pound fryer, and when pieces are browned all over return the onions to the skillet, salt and pepper to taste, add 4 ounces dry red wine, and a large tomato, chopped. Cook all together until chicken is tender, and serve at once.

One of the most savory chicken dishes we had in Italy was served at the Hotel Continental in Milan. The Maître D characterized it merely as chicken with prosciutto ham and white wine, but it deserved a far greater build-up.

CHICKEN WITH PROSCIUTTO HAM AND WHITE WINE

2 2-lb. broiler chickens	6 little green onions
Salt	½ cup diced prosciutto ham
Freshly ground pepper	24 small mushroom caps
3 oz. olive oil	½ tsp. oregano
1 clove garlic	3 oz. dry white wine
1 oz. brandy	

Disjoint 2 tender broilers weighing about 2 pounds each, and season with salt and freshly ground pepper to taste.

In a large iron skillet put 3 ounces pure olive oil, and add 1 minced and crushed clove garlic. When the oil is hot, put in the chicken pieces, and sauté briskly over a brisk flame. When the pieces are golden brown on all sides turn down the flame and add 6 little green onions (bulbs and tops), chopped, ½ cup Italian prosciutto ham (or ordinary lean ham), diced, 24 small mushroom caps, halved, ½ teaspoon oregano, 3 ounces dry white wine, and 1 ounce brandy. Blend well, then simmer for about 25 minutes, or until chicken pieces are tender.

Remove pieces to hot platter. Turn up flame under skillet a little, and let wine sauce reduce about half. Then pour over chicken and serve.

One of Rome's very lovely, and very old restaurants is Ranieri's, on the Via Mario de Fiori, not far from the American Express. It is a delight if you want an old world atmosphere, quiet but perfect service, and superb food.

The restaurant was founded one hundred and twenty years ago, and about eighteen years later was acquired by Giuseppe Ranieri, who had been chef to the Emperor Maximilian of Mexico. One of the specialties of the restaurant is *Pollo alla Massimiliano,* in obtaining the recipe.

POLLO ALLA MASSIMILIANO
(Chicken Maximilian)

1 *tender young broiler*	1 *clove garlic*
Olive oil	*Butter*
Salt and pepper	4 *tsp. dry vermouth*
1½ *oz. brandy*	

Have a young and tender chicken split in half for broiling. Anoint it with the finest olive oil, season with salt and pepper to taste, and sprinkle with a half clove garlic, finely minced. Put the two halves on a broiling pan, dot each with butter, and put about a teaspoon of dry vermouth in each cavity. When bone side is nicely browned turn chicken pieces, again sprinkle with the finely minced garlic, dot with butter, and pour over the halves the same amount of vermouth. Broil until skin side is browned and tender.

Place chicken halves in a hot fireproof serving dish with their juices, bring to the table, and pour about 1½ ounces of brandy, flaming, over chicken. When flames die out, serve at once.

Verona is another of Italy's many unforgettable cities. It has beauty, atmosphere, scores of fascinating historical buildings, and gaily busy streets and squares.

You can visit the home of the Capulets, and, going through Juliet's bedroom, stand on the balcony under which, it is said, Romeo serenaded her. Following the immortal love story to the end, you can visit the Capuchin Cloisters. There, you can stand before the altar of the little church where Romeo and Juliet were married, and visit the chamber where Juliet lay in her feigned death sleep. Finally, you may view the tomb where Romeo and Juliet lay buried.

You can sit at a sidewalk table of the Ristorante Tre Corone, on the happily thronged Piazza Bra, and while you sip an apéritif, you can gaze at the amazingly well-preserved Roman Amphitheater, scarcely a stone's throw away. It was built in the 1st century, A.D., and yet operas are still given there.

Verona has two other restaurants that are gastronomic gems— the Tre Corone, and the Dodici Apostoli (the Twelve Apostles). Giorgio Gioca, the proprietor of the latter, gave me the recipes of two of the marvelous dishes served to us there.

POLLO DI VALDARNO AL CARTOCCIO
(Chicken Cooked in Parchment)

1 2½-lb. chicken	2 pinches dried rosemary
2 slices bacon	Chopped parsley
Olive oil	2 juniper berries, crushed
1 clove garlic	Salt and pepper
2 leaves sage	2 mushrooms
	Spanish sauce

SPANISH SAUCE

2 *tbsp. butter*	¼ *lb. minced lean beef*
1 *clove garlic*	2 *cups Italian tomatoes*
1 *onion*	1 *tbsp. minced parsley*
½ *green pepper*	*Cayenne pepper*
1 *stalk celery*	1 *tsp. salt*
6 *pitted green olives*	2 *oz. dry sherry*

Clean and wash a 2½ pound chicken, and cut it in half. Take a sheet of parchment large enough to contain half a chicken, and grease it with olive oil. In the center place a slice of bacon, ½ clove garlic, chopped, a leaf of sage, a pinch dried rosemary, a sprinkling of chopped parsley, and a crushed juniper berry. Then arrange over the bacon and herbs a half chicken, and dust it with salt and pepper. Spoon over the chicken a covering of Spanish sauce, and cover this with 1 mushroom, thinly sliced. Place a second piece of parchment over the chicken, and fold the two halves together tightly so that no juices can escape. Follow the same procedure with the second chicken half, and put the 2 wrapped halves in a moderate (350 degrees) oven, and cook for 1 hour. Serve very hot, splitting the parchment wrappings at the table.

To make the Spanish sauce put 2 tablespoons butter in a saucepan and add 1 clove garlic, finely chopped. When butter is hot add 1 onion, ½ green pepper, and 1 stalk celery, all chopped, and 6 green olives, pitted and chopped. When vegetables are tender add ¼ pound lean beef, minced, and stir well until meat is all browned. Then add 2 cups canned Italian tomatoes, 1 tablespoon minced parsley, a slight sprinkling cayenne pepper, 1 teaspoon salt, and 2 ounces dry sherry. Simmer, uncovered, about 30 minutes, until sauce is thick and not too much moisture left. Use excess sauce with scrambled eggs.

Bologna is another of Italy's fascinating cities. It is very old, with miles and miles of brick arcaded streets; an unfinished church that had been planned to outdo St. Peter's in Rome; another church that contains the bones of the founder of the Dominican order (his coffin was actually X-rayed, and you can see an enlarged X-ray picture of the bones); and still another church that is really seven churches in one!

But the glory of Bologna is its cooking, which is famous all over the world. Bolognese fare is not for delicate nibblers—it is rich and lusty, and its mélange of flavors constantly keeps one's taste buds jumping with joy.

Our cultural and gastronomic guide about Bologna was Professor Keith di Pollo, an American whose family lives in San Mateo and Palo Alto, California, but who teaches dramatics at one of the universities in Bologna. Our first dinner was at Al Pappagallo, in company with a noted Bolognese writer and authority on food, Alessandro Cervellati.

Al pappagallo is known over a good part of the world. Its entrance is under one of the few remaining wooden arcades in Bologna, and the outside looks very ancient. But inside it is bright and gay. From its vaulted ceilings hang four huge crystal chandeliers, and its clientele is quite cosmopolitan. And what food! Our dinner started off with *Tortellini alla Bolognese,* our entree was *Suprema di Pollo alla Zurla,* and our dessert was a magnificent ice cream concoction called *Gelati alla Pappagallo.* Signor Zurla gave me the recipe for the chicken breasts.

SUPREMA DI POLLO ALLA ZURLA
(Chicken Breasts à la Zurla)

4 *filets chicken breasts*	4 *slices cooked ham*
Flour	*Sliced mushrooms*
Salt and pepper	*Butter*
2 *tbsp. butter*	*Grated Parmesan cheese*
1½ *oz. Marsala wine*	4 *tbsp. condensed chicken*
	bouillon

Remove the breasts from a young and tender chicken and divide them into 4 filets, after removing the skin. Flatten filets a little, and dust them lightly with flour, sprinkling them with salt and pepper to taste. In a large skillet melt 2 tablespoons butter, put in the breasts, and cook them gently (the butter must not blacken or brown) on both sides for about 10 minutes. Then pour over them about 1½ ounces Marsala wine. After it has bubbled and amalgamated with the butter, lay a thin slice cooked ham over each filet, cover each ham slice with a layer of thinly sliced mushrooms previously cooked for 5 minutes in a little butter, and over mushrooms put a thin layer of the best Parmesan cheese, grated. Finally, pour over each filet a tablespoon condensed chicken bouillon. Cover the skillet and cook very gently for about 7 minutes, or until cheese melts and combines with the juices in the skillet and forms a sauce. Serve immediately, for sauce must not dry out or cheese become hard.

The Villa d'Este, on the shores of Lake Como at Cernobbio, Italy, is probably the most regal, magnificent and luxurious hotel in the world. Its splendor cannot be put into words; you have to see it and live in it in order to appreciate not only its grandeur, but its beauty, its surroundings, its comforts, its service, and its food. It is indeed a foretaste of paradise.

Villa d'Este has a long and fascinating history. Built in 1568 as a cardinal's palace, through the years it became the home of Caroline of Brunswick, Princess of Wales and Queen of England; of the dowager Empress Marie Feodorovna of Russia; a hospital for wounded German soldiers; and finally the princely hostelry that it is today, presided over by a veritable prince of hosts, Signor Willy Dombré. Never have we experienced such kindness, thoughtfulness, and courtesy as he extended to us during our month's stay.

I could write a small volume on the superb food we were served at Villa d'Este. The most unusual and succulent dish we had was *Suprema di Pollo Villa d'Este*—stuffed chicken breasts. This is my adaptation of the recipe given me (in Italian) by the chef.

SUPREMA DI POLLO VILLA D'ESTE
(Chicken Breasts Villa d'Este)

4 *chicken breasts*	*Salt and pepper*
2 *medium onions*	3 *eggs*
6 *oz. butter*	4 *slices pâté de foie gras*
3 *large mushrooms*	*Flour*
8 *oz. Béchamel (or rich*	*Beaten egg*
cream) sauce	*Fine breadcrumbs*

Grated Parmesan cheese

Have ready 4 chicken breasts, each split lengthwise, but not completely through, and well pounded to obtain maximum thinness.

Make a Soubise sauce as follows: chop very finely 2 medium onions and cook them gently in 1 ounce butter until they begin to soften. Then add to pan 3 large mushrooms, finely chopped, and cook 5 minutes longer (the onions must not take on any color). Now add 6 ounces Béchamel sauce (rich cream sauce) and finish cooking slowly. Season with salt and pepper to taste, swirl in 1 ounce butter, and when blended press the whole through a fine sieve. The finished product should be fairly thick. Keep sauce warm, floating a little melted butter over top to keep any crust from forming.

At the last, just before you are ready to assemble the dish before cooking, make small thin omelets, called *crespelles*. Break 3 eggs into a bowl, salt and pepper to taste, and beat lightly. Put ½ ounce butter in a skillet, and when hot, add eggs. Stir briskly until there is a slight thickening. Then let the eggs spread over bottom of skillet, and remove from fire. This omelet, which should be quite thin, is divided into 4 parts, each part being just slightly smaller than a flattened half of chicken breast.

On the bone side of each half breast place one of the omelets. Spread over each omelet a layer of the Soubise sauce. Over the sauce place a thin slice of pâté de foie gras. Now refold each breast, moisten the edges, and press them together, so that they are in their original form.

Dust the folded breasts lightly with flour, dip them in beaten egg, and then in fine breadcrumbs. Heat 3 ounces butter in a skillet, then sauté the breasts until they are golden brown. Take the skillet off the fire, sprinkle the breasts with grated Parmesan cheese, dot with butter, and place the skillet under the broiler until the cheese begins to melt. Remove from broiler and place a breast on each of 4 hot plates. Pour over each breast a little butter previously browned, and serve immediately.

There are scores of delightful dining places in Florence, ranging from such elegant restaurants as Ristorante Oliviero in the Grand Hotel on the bank of the Arno, Sabatini's, near the *duomo,* and Paoli's, which is very old, to the trattorias, such as the Buca Lapi, and the Trattoria Sostanza.

The Ristorante Vincenzo Sabatini, on the Via Panzani, probably serves the finest food in Tuscany. And its atmosphere and decor are superb. Even though you are inside, you feel sure that you are outside in a wonderful old Italian garden, with trellises, flowers, vines, and foliage, all indirectly lighted.

George and Pat Richardson of San Francisco, who were on a world tour, and Mrs. Wood and I dined together at Sabatini's. The first course was *Lasagne Verdi.* For the main course two of us had *Petti di Pollo alla Sabatini,* and the other two had pork cutlets with a marvelous sauce. The dessert was a heavenly fresh strawberry tart.

The Italians are very fond of breasts of chicken, and it is amazing the number of different ways they can be prepared, but those at Sabatini's were a gastronomic masterpiece.

POLLO ALLA SABATINI
(Breasts of Chicken Sabatini)

2 *breasts of young chicken*	*Cubed Gruyère (or Swiss)*
Salt and pepper	*cheese*
Flour	*Finely diced pickled tongue*
1 *tbsp. olive oil*	*(or ham)*
2 *tbsp. butter*	3–4 *tbsp. tomato sauce*
3–4 *tbsp. condensed chicken bouillon*	

Cut out the two breasts of a young and tender chicken, remove the skin and all bones, and cut each breast into 2 slices. Flatten the slices as much as possible with a wooden mallet or rolling pin, salt and pepper to taste, then dust lightly with flour.

In a shallow frying pan put 1 tablespoon olive oil and 2 tablespoons butter. When hot put in the seasoned and floured slices chicken breasts and brown them lightly on both sides, turning frequently.

When slices are almost cooked cover each slice with very finely cubed Gruyère cheese and finely diced pickled tongue (or finely diced ham). Then add to the pan a thin layer of tomato sauce (3 to 4 tablespoons), and 3 to 4 tablespoons condensed chicken broth.

Place the pan in a 325-degree oven, and when cheese begins

to melt and sauce thickens (watch that it doesn't dry too much) serve immediately—two slices to each person. Serve with fresh peas, or mushrooms, or asparagus tips, and mashed potatoes.

In the Palace Hotel dining room in Brussels we had a most delightful chicken dish featuring Belgium's almost national comestible, endive. It is light, savory, and simple to prepare.

CHICKEN CASSEROLE WITH ENDIVE

4 *heads endive*	¼ *cup water*
2 *oz. butter*	4 *slices cooked chicken breasts*
1 *tsp. Maggi seasoning*	¼ *cup dry white wine*
	Buttered toast

Wash 4 heads endive carefully in cold water, wipe dry with paper toweling, and then cut each head in half lengthwise.

In an oblong casserole or baking dish which can be placed over a flame put 2 ounces of butter (½ stick) and 1 teaspoon of Maggi seasoning. When butter is melted, gently place the halved endive heads in the butter and brown lightly, about 2 minutes on each side. Then add about ¼ cup water and allow the endive to simmer, uncovered, for about 15 minutes.

Remove casserole from flame and place 4 generous slices of cooked chicken breasts over the endive, and pour ¼ cup dry white wine over the chicken. Place casserole in preheated 325-degree oven for 10 minutes, or until chicken is thoroughly heated.

Serve piping hot over buttered toast on preheated plates by arranging as follows: buttered toast, chicken slice, and 2 endive halves. If more sauce is desired, use additional melted butter with Maggi seasoning. This serves 4.

I have told about the fabulous Rijsttafel we had in the Bali Restaurant in Scheveningen, Holland, and I wish I could have given some recipes for the amazing dishes that went to make up the Rijsttafel. But it was a meal that couldn't possibly be made in an American home: I don't believe even a rather elaborately equipped American home kitchen could cope with the scores of dishes; and many of the comestibles are not available in America.

However, I did ask the manager of the Bali Restaurant if he could give me a modified Javanese dish that an American house-wife or amateur chef could prepare at home, and he came up with an Indonesian Chicken-Shrimp dish which is not at all dif-ficult. However, in place of the peanut sauce called for, which is a little difficult to make, I have substituted peanut butter, which will produce very much the same flavor.

INDONESIAN CHICKEN-SHRIMP SUPREME

1½ *cups raw white rice*	½ *tsp. mace*
3 *cups chicken broth*	½ *tsp. chili powder*
1½ *tsp. salt*	¼ *cup peanut butter*
½ *cup cooking fat*	1 *cup cooked crabmeat*
1½ *cups chopped onion*	1 *cup cubed cooked ham*
1 *clove garlic*	1 *cup cubed cooked chicken*
1 *tsp. whole cumin seed*	1 *cup chicken broth*
1 *lb. shrimp*	1 *cup chopped peanuts*
1 *tsp. ground coriander*	1 *cup shredded coconut*

3 *bananas, sliced*

Have ready 1 pound shrimp, shelled and deveined.

Put 1½ cups uncooked white rice, 3 cups chicken broth, and 1½ teaspoons salt in a 2 quart saucepan. Bring to vigorous boil, then turn heat very low, cover, and simmer for 14 minutes. Then remove saucepan from fire, but leave lid on until ready to use, at least 10 minutes.

While rice cooks heat ½ cup cooking fat in a large skillet, or Dutch oven. Add 1½ cups chopped onion, 1 minced clove garlic, and 1 teaspoon whole cumin seed. Cook, stirring occasionally, about 10 minutes, or until onions are tender.

When onions are tender, stir in the shrimp. If the shrimp are large, chop coarsely, but save a few whole for garnish. Cook onions and shrimp, stirring occasionally, about 5 minutes, or until shrimp are pink all over.

Into this mixture stir 1 teaspoon ground coriander, ½ teaspoon mace, ½ teaspoon chili powder, and ¼ cup peanut butter. Mix well, then add 1 cup cooked crab meat, cut up, 1 cup cubed cooked ham, 1 cup cut up cooked chicken, and 1 cup chicken broth. Heat until very hot, then gently stir in the hot rice. Serve in a large dish garnished with whole cooked shrimp. Have 3 side dishes, one of chopped peanuts (1 cup), another of shredded coconut (1 cup), and a third of sliced bananas (3). Each serving of chicken-shrimp mixture should be topped with helpings of peanuts, coconut, and bananas. This makes 12 servings.

Whole cumin seed, ground coriander, and mace may be obtained in jars in most large grocery stores.

The Italians are very fond of turkey. In many of the chicken breasts dishes turkey breasts are substituted. This is particularly true in Bologna. A very luxurious dish for a dinner party is a small roast turkey.

In Sorrento we stayed at the Europa Palace Hotel, which is almost on the edge of a cliff bordering on the Bay of Naples, and overlooks the little port of Sorrento. The broad and lovely terrace in front of the hotel is filled with trees and carefully tended gardens. Standing at the edge of the terrace you can look straight down a hundred feet or more to the shore of the bay, and in the distance is Mount Vesuvio.

One day for luncheon the waiter suggested a special dish of spaghettini, which he said was Enrico Caruso's favorite dish. He rather inferred that he had served it himself to Caruso when the great tenor came to Sorrento, which he did often. He said it was named after one of Caruso's favorite prima donnas, Madame Tetrazzini.

Well, I have heard the same story told in the old Vanderbilt Hotel in New York, but true or false, the dish is delicious, especially when made by an accomplished Italian chef.

TURKEY TETRAZZINI

8 *oz. spaghettini*	3 *cups cubed cooked turkey*
1 *tbsp. salt*	½ *cup chicken bouillon*
3 *quarts boiling water*	½ *cup dry white wine*
2 *tbsp. olive oil*	1 *cup light cream*
1 *cup sliced mushrooms*	*Salt and pepper*
1 *small onion, minced*	3 *tbsp. grated Parmesan cheese*

Add 1 tablespoon salt to 3 quarts rapidly boiling water. Gradually add 8 ounces spaghettini so that the water does not stop boiling. Cook, uncovered, stirring occasionally, for about 10 to 12 minutes, then drain in a colander.

Heat 2 tablespoons olive oil in a skillet, then add 1 cup sliced fresh mushrooms and 1 small onion, minced, and sauté until lightly browned. Then add 3 cups chopped cooked turkey, ½ cup each chicken bouillon and dry white wine, 1 cup light cream and salt and pepper to taste. Mix well.

In the bottom of a 2½ quart casserole, greased, arrange half of the cooked spaghettini and cover with half of the turkey mixture. Top that with the remaining spaghettini, and add the balance of the turkey mixture for the top layer. Sprinkle with about 3 generous tablespoons grated Parmesan cheese. Bake in a 350-degree oven for 50 minutes, or until lightly browned. This serves 4.

In my first book, *With a Jug of Wine*, I gave a recipe for a stuffed turkey that is a great favorite in Italy, *Tacchino Ripieno*.

In Parma we had a rather elaborate luncheon one day in the home of a charming Italian family we had met. It was a feast day in late May, and the main course was—*Tacchino Arrosto Ripieno!* It was prepared in almost the same way as the recipe in my book, but the stuffing had an additional ingredient that was wonderful. Here is the way this superlative roast turkey is prepared in Italian homes.

TACCHINO ARROSTO RIPIENO
(Italian Turkey Stuffing)

1 *cup chestnuts*	4 *pears*
½ *cup cooking oil*	*Salt*
Turkey giblets	*Pepper*
½ *cup cooked veal*	¼ *tsp. nutmeg*
½ *cup cooked ham*	½ *tsp. dried oregano*
½ *cup cooked salsiccia*	¼ *cup grated Parmesan cheese*
(*Italian pork sausage*)	1 *tbsp. strained honey*
½ *cup cooked prunes*	*Dry white wine*
½ *cup mushrooms*	2 *tbsp. olive oil*
4 *little green onions*	2 *eggs, beaten*

Pick over enough chestnuts to have 1 cup sound nuts. With a sharp, pointed knife cut an "X" on the flat side of the chestnuts. Heat about ½ cup cooking oil in a heavy skillet, and put in the chestnuts. Let them heat over a fast flame for about 3 minutes, shaking the pan and stirring the chestnuts all the while. Remove, drain, and the minute they can be handled remove the shells and inner skin.

Blanch and trim the gizzard, liver, and heart of the turkey, then put them through the meat grinder with ½ cup each of cooked veal, ham, and salsiccia (little Italian pork sausages), the chestnuts, ½ cup cooked prunes, ½ cup mushrooms, and about 4 little green onions, bulbs and tops. Add 4 peeled and cored pears, cut into cubes. Mix all well, and season with salt and freshly ground pepper to taste, and add ¼ teaspoon nutmeg, ½ teaspoon dried oregano, and ¼ cup grated Parmesan cheese. Moisten the mixture with about 1 tablespoon strained honey and just enough dry white wine to be absorbed. Mix all thoroughly, and cook in 2 tablespoons of olive oil for a few minutes. Then add 2 eggs, beaten, to bind everything together. Stuff the turkey, but don't press the stuffing into the cavities; rather, pick up the bird and shake down the stuffing so that it settles itself.

9 ◊ VEGETABLES

Vegetables are an important part of almost all European meals. Are they better than those found in America? In some instances they are, asparagus, for example. In other instances they are not, but the ingenuity of European cooks can often make an inferior vegetable taste better.

In some of the great markets of Europe, such as Les Halles in Paris, and the great market in the old town of Nice, the vegetables are a beautiful sight to behold. They are beautifully arranged, and are garden fresh. You will almost gasp at the great pyramids of vegetables, and the artistry with which they are displayed.

Each little town, too, has its open air market, and the vegetables displayed there have probably been picked early the same morning that they are offered for sale. They may not be beautifully arranged, but they have a freshness and taste that are irresistible. In Beaulieu the vegetable and flower market was set up in the town square, and for some time I avoided patronizing it. But one Saturday morning I did some shopping at the open air market, and I'll never forget the tiny little Brussels sprouts that I bought. I have never tasted any so succulent, or with such taste-teasing flavor, even in Brussels.

The Italians are very fond of artichokes, which are called *carciofi,* and the globe artichoke is one of the staple vegetables of Italy. They are esteemed, from the large green ones down to the very tiny ones. These latter are preserved in oil, and eaten as hors d'oeuvres. The famous Roman dish is *Carciofi alla Romana,* in which the whole green ones (so tender that the entire artichoke can be eaten) are stewed in olive oil and garlic.

This recipe, from Rome, approximates the *Carciofi alla Romana,* but makes allowance for the not so tender, but equally delicious American artichoke.

ARTICHOKES COOKED IN OIL AND GARLIC

Prepared green artichokes	2 *cloves garlic, minced*
Boiling water	½ *tsp. lemon juice*
3 *tbsp. olive oil*	¼ *tsp. salt*

Before cooking wash the artichokes well, trim the stems to 1 inch, pull off tough outer leaves, and, with scissors, snip off the tips of remaining leaves. Place artichokes upright in a deep saucepan containing 1 inch of boiling water to which has been added 3 tablespoons olive oil, 2 minced cloves garlic, and ½ teaspoon lemon juice for each artichoke. Sprinkle each artichoke with ¼ teaspoon salt, cover pan tightly, and cook 20 to 45 minutes (depending on size), or until stems can be easily pierced with a fork. Then turn artichokes upside down to drain well.

Artichokes are a favorite vegetable in and around Nice. This is a delicious Niçoise version.

ARTICHOKES NIÇOISE

Prepared green artichokes	2 *tbsp. lemon juice*
1 *3-oz. package cream cheese*	2 *tbsp. mayonnaise*
1 *2-oz. can flat filets anchovies*	1 *small onion, finely minced*

While artichokes are cooking combine one 3-ounce package cream cheese, softened, one 2-ounce can flat filets anchovies, drained and chopped, 2 tablespoons each lemon juice and mayonnaise, and 1 small minced onion. Mix well until smooth, and dip artichoke leaves in sauce before eating. As a salad, chill cooked artichokes before serving.

This is another Italian recipe from Lombardy in which the artichokes are stuffed with ham and rice.

STUFFED ARTICHOKES

4 *green artichokes*	1 *small tomato, diced*
1 *cup diced cooked ham*	2 *tbsp. melted butter*
1 *cup cooked rice*	¼ *cup grated Parmesan cheese*
2 *tbsp. dry sherry*	½ *tsp. seasoned salt*

After washing and trimming 4 artichokes place them upside down on a board or table, and press down firmly. Then place upright and remove tiny inner leaves and choke (the fuzzy portion) from artichoke heart with a sharp knife and metal spoon. Then cook according to foregoing directions.

While artichokes are cooking combine 1 cup diced cooked ham, 1 cup cooked rice, 2 tablespoons dry sherry, 1 small tomato, diced, 2 tablespoons melted butter, ¼ cup grated Parmesan cheese, and ½ teaspoon seasoned salt. When artichokes are tender and drained fill them with the rice-ham mixture. Arrange stuffed artichokes in a 2-quart casserole and bake in a 350-degree oven 15 to 20 minutes.

The following recipe has been adapted to American homes, and jars of artichoke hearts and canned mushrooms make the preparation very simple.

ARTICHOKE HEARTS AND MUSHROOMS

1 1-lb. jar artichoke hearts	Liquid from mushrooms
2 tbsp. butter	2 tbsp. dry sherry
1 tbsp. flour	Salt
1 3-oz. can chopped	Onion salt
mushrooms	Pepper

1 tbsp. minced parsley

In top of double boiler over direct heat melt 2 tablespoons butter and blend in 1 tablespoon flour. Add liquid drained from a 3-ounce can of chopped mushrooms. Cook, stirring constantly, until mixture is thickened and smooth. Remove from heat, add 2 tablespoons dry sherry, salt, onion salt, and pepper to taste, drained mushrooms, and 1 tablespoon minced parsley. Drain 1-pound jar artichoke hearts, rinse thoroughly, and cut lengthwise in halves. Add them to mushrooms, heat well over boiling water, serve to 4.

I don't believe that there is a more popular vegetable in Europe than asparagus. If you happen to be in Rome during the asparagus season, you will revel in the wild asparagus of the Roman countryside, called *asparagi di campo*. But never eat it with anything but melted butter, lest its exquisite flavor be masked. In northern Tuscany they grow really gigantic asparagus. It hasn't the flavor of French or English asparagus, but it's quite a dish when cooked with Parmesan cheese.

In Germany, in the spring, asparagus holds sway. Partaking of the "king of vegetables" has assumed a ceremonious importance—it is more than a meal. As soon as the first shoots have ripened a veritable pilgrimage starts to Schwetzingen, not far from Heidelberg, the largest asparagus producing center in West Germany, besides Brunswick. One should stroll through the asparagus market before finally sitting down to a delicious treat in one of the small hotels. Whole, with drawn butter, is the only way asparagus is served there.

In the Ticino Canton of Switzerland the small green field asparagus is never missing from tables when it is in season. It is usually steamed, and served with a fried egg. Especially good asparagus is grown on the fertile sandy bed of the Rhone valley in Canton Valais. One of their very special dishes is "Swiss Crest" asparagus, and it is not only delicious, but picturesque.

SWISS CREST ASPARAGUS

2 lbs. fresh asparagus	Rolled thin slices boiled ham
Salted boiling water	Slices ripe tomatoes
Mayonnaise	

Wash and snap off the tough stems of 2 pounds asparagus, and cook in salted boiling water until tender. Drain, and let cool. Divide the stalks of asparagus into 4 equal parts and place them on a large platter, forming a cross, leaving a space in the center of the cross. Fill the gaps between the arms of the cross with rolled, thin slices boiled ham (or rolled prosciutto ham). Surround with slices ripe tomatoes. Last, fill the space in the center of the cross with mayonnaise. Serve cold.

An unusual combination found in Switzerland is asparagus with new potatoes.

ASPARAGUS WITH NEW POTATOES

2 *lbs. asparagus*	*Cooking water of asparagus*
2 *lbs. new potatoes*	*Salt*
Boiling salted water	¼ *tsp. dried fines herbes*
1 *oz. butter*	1 *small onion, minced*
1 *oz. flour*	1 *cup cream*

Wash and prepare 2 pounds asparagus. Cut each stalk into 3 pieces, and cook in boiling salted water until tender. Boil 2 pounds new potatoes in salted water, and when tender peel at once and cut each potato into slices about ¼ inch thick.

Make a sauce with 1 ounce each of butter and flour, the cooking water of the asparagus, salt to taste, ¼ teaspoon dried *fines herbes,* and cream (about 1 cup each asparagus water and the cream), and 1 small onion, minced. This is really a Béchamel sauce. When sauce is finished, mix into it the asparagus and potatoes, allow all to heat well, and serve very hot. This is an excellent accompaniment to ham.

Another marvelous asparagus dish from Switzerland is asparagus in white wine, au gratin.

ASPARAGUS IN WHITE WINE, AU GRATIN

2 *lbs. asparagus*	2 *oz. dry white wine*
Boiling water	*Salt and pepper*
3 *oz. melted butter*	2 *oz. grated Gruyère cheese*

Wash and prepare about 2 pounds asparagus, and cook in boiling water until tender. Then drain and place stalks in a baking dish. Pour 3 ounces melted butter over asparagus and 2 ounces dry white wine. Salt and pepper lightly, and sprinkle generously with grated Gruyère cheese (about 2 ounces). Place in a 425-degree oven for about 10 minutes, or until cheese lightly browns. Remove and serve hot.

I got this recipe for a savory luncheon dish using asparagus rolled in ham from Provence.

ASPARAGUS HAM ROLLS

16–24 *stalks fresh asparagus*   ½ *cup dry white wine*
4–6 *slices boiled ham*   1 *cup chopped ripe olives*
Salt and pepper   2 *oz. butter*
Melted butter   ⅓ *cup flour*
1 *small onion, minced*   1 *tsp. salt*
1½ *cups rich milk*   ½ *cup grated Parmesan cheese*

Cook 16 to 24 fresh asparagus stalks until tender-crisp. Arrange stalks on 4 to 6 large pieces of boiled ham, using 4 stalks per slice. Sprinkle with salt and pepper, brush with melted butter, and roll slices over to enclose the stalks, fastening with a toothpick. Arrange the rolls in a shallow, oblong casserole or baking pan, and cover with a cheese and olive sauce. Bake in a 350-degree oven for 20 to 25 minutes.

To make the cheese-olive sauce put 1 small onion minced into 1½ cups rich milk and ½ cup dry white wine. Add 1 cup coarsely chopped pitted ripe olives. Melt 2 ounces butter, and blend in ⅓ cup sifted flour and 1 teaspoon of salt. When smooth, add the milk mixture slowly, and cook until thickened and smooth—about 10 minutes. Then stir in ½ cup grated Parmesan cheese. When cheese is melted, pour sauce over asparagus rolls and bake as directed. This serves 4 to 6.

At the Queen's Hotel in Chester we had an out-of-the-ordinary delectable. It was almost a Welsh rabbit poured over asparagus stalks, and made a delightful light luncheon dish.

ASPARAGUS RABBIT ROYAL

1 *lb. fresh asparagus*   ½ *tsp. Worcestershire sauce*
1 *tbsp. butter*   ¾ *cup beer*
2 *cups grated sharp Cheddar*   1 *well-beaten egg*
   cheese   4 *slices toast*
½ *tsp. dry mustard*   *Salt and pepper*
                    Paprika

Melt 1 tablespoon butter over a low heat, then add 2 cups grated sharp Cheddar cheese (about ½ pound) and cook until cheese is melted. Then add ½ teaspoon each of dry mustard and Worcestershire sauce, and ¾ cup beer. Blend all well. Next, add a small amount of the cheese mixture to 1 well-beaten egg and mix well. Then add this to the remaining cheese mixture and cook, stirring constantly, until thickened.

Cook 1 pound of white asparagus until tender, then drain. Arrange stalks on 4 slices of toast, cut in strips, sprinkle with salt and pepper, top with the cheese sauce, and dust with paprika. This serves 4.

During our tour of the Continent I don't remember ever having seen an avocado on menus. They are to be found in England, but they are very expensive. I remember browsing through the grocery department of Harrod's, London's finest department store, and seeing avocados. They were beautiful to look at, and were carefully displayed nested in shredded paper. But the price was amazing—about a dollar and a half each, as I recall!

However, we did have two delicious luncheon dishes in London featuring avocados. One was at the Savoy Hotel, and the other at the Dorchester Hotel, both of which are among London's top hotel restaurants.

AVOCADO STUFFED WITH CHICKEN AND MUSHROOMS

2 cups finely diced chicken meat	Salt
	Freshly ground pepper
½ cup diced mushrooms	3 large ripe avocados
1 oz. butter	1 lightly beaten egg yolk
1 oz. dry sherry	Grated Parmesan cheese
1½ cups rich cream sauce	Melted butter

Sauté 2 cups finely diced chicken meat and ½ cup diced mushrooms lightly in a skillet containing about an ounce of butter. Then add 1 ounce dry sherry wine, and cook until liquid is completely reduced. Then add 1 cup rich cream sauce to chicken-mushrooms, season to taste with salt and freshly ground pepper, and mix thoroughly.

Split 3 large ripe but firm avocados in half lengthwise, remove pits, and sprinkle with lemon juice (to prevent discoloration). Stuff center of avocados with chicken-mushroom mixture, and transfer to baking sheet.

Add 1 lightly beaten egg yolk to ½ cup rich cream sauce, and top stuffed avocados with this sauce. Sprinkle grated Parmesan cheese (about 2 tablespoons) over stuffed avocados, drizzle a little melted butter over each, and bake in preheated 450-degree oven to golden brown. Serve with half a spiced peach and fried Julienne potatoes.

In this delectable the avocado is stuffed with crabmeat.

AVOCADO STUFFED WITH CRABMEAT

3 *large avocados*	*Salt*
Lime juice	*Freshly ground pepper*
1 *cup flaked crabmeat*	*Cayenne pepper*
1 *cup rich cream sauce*	1 *tsp. minced onion*

1 *cup grated sharp Cheddar cheese*

Cut 3 large ripe but firm avocados in half lengthwise, remove pits, and sprinkle with fresh lime juice.

Combine 1 cup flaked crabmeat and 1 cup rich cream sauce. Season to taste with salt, freshly ground pepper, a pinch cayenne pepper, and 1 teaspoon minced onion. Fill the cavities of the avocado halves with the crab mixture, and top with finely grated sharp Cheddar cheese, using about 1 cup. Place stuffed avocado halves in a shallow baking dish with ½ inch water in the bottom. Bake in a 350-degree oven for 15 minutes, or until cheese melts and the avocados are heated through.

Although Belgium is a very small country it has a most distinctive cuisine. With fertile farm lands and an extensive coast line, its produce, poultry, meats, and fish are of exceptional excellence, and Belgian cooks make the most of their opportunities. Some of their dishes are famous throughout Europe, such as *La Waterzoie* and *La Carbonnade Flamande*. Recipes for both of these dishes are detailed in this book.

Two other delicacies which are native to Belgium, and also famous throughout the world are *Chicorees de Bruxelles* (endive) and *Choux de Bruxelles,* which we know as Brussels sprouts.

If you think that Brussels sprouts are miniature cabbages designed by nature for Lilliputians, you're very wrong! While they are of the cabbage family, they have a delicious and delicate flavor that is quite different from that of cabbages. Unlike cabbage, they are a delightful accompaniment to almost all meats, fish and poultry, and are easily adaptable to both plain and gourmet dishes.

From the Leige-Ardennes countryside of Belgium comes this recipe for Brussels Sprouts with Green Grapes.

BRUSSELS SPROUTS WITH GREEN GRAPES

1 *lb. Brussels sprouts*	1 *cup seedless grapes*
Lukewarm salted water	2 *tbsp. butter*
1½ *cups chicken bouillon*	⅛ *tsp. pepper*

Soak 1 pound fresh Brussels sprouts in lukewarm heavily salted water for 10 to 15 minutes. Then drain them and remove any loose or yellow leaves. Bring 1½ cups chicken bouillon to a boil in a large saucepan and add the sprouts. Cover and cook over a low heat for 15 to 20 minutes, or until sprouts are almost tender. Then stir in 1 cup seedless green grapes, 2 tablespoons butter, and ⅛ teaspoon pepper. Cook for 5 to 7 minutes longer, drain, and serve to 4. Incidently, the drained-off stock may be used to good advantages in soups or sauces.

At a rather pretentious but most interesting restaurant in Brussels we had Brussels Sprouts au Gratin, which was a very toothsome dish. It was an accompaniment for some delicious, done-to-a-turn roast lamb.

BRUSSELS SPROUTS AU GRATIN

1 *quart fresh Brussels sprouts*	¼ *cup butter*
Lukewarm salted water	¼ *cup flour*
2 *cups chicken bouillon*	½ *cup grated Swiss cheese*
⅛ *tsp. nutmeg*	2 *tbsp. dry white wine*
Freshly ground pepper	½ *cup fine breadcrumbs*
Milk	2 *tbsp. butter*

Prepare 1 quart fresh Brussels sprouts for cooking as in the preceding recipe. Combine 2 cups chicken bouillon, ⅛ teaspoon nutmeg, and freshly ground pepper to taste in a large saucepan and bring to boil. Add the Brussels sprouts, cover, and simmer for 10 to 15 minutes, or until sprouts are just tender. Drain liquid from sprouts and add enough milk to make 2 cups, and reserve mixture.

Melt ¼ cup butter in another large saucepan and blend in ¼ cup flour. Gradually add the reserved liquid and cook over low heat, stirring constantly, until thickened. Then add ½ cup grated Swiss cheese and continue cooking until cheese is melted. Then add 2 tablespoons dry white wine and the cooked sprouts. Mix very gently then turn the whole into a greased 1½ quart shallow baking dish. Sprinkle the top with ½ cup fine dry breadcrumbs, and dot the top with 2 tablespoons butter. Put into the broiler, 4 to 5 inches from the heat source, and broil for 2 to 3 minutes, or until golden brown. This serves 4.

Incidentally, puréed Brussels sprouts (cooked and forced through a sieve) mixed with mashed potatoes is an excellent accompaniment to roast beef. And a surprisingly good dish is cooked Brussels sprouts covered with a batter, fried in deep fat, and served with tomato sauce.

Eggplant has the same Italian and French name—*aubergine*. It has been cultivated in Italy since the fifteenth century, and I don't know for how long in France.

The Balkan countries, such as Turkey, Armenia, and Greece, do terrific things with eggplant. In my two preceding Jug of Wine books there are recipes for *Iman Bayeldi* (stuffed eggplant from

Turkey) and *Moussaka,* the great eggplant and veal dish from Greece. But neither in Italy nor in France does one find comparable culinary masterpieces utilizing eggplant.

However, I did come across a delicious eggplant dish in Naples, at a very lovely restaurant, Bersagliera, fronting on the Borgo Marinaro, the tiny port to the east of the Castel dell'Ovo, and directly across from our hotel, the Royal. If I recall correctly, its Italian name was *Melanzane alla Parmigiana.*

MELANZANE ALLA PARMIGIANA
(Eggplant Pie)

1 *No. 2 can tomatoes*	*Salt and pepper*
2 *tbsp. olive oil*	2 *lbs. eggplant*
2 *tbsp. tomato paste*	*Beaten eggs*
2 *tbsp. dry Marsala (or dry*	*Fine breadcrumbs*
sherry)	*Hot olive oil*
2 *small cloves garlic*	*Grated Parmesan cheese*
Pinch fennel seeds	*Mozzarella cheese*

In a saucepan combine contents of a No. 2 can tomatoes with 2 tablespoons each olive oil, tomato paste, and dry sherry, 2 small cloves garlic, finely minced, a pinch fennel seeds, and salt and pepper to taste. Let mixture simmer, uncovered, for about 30 minutes.

Wash, dry, and cut about 2 pounds eggplant into ⅜ inch slices. Dip slices in beaten eggs, cover with fine breadcrumbs, and fry in hot olive oil until soft and golden brown on both sides. Then drain on absorbent paper.

Put a film of olive oil in bottom of round baking dish. Place layer eggplant slices on bottom, cover with tomato sauce, and liberally sprinkle with grated Parmesan cheese. Repeat layers until eggplant slices and sauce are used up. Cover top layer with thin slices mozzarella cheese, and bake in 350-degree oven until cheese is lightly browned (about 15 minutes). Cut in wedges and serve to 4 while hot.

I am exceedingly fond of Belgian endive, but I like it best as a salad. Even though it is usually expensive in America (sometimes as high as $1.85 a pound), we have an endive salad at least twice a week when it is in the market. I usually buy 2 heads, split each in half, and lay the halves on a bed of watercress. Over it I pour a little true French dressing, and I know of no salad that is tastier to go with meats, chicken or fish.

In London, however, we had endive cooked as a vegetable, and served with a delicious steak at Vine. This is a charming restaurant on Piccadilly Place, by the side of the Piccadilly Hotel. It is run by the Bentley Brothers (those oyster farmers I have mentioned previously), and the Scotch beef and English lamb are superb. Steaks are beautifully grilled right before your eyes, and the prices are most moderate. This is the way they did the endive.

ENDIVE WITH WALNUTS

1 *large or 2 small heads endive*	*Salt and pepper*
per person	¼ *cup beef bouillon*
2 *oz. butter*	1 *tsp. (or more) walnuts*
¼ *tsp. dried basil*	*Hot melted butter*

Allow 1 large head of endive cut lengthwise in half, or 2 small heads, for each serving. Crisp the endive in ice water before using, then dry gently in a paper towel.

In a large shallow heavy pan, over a medium flame, melt 2 ounces butter, and add ¼ teaspoon dried sweet basil. Arrange the endive heads carefully in the pan, season lightly with pepper, and brown lightly 2 minutes on each side. Then add ¼ cup condensed beef bouillon, and allow the endive to simmer gently, uncovered. Watch carefully to prevent scorching. As the bouillon evaporates, gradually add a little more. Repeat this process for 20 to 25 minutes, or until the endive is tender, but not overcooked, and most of the liquid has been absorbed. If more sauce is desired, however, add additional beef bouillon and simmer 2 minutes more before serving.

Serve the endive piping hot on preheated plates. Garnish each serving with 1 teaspoon (or more) of walnut meats browned in hot melted butter.

One of the most intriguing light luncheon dishes we had in France was at the Palace Hotel in Nice, where we lived for a month while Mrs. Wood recuperated from an attack by a *voleur* (a purse-snatching thief) we encountered on the Quai des États Unis two nights after our arrival in Nice. For three weeks we had to have all our meals served in our rooms, and the food, and the service, were incomparable. One day Mrs. Wood had a yen for mushrooms, and the chef came up with this delectable.

BAKED MUSHROOMS WITH ROQUEFORT CHEESE

2 *lbs. large fresh mushrooms*   ¼ *tsp. minced chives*
½ *cup Roquefort cheese*   2 *tbsp. butter*
1 *cup fine breadcrumbs*   ¼ *cup sherry*
                       ½ *cup heavy cream*

Wash 2 pounds large fresh mushrooms and remove stems. Place a small piece Roquefort cheese in each cavity. Cook 1 cup fine dry breadcrumbs and ¼ teaspoon minced chives in 2 tablespoons butter just long enough to coat crumbs nicely. Then toss crumbs with remaining crumbled Roquefort cheese (½ cup less pieces used in cavities). Place layer of crumbs in a buttered casserole, then lay mushrooms, cavity side up, on crumbs. Drizzle ¼ cup dry sherry over all, and sprinkle with remaining cheesed crumbs. Pour ½ cup heavy cream carefully on mixture, cover casserole, and bake at 375 degrees for 25 minutes. Serves 6.

10 ⚬ POTATOES, PASTAS, AND RICE

Potatoes is potatoes, if I may paraphrase the title of Ellis Parker Butler's well-known book, *Pigs is Pigs*. You will encounter them all over Europe, boiled, fried, baked and mashed. They can be exceedingly good, and they can be pretty dreadful, depending upon the product, the cook, and the country.

The great potato country in Europe is Ireland, and you will always find potatoes on the menus. As a matter of fact the majority of the Irish believe that a day without potatoes is a day without nourishment.

In Ennis, Ireland, about 16 miles from Shannon Free Airport, we stopped at the Old Ground Hotel. It is a beautiful old inn, surrounded by gorgeous flower gardens, and the sort of place you would dream about staying in in Ireland. There was a timbered cocktail lounge presided over by a lovely young girl named Josie (who taught me some Gaelic toasts in return for my teaching her how to make an American dry martini), and a charming dining room serving superlative food. One night, at my request, the chef made the renowned Irish potato dish, Colcannon. This is a potato dish never to be forgotten.

The recipe is in my second book, *More Recipes With a Jug of Wine*, but no cookbook on the British Isles and Europe would be complete without the recipe for Colcannon.

COLCANNON

Tender green cabbage leaves	1¾ *lbs. new potatoes*
Water	1 *quart water*
15 *little green onions*	½ *tsp. salt*
1½ *cups milk*	¼ *tsp. dried basil*
½ *tsp. salt*	*Salt and pepper*
3 *tbsp. butter*	*Melted butter*

207

Boil tender green cabbage leaves (enough to make about 2 cups when chopped) in water for about 5 minutes. Then drain and chop finely. Also chop about 15 good-sized spring, or little green, onions (utilizing the bulbs and tops) and put them to soak in the milk to which the salt has been added. Then put them on to boil in the milk, adding the butter, and simmer slowly until tender.

Peel and slice about 1¾ pounds of new, or red, potatoes, put them in a pan, cover with 1 quart of water to which ½ teaspoon of salt and ¼ teaspoon of dried basil has been added, and boil until the potatoes are tender. When they are, drain them and begin mashing. Gradually add the chopped onion and milk, and the chopped cabbage leaves, pounding them into the potatoes. Keep mashing and stirring until the potatoes become fluffy, and the onion and cabbage leaves are entirely absorbed. In Ireland they use a wooden masher, or pestle, and call this "beetling." Pepper and salt to taste. To keep the potatoes in the pan hot while mashing, put the pan in a larger pan with scalding water.

Serve Colcannon hot on individual plates. Make a depression in the center of each portion and fill the cavity with melted butter. Eat with a spoon, from the outside in, dipping a spoonful of Colcannon into the melted butter.

France has a great many notable potato dishes. It was a Frenchman, Parmentier, who first grew the potato as a food in France, and today his name is immortalized in connection with potato dishes.

The different provinces in France have their own potato specialties. Lyonnaise potatoes are world famous, being cooked with onions or shallots. Parisienne potatoes are tiny little new potatoes about the size of a walnut, and are sautéed in butter and sprinkled with parsley. In the province of Dauphiné they cook thinly sliced potatoes with milk, egg, and grated cheese, baked in the oven.

In the province of Auvergne, in central France, they have a mashed potato dish that is terrific, made with cheese.

POMME DE TERRE AUVERGNE
(Mashed Potatoes with Cheese)

Boiled potatoes	*White pepper*
Butter	*Hot thin cream*
Pinch dried rosemary	*Grated Gruyère cheese*
Salt	*Melted butter*

Boil the potatoes in their skins. When done, peel them and put them through a ricer into a clean, warm saucepan. Add melted butter, to which a pinch of dried rosemary has been added, and salt and white pepper to taste. Then add, little by little, the hot, thin cream, until the mashed potatoes are about the consistency of thick cream. Then beat in enough grated Gruyère cheese to bring the mashed potatoes to the normal consistency. Put the mashed potatoes into a greased baking dish, sprinkle more grated Gruyère cheese on top, and cover with melted butter. Put the baking dish in a moderate oven, and when lightly browned, remove, and serve.

The famous Swiss potato dish is Rosti Potatoes. They are really fried potatoes, but what fried potatoes! We had them on a number of occasions in Zürich (the first time at the Veltliner Keller to accompany *G'schnetzlets*), and I made them frequently in our apartment at the Residence Im Park, in Zürich.

ROSTI POTATOES

4 *cups cold boiled potatoes*	1 *tbsp. bacon drippings*
3 *tbsp. butter*	*Salt and pepper*
4 *tbsp. chopped chives*	

In a heavy skillet melt 3 tablespoons butter and 1 tablespoon bacon drippings. When hot add 4 cups cold boiled potatoes peeled and coarsely grated, salt and pepper to taste, and 4 tablespoons chopped chives. Cook over hot flame, mixing with a fork, until they are lightly browned. Then lower flame, press potatoes into a smooth cake, neatly trimmed, and continue cooking until a crisp brown crust forms on bottom. Put plate over potatoes, reverse skillet, and serve potatoes browned side up.

Another delicious Swiss potato dish is sort of a potato pie, and is somewhat similar to the French *Pommes de Terre Dauphinoise*. It is one of the most savory potato dishes I have ever tasted.

POTATO CHEESE PIE

¼ *lb. butter*	2 *large eggs*
5 *medium potatoes*	1 *tsp. chopped chives*
Salt and pepper	6 *slices liverwurst sausage*
	¼ *lb. Gruyère cheese*

Melt ¼ pound butter in a frying pan and add 5 medium potatoes, peeled and sliced 1/16 inch thick. Season to taste with salt and pepper. Fry on top of range or place in a 375-degree oven until potatoes are tender. To 2 large or 3 small beaten eggs add 1 teaspoon chopped chives, and pour evenly over potatoes.

Arrange 6 slices liver sausage over potatoes, and cover these with ¼ pound Gruyère cheese, sliced thin. Place in a hot oven or under broiler until cheese melts to a golden brown. Cut in pie-shaped wedges, and serve hot to 6.

I don't care what anyone else thinks or says—to me, pastas are the greatest glory of Italy.

There are two distinctions to be made regarding Italian pastas. There are the homemade pastas (or pastas freshly made in restaurants) and the mass-produced pastas which are dried in the factory and are sold by the pound (in America, they are usually sold by the package).

There are some pastas that the American cook just can't make, such as tortellini, tagliatelle, lasagne, agnolotti, and so on. Another pasta, of which I am inordinately fond, is cannelloni, and this too is almost impossible, from the point of view of work, equipment and time.

If you want to know how to make various pastas, buy the book by Elizabeth David, *Italian Food*. Her directions are very clear and concise, and the book will tell you just what kitchen equipment you will have to have, and how to use it.

Fortunately, there are a great many Italian pastas, factory produced, that are excellent. So don't forgo Italian pastas just because you can't make or can't get the homemade varieties.

Some years ago Mrs. Wood and I had dinner in San Francisco with a dear friend, Elena Cavagnaro Dardi. She is an accomplished hostess, and a superb cook. She spends a great deal of time in Italy, and knows Italian cooking in all its aspects.

At her dinner party (she prepared the entire menu herself) she served cannelloni, and she gave me her recipe, not only for the cannelloni, but for the filling and the sauce. I present it here, for it may be a help to anyone who wants to make and serve some of the cannelloni dishes that will follow.

CANNELLONI ELENA DARDI

CANNELLONI (PASTA)

3 *cups flour*	*Few grains salt*
3 *eggs*	3 *tbsp. tepid water*
	Boiling salted water

FILLING

1 *cup spinach*	1 *clove garlic*
2 *sets calf's brains*	*Pinch nutmeg*
½ *lb. sausage meat*	2 *tbsp. olive oil*
1 *tbsp. chopped parsley*	½ *cup cracker crumbs*
1 *tsp. dried oregano*	½ *cup grated Parmesan cheese*
½ *tbsp. chopped onion*	3 *lightly beaten eggs*

SAUCE

4 *tbsp. butter*	*Salt and pepper*
½ *onion, minced*	*Small pinch dried oregano*
½ *cup flour*	*Small pinch grated nutmeg*
2 *cups rich chicken broth*	2 *egg yolks*
2 *cups hot milk*	*Grated Parmesan cheese*
	Butter

For the pasta make a paste of 3 cups flour, 3 eggs, a few grains salt and 3 tablespoons tepid water. Form into a ball and cover with a warm bowl for 15 minutes. Knead about 30 times and cover with warm bowl. Repeat this 3 times. Then roll dough out thin and cut into 3 by 3 inch squares. Put the squares, a few at a time, into boiling, salted water for 5 minutes, then remove and drain on damp towels.

For the filling cook enough spinach (or chard), to make 1 cup, squeezed very dry. Put through a food chopper twice. Parboil 2 sets calves brains for 5 minutes, cool and clean, and put through food chopper twice. Combine spinach, brains, and ½ pound good sausage meat, add 1 tablespoon chopped parsely, 1 teaspoon dried oregano, ½ tablespoon chopped onion, 1 clove garlic, minced, and a pinch of grated nutmeg. Mix all together well, then add 2 tablespoons olive oil, ½ cup each cracker crumbs and grated Parmesan cheese, 3 lightly beaten eggs, and salt and pepper to taste. Again mix well.

For the sauce, to 4 tablespoons butter heated in a heavy pot add ½ minced or grated onion and cook until transparent (not brown). Gradually add ½ cup flour and blend. Add 2 cups each rich hot chicken broth and hot milk and stir until mixture thickens. Season with salt and pepper to taste, a small pinch each dried oregano and nutmeg. Finally, carefully stir in 2 egg yolks.

Butter flat baking dish. Spread on each cannelloni square some stuffing, roll up, and place rolls side by side in the dish. Cover with the sauce, and then a good layer of grated Parmesan cheese, and dot top with butter. Place in a 350-degree oven and heat until sauce bubbles at edges, 30 to 45 minutes. Serve from the dish in which it was cooked.

As long as I live I will never forget a luncheon we had at Ravello, on our way, via the Amalfi Drive, from Sorrento to Salerno, in the Hotel Caruso Belvedere.

We had left the lovely and peaceful Hotel Europa Palace at Sorrento in the morning, eagerly anticipating the scenery of the Amalfi Drive. Without question, this road is the most amazing and beautiful in the world, and in spite of its serpentine twistings, it is a good road, and easy to drive if you keep your speed low. In most places the road is carved out of granite cliffs, but it also passes through sleepy fishing villages, such as Positano, which has houses built up from the sea to a considerable height on the mountainside, looking as though they were pasted on it.

We got into Amalfi about 2:30, and decided to make a detour to Ravello, a village on a promontory a thousand feet above the sea, back of Amalfi. And what a reward awaited us!

We drove up to the Caruso Belvedere, parked our car, and once we were inside we were greeted by Signor Caruso. He led us out to the dining terrace, and for several minutes we were speechless, drinking in the unbelievably beautiful and breathtaking view.

Far below us, and stretching out for miles was the Mediterranean coast line, with the villages of Maiori and Minori close by, glistening in the brilliant sunshine. Then a table was laid for us, in a little while we were served superb cannelloni, accompanied by a bottle of Grand Caruso Rosé (which is a product of the Caruso vineyards). For dessert we had the world-famous Caruso's Chocolate Soufflé, the like of which we have never experienced. It was truly divine. Before we left Signor Caruso gave us the recipes for both the cannelloni and the soufflé. The latter has become so renowned and sought after that it has been printed in English on cards.

For the cannelloni you can either follow Elena Dardi's recipe, or you can make little thin unsweetened pancakes, which do very well as a substitute for the cannelloni.

CANNELLONI CARUSO

24 *little thin pancakes*   *or*   18 *cannelloni*

MEAT SAUCE

3 *oz. bacon*	3 *tsp. concentrated tomato*
½ *oz. butter*	*purée*
1 *carrot*	3 *oz. dry white wine*
1 *onion*	*Salt and pepper*
1 *small stalk celery*	1 *cup condensed beef bouillon*
¾ *lb. ground lean beef*	*Pinch grated nutmeg*

¼–½ *cup cream*

FILLING

2 *cups rich cream sauce*	¼ *cup finely diced ham*
2 *tbsp. grated Parmesan cheese*	¼ *cup finely diced mozzarella*
2 *egg yolks*	*cheese*
¾ *cup above meat sauce*	*Juice from above meat sauce*
½ *lb. ricotta cheese*	*Butter*
¼ *cup finely diced salami*	*Grated Parmesan cheese*

Cut 3 ounces bacon into very small pieces and brown them in a skillet slowly in ½ ounce butter. Then add 1 carrot, 1 onion, and 1 small stalk celery, all finely chopped. When they have browned put in the skillet ¾ pound ground beef, lean, and keep mixing until it has all browned evenly. Then add 3 teaspoons concentrated tomato purée and 3 ounces of dry white wine. Season with salt and pepper to taste and a pinch grated nutmeg and 1 cup condensed beef bouillon. Cover the skillet and simmer very gently for 45 minutes to 1 hour. At the last add about ¼ to ½ cup cream (the sauce should be thick) and let heat through.

To 2 cups rich cream sauce add 2 tablespoons grated Parmesan cheese, 2 egg yolks, ¾ cup of the meat sauce, ½ pound ricotta cheese (or cream cheese), ¼ cup each finely diced salami, finely diced ham, and finely diced mozzarella cheese. Mix all this well together and place on the pancake rectangles. Roll them up and place them side by side in a buttered baking dish containing a thin layer of the juice from the meat sauce. Dot them with butter, spread a few spoonfuls of the meat sauce over them, and sprinkle very generously with grated Parmesan cheese. Put in a 400-degree oven for about 10 minutes, and serve immediately, to 6.

Not the least of Rome's fabulous attractions are its many and varied restaurants. They range from the ultra-ultra-luxurious and fashionable to the small side street trattorias (where the food is often better and more authentically Italian).

Rome's two smartest restaurants are the Palazzi (on the outskirts of the city) and the Hostaria Dell'Orso, near the Umberto Bridge. The first occupies the magnificent modernistic villa Mussolini built for his mistress, Clara Petacci, and commands a breath-taking view of the city of Rome. You need to be smartly dressed to get into this palatial restaurant, and a fistful of those huge ten thousand lire notes to get out!

Equally smart is the Hostaria Dell'Orso, also known as the House of the Bear, which occupies a 15th century building in which Dante is said to have once lived. It is very luxurious, and, like the Palazzi, the food is tops, albeit the cuisine in both restaurants is "Continental" rather than strictly Italian.

The most delightful and fascinating restaurant we found in Rome was La Biblioteca on the Largo Teatro Valle. It is a huge place located in a basement, but you are not aware of its size because it is divided up into about nine vaulted rooms. From floor to ceiling the walls of each room are lined with bookcases ("Biblioteca," you see, means "library"). But behind the grilled bookcase doors are not books, but upright wine bottles!

It is a gay place, where the patrons sing after dinner, and dance later to excellent small orchestras. The food is superlatively good, and the wines lovely (they don't come, by the way, from the upright bottles in the "library").

From a seafood trolley we selected *datteri di mare* to start with. These look exactly like large dates, but when they are opened a small, oblong-shaped oyster nestles inside the shell. A sauce is sprinkled over the oysters and they are slipped under the broiler for a few moments, then served. They were a delicious new experience.

Our second course was one of the restaurant's specialties, *Cannelloni Deliziosi alla Valle* (In Italy, after you have had cannelloni three or four times, you vow you will try other pastas, but you aways fall for the cannelloni, because they are always superb).

CANNELLONI DELIZIOSI ALLA VALLE

½ lb. spinach
½ lb. ricotta cheese
Salt and pepper
¼ cup grated Parmesan cheese
1 tbsp. finely chopped chives

Generous pinch grated nutmeg
2 beaten eggs
Cannelloni rectangles (or little thin pancakes)
Chicken bouillon
Béchamel sauce
Grated Parmesan cheese

For the filling cook ½ pound spinach, drain it, and press it until it is as dry as possible. Then put it through a food grinder (or chop it very fine). Next mix it with ½ pound ricotta cheese (or cream cheese), salt and pepper to taste, ¼ cup grated Parmesan cheese, 1 tablespoon finely chopped chives, a generous pinch grated nutmeg, and 2 beaten eggs. Mix all lightly but thoroughly.

Have ready your cannelloni rectangles which have been cooked in boiling water and drained, or small, thin, unsweetened French pancakes about the same size. Fill them lightly with the spinach-cheese mixture, roll them up, and place them side by side in a greased shallow baking dish, into which a film of chicken bouillon has been poured. Cover the cannelloni with a Béchamel sauce, and sprinkle the whole liberally with grated Parmesan cheese. Put in a 350-degree oven until they are well heated through, about 10 to 15 minutes.

Fettuccine (egg noodles cut in long, narrow strips) is a specialty of Roman restaurants. It reaches the height of deliciousness in Alfredo's famous restaurant. Tagliatelle are egg noodles, also cut in long, narrow strips, boiled, and served with various sauces. Tortellini is the glory of Bolognese gastronomy, inspired, according to legend, by a cook's vision of the navel of Venus. It is a pasta, round in shape with an indentation in the center, and served in broth, or dry with various sauces. Incidentally, tortellini are made with ground meat, and tortelloni are made with ricotta cheese and minced parsley.

As I mentioned previously, one restaurant in Rome that must not be missed is Alfredo all' Augusteo. Alfredo's great specialty, *Maestrissime fettuccine all'Afredo,* is something you will dream about for days afterward. Yet it can be prepared in any home by even a novice cook. Here is how.

FETTUCCINE ALL'ALFREDO

Fettuccine	*Hot Melted Butter*
Boiling salted water	*Finely grated Parmesan cheese*

Cook your fettuccine in boiling salted water until it is *al dente* (firm to the bite). Put it on a very hot platter as you take it out of the kettle. Pour over it hot melted butter in a very generous quantity, and a generous quantity of very finely grated Parmesan cheese. With great rapidity whisk the fettuccine about with a fork and spoon until everything is blended, and serve immediately on heated plates. The secret of this dish is serving it piping hot, in spite of the mixing of the fettuccine, butter, and cheese.

I think Mrs. Wood and I, while staying in Naples, really "discovered" two of the most delightful and charming seaside restaurants we have ever encountered.

One morning we departed from Naples on a very modern and streamlined little steamer, and two hours later we landed at the Emerald Isle, as the Island of Ischia is called, for it is clothed in vines, exotic vegetation, olive trees, and pine woods cover its mountains. Incidentally, as we came into the harbor, we passed close to the barge of Cleopatra that was used in the motion picture.

At dock side we hired an open car and started our tour of the island. We passed through white villages of Moorish appearances, and here and there an ultra-modern luxury hotel on the seashore. Finally we arrived at the terraced Ristorante San Montano, at the water's edge on a sandy beach, near the village of Lacco Ameno. It was on a sheltered little cove; very modern and elegant. We were the only tourists; the rest of the patrons were from motor cruisers moored in the cove. Our luncheon was simple, but oh, so delicious! *Spaghetti alle Vongole* and *Calamaretti e Scampi alla Strecche.* This was accompanied by a lively chilled Ischia white wine.

A few days later we took a steamer from Sorrento to Capri, aptly named the Island of Dreams. Its coast line is honeycombed with fairy grottos, the most famous of which is the Blue Grotto. Its blissful scenes under sub-tropical vegetation form heavenly pictures framed between a sky that is always clear, and a deep, blue, crystal-clear sea. The piazza of the city of Capri is a fascinating place, always crowded, and ringed with all sorts of shops displaying all sorts of wares. Later, traveling a long, winding road up the mountain we came to Anacapri. This is where Axel Munthe built his famous Villa San Michele. We spent two hours there, entranced by the furnishings, the works of art, the gardens, and the panoramic views.

For luncheon, our driver took us to the Ristorante Onda d'Oro, a lovely little terraced restaurant overlooking the beach of the Marina Piccola. Again we were the only tourists. And our meal? It was identical with that we had on Ischia! That's how marvelous *Spaghetti alle Vongole* is.

Vongole are very small clams found off Italian shores, but not in America. However, any American clams can be used. If they are large, chop them coarsely; if small, leave them whole.

SPAGHETTI ALLE VONGOLE
(Spaghetti with Clam Sauce)

24 *clams in shells*	1½ *lbs. chopped ripe tomatoes*
3 *tbsp. olive oil*	(*or a 1-lb. can Italian to-*
1 *onion, minced*	*matoes*)
3 *cloves garlic*	*Clam juice*
1 *lb. spaghetti*	1 *tbsp. chopped parsley*

Wash and scrub about 2 dozen clams in their shells, and put them in a heavy pan over a brisk fire. They are to cook in their own liquid only. Cover pan to start with, then take lid off when they start to open. Remove clams from shells, and strain broth.

Heat 3 tablespoons olive oil in a heavy skillet, and when hot add 1 onion, minced, and 3 cloves (or more) garlic, minced. When onions are limp add 1½ pounds skinned and chopped ripe tomatoes (or a 1-pound can Italian tomatoes) and the clam juice. Simmer all this until it has reduced somewhat and attained a good consistency. Then add the clams, and a generous tablespoon chopped parsley. As soon as clams are hot, pour this sauce over 1-pound spaghetti, cooked *al dente,* and serve. Never use grated Parmesan cheese on this.

One night at the Continental Hotel in Milan we had a spaghetti dish that we had never experienced before. It was mixed at our table, and was called *Spaghetti alla Carbonara*. It is a simple dish to prepare, but its flavor was exquisite.

SPAGHETTI ALLA CARBONARA
(Spaghetti with Ham and Cream)

5–6 *oz. spaghetti*	½ *cup ham in julienne strips*
Boiling salted water	6 *tbsp. grated Parmesan cheese*
1 *tbsp. butter*	1 *well-beaten egg*
	½ *cup hot cream*

Cook 5 to 6 ounces spaghetti in boiling salted water until *al dente*. In the meanwhile put 1 tablespoon butter in a skillet and in it cook ½ cup ham cut in short julienne strips on a low fire until ham is very hot. Combine drained spaghetti and ham, and bring to table very hot.

At the table have mixed together well about 6 tablespoons grated Parmesan cheese, a well-beaten egg, and ½ cup hot cream. Put spaghetti and ham in chafing dish over low heat, and pour over this cream-cheese-egg mixture. Mix everything well and serve at once to 2.

On our way from Rome to Naples we spent the night in the little seaside town of Terracina, at the Grand Hotel Palace. It was a charming, modern hotel, overlooking the sea, and close by the ancient but impressive ruins of the famous Temple of Jupiter Auxur, 750 feet about the level of the city.

For dinner we had what they told me was a special Neopolitan dish of spaghetti, and it was indeed very special, containing fresh shrimp. This is the recipe the manager obtained for me from the chef.

SPAGHETTI WITH SHRIMP

¼ *cup olive oil*	8 *oz. spaghetti*
½ *cup chopped onions*	3 *quarts salted boiling water*
6 *oz. tomato paste*	1 *lb. fresh shrimp*
¾ *cup rosé wine*	1 *tsp. salt*
1 *tsp. salt*	½ *lb. mozzarella cheese*

In a saucepan put ¼ cup olive oil over low flame. When hot add ½ cup chopped onions and cook until tender but not brown. Then add 6-ounce can tomato paste, ¾ cup rosé wine, and 1 teaspoon salt. Mix thoroughly, cover, and cook over low heat for at least 20 minutes, stirring occasionally.

Meanwhile cook 8 ounces spaghetti in 3 quarts boiling salted water until tender, about 12 to 14 minutes. Then drain in a colander.

Wash 1 pound fresh shrimp. Place shrimp, with any water clinging to them, in a saucepan and sprinkle with 1 teaspoon salt. Cover and cook over low flame until shrimps are pink, about 5 minutes, stirring occasionally. Drain, remove shells, and black vein.

In a 2-quart casserole arrange a layer of cooked spaghetti. Then cover with a layer of shrimp, then a layer of sauce. Cover with thin slices of mozzarella cheese. Repeat layers until all ingredients are used, finishing with cheese (you'll need about ½ pound mozzarella altogether). Bake in moderate oven 20 minutes, and serve, piping hot, to from 4 to 6.

Contrary to general opinion pastas in one form or another are not served daily throughout Italy. The tourist can get pastas almost everywhere in the country, but in the Northern provinces, such as Lombardy, Piedmont, and Veneto, rice takes the place of pastas among the Italians.

The risotto is the favorite form of rice dish in Northern Italy, and probably the most famous risotto is Risotto alla Milanese. The American who is accustomed to dry, white, flaky rice as cooked and served by the Chinese is in for a surprise when he or she is first served a risotto, for the rice in this dish is served in a perfect state of creaminess, yet it is slightly *al dente* at the core. But on the other hand a risotto is never mushy.

A risotto may be served as a first course, or a main course; it should never be served to accompany meat or chicken or seafood. If meat, poultry, seafood or game are to be served, these are integrated into the risotto.

The first night that we arrived in Milan we were dinner guests of Italian friends at one of Milan's outstanding restaurants, Savini's. This restaurant is located in the amazing Galleria Vittorio Emanuele II, one entrance of which opens off the Piazza del Duomo. The longer arm of the arcade is 643 feet long, while the shorter is 345 feet long, and their width is 47 feet. The central octagon has a diameter of 140 feet, and the dome reaches a height of 160 feet. The whole Galleria is under glass, and contains numerous shops and cafés which are among the best in the city. It is one of the most frequented places in Milan in the late afternoon and evening.

Naturally, we had Milan's most famous dish, Risotto alla Milanese. This is the recipe that was given me.

RISOTTO ALLA MILANESE

3 *oz. butter*	3 *oz. dry white wine*
1 *finely minced onion*	4 *cups chicken bouillon*
1 *oz. beef marrow (optional)*	¼ *tsp. powdered saffron*
1½ *cups long grain rice*	⅓ *cup grated Parmesan cheese*

Into a large heavy skillet put 2 ounces butter, and when it is hot, but not brown, sauté a very finely minced onion in it for about 10 minutes (an ounce beef marrow added at this time gives a rich quality to the risotto). Then add 1½ cups well-washed long grain rice. Stir constantly with a wooden fork until rice is thoroughly impregnated with butter, but don't let rice brown. Next add about 3 ounces dry white wine (or dry Marsala wine). Let rice cook over a moderate flame until the wine has almost been absorbed. Then begin adding simmering chicken bouillon, about a cupful at a time. As the bouillon is absorbed add another cup (you will need about 4 cups bouillon total). Cook for 20 to 30 minutes, and during the latter part of cooking stir rice continuously with a wooden fork so that it will not stick to bottom of utensil.

Dissolve ¼ teaspoon powdered saffron in ¼ cup hot chicken bouillon, and add this to the rice. Next stir in an ounce butter and about ⅓ cup grated Parmesan cheese. Serve risotto as soon as cheese melts. This serves 4.

At the Villa d'Este we had a *Risotto alla Certosina*, a risotto with shrimp, peas, and mushrooms. It was magnificent.

RISOTTO ALLA CERTOSINA
(Risotto with Shrimps, Peas and Mushrooms)

1½ *oz. butter*	1 *tbsp. olive oil*
½ *finely minced onion*	*Bit of garlic*
¾ *cup long grain rice*	1 *oz. brandy*
1½ *oz. dry white wine*	½ *cup cooked peas*
2 *cups water*	1 *large tomato*
12 *cooked, shelled shrimp*	½ *oz. butter*
1 *tbsp. butter*	¼ *cup grated Parmesan cheese*

Make a white risotto (the same as Milanese, but without the beef marrow or saffron, and using water instead of stock) in the quantity of one half the foregoing recipe.

In the meantime heat 12 cooked and shelled shrimp (if shrimps are large, cut them into medium sized pieces) in 1 tablespoon each butter and olive oil, to which a bit of garlic has been added. When shrimps are brown flambé them with about 1 ounce brandy. Then add ½ cup cooked peas and a large tomato well cut up. Let all cook for a few minutes together. Then add to the risotto, and stir in the final butter (½ ounce) and ¼ cup grated Parmesan cheese. This serves 2.

The Dodici Apostoli, where we had the wonderful chicken baked in parchment which I detailed in a preceding chapter, is a restaurant you should not miss if you are in Verona. It is very old, but the walls have gay frescos, and although it is tucked away in a little alley that takes a bit of doing to find, you will eventually find it, as we did, by asking a number of different people.

Our first course was a *Risotto con Funghi,* and there wasn't a morsel left on our plates.

RISOTTO CON FUNGHI
(Risotto with Mushrooms)

1½ cups rice	2 tbsp. olive oil
1 tbsp. minced onion	⅓ lb. sliced mushrooms
1 oz. butter	Salt
5 cups chicken bouillon	1 tbsp. minced parsley
1 large clove garlic	Curls of butter

Brown 1½ cups rice with 1 tablespoon minced onion in 1 ounce butter. Then add 5 cups boiling chicken bouillon little by little, and let rice cook about 18 minutes.

In the meantime cut 1 large clove garlic in slivers, and brown in 2 tablespoons olive oil. Then put in ⅓ pound sliced mushrooms and salt to taste, and cook over a lively fire for 10 minutes.

When rice has cooked to a creamy consistency, yet is al dente, add the mushrooms and garlic and juices, and 1 tablespoon minced parsley. Serve in the dish topped by some curls of butter.

We had another delicious risotto at the Brufani Palace Hotel in Perugia. It was called Risotto alla Montefalchese, and Signor Nando Curti, who has given me the recipe for the delectable Chicken Arrabbiato, also gave me the recipe for his risotto.

RISOTTO ALLA MONTEFALCHESE
(Risotto with Ham, Mushrooms and Chicken Livers)

6 oz. butter	4 oz. diced raw chicken livers
2 minced onions	1 sweetbread
2¼ cups raw rice	2 bay leaves
7½ oz. dry Marsala wine	Generous pinch sage
8 cups hot chicken bouillon	8 oz. peas
2 oz. minced raw ham	Salt and pepper
½ cup sliced mushrooms	1 cup beef gravy

Melt 2 ounces butter in a deep, heavy, skillet and add a minced onion. When it begins to brown add 2¼ cups raw rice, and let it cook until it begins to take on a golden color. Then add 3 ounces

Marsala wine. When the wine has been absorbed by the rice, add 8 cups hot chicken broth. (Pour in 2 cups at a time, allowing the rice to absorb each addition.) When the rice is done it should be slightly dry, but not too soft.

In the meantime make the sauce. In a saucepan put 4 ounces butter, and when melted and hot add a minced onion, and 2 ounces raw ham, minced (prosciutto if obtainable). When well browned add ½ cup thinly sliced mushrooms, 4 ounces diced raw chicken livers, 1 sweetbread that has been parboiled, skinned and diced, 3 ounces Marsala wine, 2 bay leaves, crumbled, a generous pinch dried sage, and lastly 8 ounces peas, which have been partially cooked. Mix everything well, and let it cook slowly over a gentle heat until meat and vegetables are well integrated and reduced. Add salt and pepper to taste, 1½ ounces Marsala wine, and about 1 cup beef gravy. Simmer for about 10 minutes.

Stir half of the above sauce into the risotto, and mix gently. Serve remaining half of sauce separately in a jug.

Not far from the Lake of Constance is the Swiss town of St. Gall, capital of Canton St. Gallen, and center of the Swiss textile and embroidery industry. Like all Swiss towns there is a profusion of flowers everywhere—along the streets, on barns, houses, factories, and office buildings.

In St. Gall there is a little hotel called the Im Portner, which is one of the famous eating places in Switzerland. Its chef de cuisine is Walter Fehlman, and one of his specialties is Risotto Casmir. This is his recipe to serve 4.

RISOTTO CASMIR
(Risotto with Curry Sauce)

4½ oz. butter	Salt and pepper
1½ cups raw white rice	Curry powder
3 cups boiling consommé	½ cup onion, chopped
Grated Parmesan cheese	2 oz. chopped fresh mushrooms
10 oz. chopped lean veal	1 slice pineapple
½ sweet red pepper	

CURRY SAUCE

1 lb. veal bones   1½ oz. curry powder
1 apple   Water
            ½ cup cream

Melt 1½ ounces butter in a deep saucepan, and when hot add 1½ cups white rice. Mix the rice well with the butter so that every grain is coated. Then add 3 cups boiling consommé. Mix well with a wooden spoon and bring to a fast boil. Then cover, lower the flame to the lowest possible point, and let simmer for 15 to 20 minutes, or until rice is tender and the consommé has been absorbed. Then melt 1 ounce of butter in it and sprinkle generously with grated Parmesan cheese. Put in a warm oven to keep hot.

In a skillet melt 1 ounce butter, and when hot add 10 ounces chopped veal which has been sprinkled with curry powder, and salted and peppered to taste, and ½ cup chopped onions. Fry gently until onions are transparent and veal is cooked. In another skillet melt 1 ounce butter, and when hot add 2 ounces chopped fresh mushrooms, 1 slice pineapple, diced, and ½ sweet red pepper, cut in strips. Fry these gently until mushrooms are done, about 6 minutes.

Spread the rice out on a hot platter, with a long trough down the center. The veal and the onions are placed in the trough, and the mushrooms, pineapple and pepper mixture is spread over that. The Risotto Casmir is served with a curry sauce, and this is the way Walter makes it.

Put 1 pound veal bones in a kettle, 1 pared, cored and sliced apple, and 1½ ounces curry powder. Cover the veal bones with water and boil for 1 hour. Strain the broth, and add ½ cup of cream to thicken sauce.

The Swiss canton of Ticino borders on Italy, and the food has an Italian flavor. It is a land of palms, mimosa, spices, laurel, fennel and rosemary, and olive oil, pastas, and the melodious tones of the guitar. Ossobuco, fritto misto, and polenta are as popular in the canton as they are in Italy. And their risotto with mushrooms is delicious.

RISOTTO WITH MUSHROOMS

1–2 *onions*	*Water*
2 *oz. butter*	1 *quart consommé*
1 *lb. raw white rice*	2 *small packets saffron*
1½ *oz. dried mushrooms*	*Salt and pepper*

Grated Parmesan cheese

Chop 1 to 2 medium onions fine, and fry lightly in 2 ounces butter, without letting onions become brown. Remove onions with a skimming ladle and put 1 pound white rice into the butter in which onions were fried. Stir gently to help butter penetrate rice. Coarsely chop 1½ ounces dried mushrooms (which have previously been soaked in lukewarm water to make them swell, then drained) and add them to rice. Heat 1 quart consommé and season with 2 small packets saffron, and salt and pepper to taste. Add to rice, and cook gently until rice is tender and absorbed all liquid. Serve with grated Parmesan cheese.

In America it is almost a "must" to team up certain foods, such as ham and eggs, coffee and doughnuts, corned beef and cabbage, and mustard and hot dogs. In England, there is also a team that is practically a "must," roast beef and Yorkshire pudding.

Unfortunately, I never found a light and delicious Yorkshire pudding in England. I must admit that I never had one in a private home, but those that I had in London restaurants were invariably tough as shoe leather, or a soggy mess that was repulsive.

However, here is a recipe that is easy to make, and the method is foolproof. It comes out crisp and brown, like popovers, and with absolutely no sogginess. By the way, don't let the amount of pepper bother you. 1 teaspoon is correct.

YORKSHIRE PUDDING

1½ *cups sifted flour*	1 *tsp. grated nutmeg*
1 *tsp. salt*	4 *eggs*
1 *tsp. pepper*	1½ *cups scalded milk*

½ *cup beef fat drippings*

Mix together the flour, salt, pepper, and nutmeg. To this add the beaten eggs (a quarter of the mixture at a time), and the milk, added little by little. Stir well and beat again with a rotary beater. Cover with a cloth and chill in refrigerator for at least 2 hours.

When the roast is done and taken out of the oven, put ½ cup of drippings into a shallow pan, and set pan in oven to become sizzling hot. Then beat the chilled batter vigorously, and pour it into the pan of hot fat. It should be about ½ inch deep in the pan. Bake in a 450-degree oven for about 15 minutes, or until pudding has risen. Then reduce heat to 300 degrees, and bake 15 minutes longer, or until pudding is crisp and brown. To serve, cut pudding in squares, and place around the roast on the platter.

11 ≉ SALADS AND SAUCES

I have found that salads, as Americans know them, do not enjoy anywhere near the popularity in France that they do in America. On most of the restaurant menus the only salad listed is "*Salade de Saison.*"

One notable exception is in Nice, where *Salade Niçoise* is a famous specialty. Many Nice restaurants serve it, but to my mind it reaches its peak of perfection at the superlative Restaurant Reynaud, facing the Mediterranean on the Quai des États-Unis.

In chatting with Monsieur Reynaud, he told me three rules that must be followed in making *Salade Niçoise*. First, it should never contain anything that has been cooked. Second, the tomatoes, which are a "must," should be cut in quarters, never sliced, and third, a genuine *Salade Niçoise* must be laced generously with *pissala*, which is anchovies ground to a paste in a mortar, and moistened with olive oil.

SALADE NIÇOISE

Tomatoes	*Beets*
Spanish onions	*Black olives*
Little green onions in season	*Anchovy filets*
Green sweet pepper	*Baby lima beans*
Yellow sweet pepper	*Pissala*
Red sweet pepper	*Wine vinegar*
Celery	*Olive oil*
Radishes	*Salt and pepper*
Baby artichokes	*Dijon mustard*
Hard-cooked eggs	

At Restaurant Reynaud the waiter brings to your table a huge bowl filled with chilled vegetables. From this bowl into another

229

bowl go quartered tomatoes, thin slices of sweet Spanish onions (or little green onions in season), sliced green, yellow and red sweet peppers, celery, radishes, tiny baby artichokes, sliced beets, pitted Italian black olives, square pieces of anchovy filets, and, in season, tiny baby *fèvettes* (in America use tiny baby lima beans). The whole thing is generously laced with *pissala,* then a dressing of wine vinegar, olive oil, salt and pepper, and a little Dijon mustard is dabbed over the salad, and it is gently tossed. It is then heaped upon your plate, and garnished with quartered hard-cooked eggs (the only cooked ingredient allowed!). *Salade Niçoise* is an experience that your eyes and your taste buds will never forget.

In and around Nice Italian pastas are very popular. Macaroni, cannelloni, ravioli, and gnocchis are found on many restaurant menus. I had a macaroni-lobster salad that was simply superb.

MACARONI-LOBSTER SALAD

2 *cups elbow macaroni*	½ *tsp. dried basil*
Boiling salted water	1 *tsp. salt*
9-*oz. package frozen artichoke*	¼ *tsp. pepper*
hearts	½ *cup French dressing*
5 *oz. cooked lobster meat*	⅓ *cup mayonnaise, or aioli*
¼ *cup sliced radishes*	*sauce*

Lettuce

Cook 2 cups (8 ounces) elbow macaroni in the usual way, then drain, rinse with cold water, and drain again.

Cook a 9-ounce package frozen artichoke hearts as directed on package, and drain, if necessary. Combine the macaroni, 5 ounces cooked lobster, ¼ cup sliced radishes, ½ teaspoon dried basil, 1 teaspoon salt, and ¼ teaspoon pepper. Then toss lightly and chill. Also combine ½ cup French dressing with ⅓ cup mayonnaise and blend well. If you want to be very Niçoise, you'll use *Aioli* sauce (see page 237) instead of mayonnaise.

To serve, combine the macaroni mixture and the French dressing mixture, toss lightly but thoroughly. Arrange lettuce on 4 salad plates, and top with the salad.

On one of the rare occasions when we ate a light lunch by choice, we had a most delicious and refreshing salad at the Hotel Milano Excelsior in Bologna. This is how it was made.

BOLOGNA SALAD

1 *clove garlic*	*Salt and pepper*
½ *cup olive oil*	1 *cup in all of:*
1 *cup bread cubes*	*Mortadella sausage*
1 *small head lettuce*	*Bologna sausage*
1½ *tsp. Worcestershire sauce*	*Salami*
¼ *cup grated Parmesan cheese*	*Parma ham*

¼ *cup lemon juice*

Let a clove garlic, thinly sliced, stand in ½ cup olive oil for several hours. Then remove garlic and heat half of the garlic-flavored oil in a skillet. Lightly brown 1 cup bread cubes in the oil, then drain them on absorbent paper. Break a head of chilled, tender lettuce into bite-size pieces in a salad bowl (use enough lettuce to make about 1½ quarts). Sprinkle in 1½ teaspoons Worcestershire sauce, ¼ cup grated Parmesan cheese, and salt and pepper to taste. Then add 1 cup cold cuts cut into thin strips (we had mortadella, Bologna, two different kinds of salami, and Parma ham), ¼ cup lemon juice, and the remaining garlic-flavored oil. Toss thoroughly, and serve immediately to 5 or 6.

As befits the largest city in the world, London has a great variety of foreign restaurants. No matter what your nationality, you can probably find a restaurant in London that will serve you food from your native land.

We dined at eight or ten foreign restaurants while we were in London, and in each case the food was excellent, and really prepared according to the cuisine of the country. One night we went to the Akropolis, a Greek restaurant in Soho, and our main course, *Moussaka,* was perfectly prepared. With our dinner we had a light but delicious salad, which is well worth detailing here.

GREEK SALAD

3 *small cucumbers*	½ *cup olive oil*
16 *radishes*	1 *tsp. salt*
1 *cup celery hearts*	1 *cup tarragon wine vinegar*
½ *cup coarsely chopped wal-*	2 *tbsp. lemon juice*
nuts	½ *tsp. dried salad herbs*
½ *tsp. dried chervil*	*Watercress*
¼ *cup crumbled feta cheese*	*Green stuffed olives*

Ripe olives

Combine 3 small cucumbers, cut in ½ inch slices and diced, 16 crisp radishes, sliced, 1 cup celery hearts, chopped, and ½ cup walnuts, coarsely chopped. Sprinkle over this combination ½ teaspoon dried chervil and ¼ cup crumbled feta cheese, and mix gently.

Prepare a dressing of ½ cup olive oil, 2 teaspoons salt, 1 cup tarragon wine vinegar, 2 tablespoons lemon juice, and ½ teaspoon dried salad herbs. When well blended, pour over the salad ingredients and toss until everything is well coated. Serve on a bed of watercress and garnish with green stuffed and ripe olives. This serves 4.

This is an English recipe for a delightful avocado salad.

AVOCADO SALAD

2 *medium tomatoes*	½ *green pepper*
½ *small onion*	2 *medium avocados*
2 *stalks celery*	¼ *cup mayonnaise*
½ *cup diced cucumber*	*Cupped lettuce leaves*

Peel and dice 2 medium tomatoes, chop ½ small onion and 2 stalks celery, dice or slice enough cucumber to make ½ cup, and dice ½ green pepper. Last of all peel and dice 2 medium-sized ripe but firm avocados. Toss all the ingredients together lightly with about ¼ cup mayonnaise (more, if you prefer it). Serve the salad on cupped lettuce leaves.

The subject of sauces is a vast and complicated one. French sauces are usually involved and very elegant, and the French utilize *fumets* and meat glazes and flavored butters extensively. French sauces are thickened by roux, egg yolks, cream, and reducing over a flame. Italian sauces, on the other hand, are far less complicated. Their foundations are usually olive oil and wine, and are thickened with breadcrumbs, cheese and purées. The Germans are fond of sweet-sour sauces.

The most famous sauce in all of Italy is *ragù*, which is the true name of Bolognese sauce. I don't believe there has been a single restaurant we have eaten in throughout our travels that has not listed one pasta or another *alla bolognese* (with Bolognese sauce). Its form varies with different chefs, and so does its flavor, but it is at its supreme best in the restaurants of Bologna. We had it in the two top restaurants in Bologna—Al Pappagallo, and Ristorante Nerina, and it was unforgettable.

Most Bolognese prefer *ragù* with Lasagne Verdi. In this dish the sauce alternates with layers of lasagne, and the whole is baked in the oven. But for spaghetti, tagliatelle, tortellini, and other pastas, the sauce is mixed with the very hot pasta in a heated dish, and a lump of butter is added before serving.

I obtained two recipes for a true Bolognese sauce; one from Signor Zurla, of Al Pappagallo, and one from the Nerina Restaurant. There is very little difference between the two, yet each is distinctive. I have combined them, and I don't believe that you will get a sauce like it in the vast majority of American restaurants, yet you can make it easily in your own home. Just be sure that you use the very best and freshest of ingredients.

BOLOGNESE RAGÙ SAUCE
(A rich meat sauce)

1 *tbsp. butter*	4 *tsp. concentrated tomato*
3 *oz. bacon*	*purée*
1 *carrot*	½ *cup dry white wine*
1 *onion*	*Salt*
1 *stalk celery*	*Freshly ground pepper*
½ *small green pepper*	*Pinch grated nutmeg*
½ *lb. ground lean beef*	1 *cup condensed beef bouillon*
¼ *lb. ground veal*	¼ *lb. fresh mushrooms*
¼ *lb. chicken livers*	*Butter*
1 *cup cream*	

Melt 1 tablespoon butter in a saucepan and add to it 3 ounces bacon cut into very small pieces. Cook slowly until lightly browned, then add 1 carrot, 1 onion, 1 stalk celery, and ½ small sweet green pepper, all finely chopped. When vegetables are lightly browned put in ½ pound ground lean beef and ¼ pound ground veal. Stir all with a fork until the meat browns evenly. Next add ¼ pound chicken livers, chopped, and after everything has cooked 4 or 5 minutes add 4 teaspoons concentrated tomato purée, and then ½ cup dry white wine. Season to taste with salt and freshly ground black pepper and a pinch grated nutmeg, and add 1 cup condensed beef bouillon. Cover the pan and simmer the sauce very gently for about 15 minutes. Then add ¼ pound thinly sliced mushrooms which have previously been cooked in butter for 5 minutes, and simmer the sauce for another 10 minutes. For a very smooth sauce, at the last minute add 1 cup of cream to the sauce, let it heat, and serve with pastas or combine with lasagne. The above recipe makes about 4 cups of sauce.

Under normal circumstances you would scarcely expect to find luxurious dining rooms, serving the most sophisticated gourmet food (Malossol caviar, Chateaubriand steaks, flambéed pheasants, etc.) in a restaurant that prominently features self-service counters where pedestrians can stop for a quick snack, lunch counters, and buy them table service at popular prices. Yet all that is what you will encounter at the Movenpick restaurant in Dreikonighaus in Zürich. (Incidentally, "Movenpick" to the Swiss describes the action of a gull swooping down to pick up food—a sort of eat and run action.)

The place is utterly amazing. Sigrid Fitze, the public relations director of the Movenpick chain (5 restaurants in Zürich, and 1 each in Lucerne, Berne, and Geneva) took Mrs. Wood and me on a complete tour of Dreikönighaus. It was a miracle of design, decor, maintenance, sanitation and efficiency. In the kitchens, refrigeration, dishwashing and service areas, stainless steel is everywhere.

The three luxury dining rooms are the Crystal Room, the Pearl

Room (oyster shells are imbedded into cement with the pearl side out, to form the walls), and the Grill, or Rotisserie Room, with its great copper grill, and elegant draperies.

We had excellent martinis in the intimate cocktail room, then, in the Grill, we had scampi broiled on skewers with a delicious sauce, superb steaks (which are selected, cut, and weighed at the table) with an exquisite herb-butter sauce, and a cherry and raspberry sauce, flambéed, over ice cream.

The herb butter (*Krauterbutter*) was the most delicious steak spread I have ever tasted. Making it in large quantities, as they do at Movenpick's, the best the chef could do for me was to reduce it to a quantity to serve 20 to 25 persons.

KRAUTERBUTTER
(Steak Sauce)

1 *tbsp. chopped garlic*	1 *tbsp. mustard*
18 *oz. butter*	2 *tsp. Cognac*
1 *tsp. salt*	2 *tsp. sherry*
1 *tsp. fresh lemon juice*	⅕ *bottle catsup*
1 *tsp. meat extract*	1¾ *oz. onions*
1 *tsp. paprika*	2 *tbsp. fresh parsley*
1 *tsp. pepper*	1½ *tsp. dried tarragon*
1½ *tsp. Worcestershire sauce*	1 *tsp. filet of anchovy*

Blend 1 tablespoon chopped garlic with 18 ounces butter until smooth and foamy. In a bowl mix together 1 teaspoon each salt, fresh lemon juice, meat extract, paprika and pepper, 1½ teaspoons Worcestershire sauce, 1 tablespoon mustard, 2 teaspoons each Cognac and sherry, and ⅕ bottle catsup. Also chop 1¾ ounces small onions, 2 tablespoons fresh parsley, 1½ teaspoons dried tarragon, and 1 teaspoon filet of anchovy. Add the contents of the bowl and chopped ingredients to the garlic butter, and again blend the whole well. Chill in refrigerator until mixture has firmed up, then make a roll of it (about 2 inches in diameter) in wax paper. Again chill until ready to serve, then cut in slices about ½ inch thick, and place a slice on each serving of steak.

The balance can be refrigerated, and kept for some time, for use on other dishes.

There are a number of bistros and restaurants in Paris that specialize in charcoal broiling. Steaks are broiled over a grill, chickens are roasted on a spit.

The night we went to the Folies Bergère we had dinner at a charming little restaurant almost across the street from the theatre. Its name was *Auberge du Père Louis,* and the first sight that greeted you after entering was a huge fireplace with chickens roasting on spits.

Mrs. Wood had a half chicken, and I had an entrecôte with a wonderful sauce over it, a sauce Provençale.

SAUCE PROVENÇALE

⅓ cup olive oil	4 oz. condensed consommé
¼ cup chopped mushrooms	2 oz. tomato paste
3 anchovy filets	2 oz. dry red wine
2 small cloves garlic	Cayenne pepper
1 medium onion	1 tbsp. chopped fresh parsley

Heat ⅓ cup olive oil in a saucepan and add ¼ cup fresh mushrooms, chopped, 3 anchovy filets, chopped, 2 small cloves garlic, minced, and 1 medium onion, finely chopped. Cook about 5 minutes over a low flame, stirring almost constantly, until mixture is soft, but not browned. Combine 4 ounces condensed consommé, 2 ounces each tomato paste and dry red wine, tiny pinch cayenne pepper, and 1 tablespoon chopped fresh parsley. Add this to the mushroom-anchovy-onion mixture, stirring from bottom of pan, until mixture boils. Lower flame at once, and simmer gently for 15 minutes, stirring occasionally and keeping saucepan covered. Pour sauce over beef before slicing. Spoon sauce over slices.

In giving the recipe for the lobster-macaroni salad I suggested that you use an *aioli* sauce in preference to a mayonnaise. And if you are fond of garlic, you'll love it. *Aioli* is the Provençal version of mayonnaise.

AIOLI SAUCE

6 *cloves garlic*	4 *tbsp. olive oil*
1 *egg yolk*	1 *tbsp. lemon juice*
½ *tsp. pepper*	1 *tbsp. tepid water*
	1 *cup olive oil*

Finely chop 6 cloves peeled garlic and mash them to a pulp in a mortar. With a wire whisk stir in 1 egg yolk and ½ teaspoon pepper. Then, very slowly, beating all the while, add about 4 tablespoons olive oil, almost drop by drop. Then put mixture into an electric blender, slowly add 1 tablespoon each lemon juice and tepid water while blender is operating, then add 1 cup olive oil and let blender operate for about 1 minute. Chill thoroughly.

12 ⇒ EGGS
AND CHEESE

EGGS

A pinch of this, a suggestion of that, and a wee bit more of something else, plus a generous dash of imagination, is all that it takes to create something new in the kitchen.

While the above recipe applies to all cookery, it is particularly true of egg cookery, for the egg is the most versatile of foods. The late George Rector, famous restaurateur, said that he understood there were 742,376 ways of preparing eggs! But he admitted that he had never been able to check the accuracy of that figure!

In France, eggs with breakfast is unthinkable! But with luncheon the egg really comes into its own. The genius of French chefs can transform ordinary fried eggs, poached eggs, scrambled eggs, and omelets into masterpieces of succulence, beauty and elegance. Even at dinner omelets, eggs en gelée, and stuffed eggs are offered as hors d'oeuvres.

I had one of the most unusual egg dishes in Burgundy. I say unusual, for the eggs were poached in a red wine sauce, and red wine is not supposed to go with eggs, but it did, beautifully.

POACHED EGGS, VIN ROUGE

2 *tbsp. butter*
1 *onion*
½ *clove garlic*
2 *tbsp. chopped celery*
1 *small bay leaf*
Salt and pepper
Pinch dried thyme

1 *tbsp. chopped fresh parsley*
4 *tsp. flour*
1 *cup hot chicken bouillon*
1 *cup warm dry red wine*
6 *eggs*
6 *slices bread*
Butter

Put 2 tablespoons butter in a heavy saucepan. When hot add 1 onion, chopped, half a clove garlic, and 2 tablespoons finely chopped celery. Sauté over a low flame until tender, but not brown. Then add a small bay leaf, salt and pepper to taste, a pinch dried thyme, and a tablespoon chopped fresh parsley. Sprinkle in about 4 teaspoons flour, and blend well. Then add 1 cup each hot chicken bouillon and warm dry red wine, stirring constantly until sauce is smooth. Simmer over a low flame for about 15 minutes.

While sauce is simmering toast 6 slices bread. Cut a circle about 2 inches in diameter out of the center of each slice. Then butter the slices and keep warm.

When sauce has cooked the required length of time strain it into another skillet and bring it to a boil. Then slip into the sauce 6 eggs, one at a time, and poach about 2 or 3 minutes. Carefully remove eggs with a skimmer to the centers of the prepared toast slices, then pour sauce over them, and serve immediately.

On our way back to Milan from Venice we stopped at the proud and noble city of Vicenza. The wealthy men of the past built nearly one hundred palaces there, which has caused Vicenza to be called a Venice on land.

We saw one of the most amazing theatres there, called the Teatro Olimpico. It was opened in 1583, and performances are still being given there. The stage has superimposed niches, columns, and statues, and three streets in perspective, painted in false relief, give the impression that you are looking for blocks down the streets.

We stopped at the Jolly Hotel, and enjoyed its dining terrace facing the park (all the Jolly Hotels in Italy are excellently run and managed, the rooms nicely furnished and clean, and the food is always good). One day for brunch we were intrigued by the item, *Uova in Purgatorio,* and we tried it. It was delicious, poached eggs in a tomato sauce. I presume the red of the tomatoes is supposed to represent Purgatory.

UOVA IN PURGATORIO
(Poached Eggs in Tomato Sauce)

2 *cloves garlic*	1 *tbsp. chopped parsley*
2 *tbsp. olive oil*	6 *filets anchovies*
1 *No. 2½ can tomatoes*	*Salt and pepper*

6 *eggs*

Sauté 2 finely chopped cloves garlic in 2 tablespoons olive oil. Add one No. 2½ can tomatoes, 1 tablespoon chopped parsley, 6 filets of anchovies, and pinch each of salt and pepper. Simmer over slow fire 15 minutes. Put sauce in shallow pan, bring to boil, then break in 6 eggs. Cover and let eggs poach in sauce about 3 minutes.

In German *Bauern Frühstück* means "Farmer's Breakfast." But this savory egg dish is better suited (for Americans) to brunch rather than breakfast. We had it at the Orinean Hotel in Fulda, Germany, and it really filled us up, delightfully.

BAUERN FRÜHSTÜCK
(Eggs with Bacon, Potatoes and Beer)

2 *cups cubed slab bacon*	4 *tbsp. chopped dill pickles*
2 *onions*	2 *cups diced cooked potatoes*
½ *cup dark beer*	4 *eggs*

Brown 2 cups cubed slab bacon in a heavy skillet. Then pour off all but ½ cup fat. Add to the cubed bacon 2 onions, chopped, and let them brown. Add ½ cup dark beer, 4 tablespoons chopped dill pickles, and 2 cups diced cooked potatoes. Cook a few minutes, then turn down heat and add 4 lightly beaten eggs. Cook slowly until eggs are set, then serve to 2 or 4, depending upon appetites.

One of the most fantastic and fabulous places in all of Europe is the village of Portmerrion in Northern Wales, a mile or so from the city of Penrhyndeudraeth. Placed about the hillsides facing Tremadoc Bay are Italian villas, baroque towers, chapels, a campanile, loggias, beautiful gardens, colonnades, in almost every assorted color of a rainbow. Near the edge of the waters of the bay is a rambling hotel, luxuriously furnished, and a great dining room that is glass enclosed. Our quarters were in a small villa called "Fountain Two," a most luxuriously furnished living room and bedroom, and large bath with a dressing room.

The originator and architect of Portmerrion is a charming, not-too-young man, Mr. Clough Williams-Ellis, who has his own magnificent estate a few miles away. I spent an afternoon with him, and he told me how and why he created this Mediterranean type of village. He is still working every day, improving and adding to its beauties.

The food was excellent, and for breakfast the morning we left we had a Welsh omelet. This is the recipe.

WELSH OMELET

4 *slices bacon*	4 *eggs*
1 *medium onion*	½ *cup light cream*
2 *tbsp. minced parsley*	⅛ *tsp. pepper*
1½ *tsp. salt*	1 *cup grated Swiss cheese*
	Paprika

Cut each of 4 slices of bacon in two, and fry until partially cooked. Then remove them, and add to the skillet a medium onion, finely minced, and 2 tablespoons minced parsley, and cook until onions are lightly brown. Season with ½ teaspoon salt, and spread out the onions and parsley on the bottom of an 8-inch pie tin or plate.

Beat 4 eggs lightly with ½ cup light cream, seasoning with 1 teaspoon salt and ⅛ teaspoon black pepper. Pour the egg mixture over the onions in the pie tin, and sprinkle in 1 cup of grated Swiss cheese. Arrange the bacon slices on top, sprinkle with paprika, and bake in a 350-degree oven for 15 minutes, or until eggs are set and cheese melted.

One of the best known of all Basque dishes is *Piperade,* a combination of onions, tomatoes and green peppers. It is also called a Basque omelet, and can be made as an omelet, or as scrambled eggs, which is more typically Basque.

We had it as a luncheon dish one day at a bistro not far from our hotel, Caveau Montpensier. It's wonderful.

PIPERADE
(Scrambled Eggs with Onions, Tomatoes and Green Peppers)

2 tbsp. bacon drippings (or olive oil)	Freshly ground pepper
	2 ripe tomatoes
½ clove garlic	1 slice canned pimento
1 small green pepper	Small pinch dried marjoram
1 onion	4 eggs
Salt	1 oz. dry sherry

In a heavy skillet melt about 2 tablespoons bacon drippings (or olive oil) to which ½ clove garlic, chopped, and crushed, has been added. In this sauté slowly 1 small seeded and chopped green pepper, and 1 onion, chopped, until vegetables are transparent. Then add salt and freshly ground pepper to taste, 2 ripe tomatoes, peeled, seeded and chopped, a slice canned pimento cut in strips, and a small pinch dried marjoram. Cover skillet and cook until vegetables are rather soft, about the consistency of a purée—about 20 to 30 minutes.

Combine 4 eggs, a pinch salt and pepper, and 1 ounce dry sherry. Beat lightly, then pour into the vegetable mixture, after raising heat slightly. Stir gently, as for scrambled eggs. When eggs are proper consistency (don't let overcook) serve immediately.

If *Piperade* is to be served as an omelet, stir eggs vigorously into hot vegetable mixture, then cook. When done, slide omelet onto a heated platter.

Omelets in France are nearly always superb. The reason is, I think, that only the freshest of fresh eggs are used, as well as the finest Normandy butter and cream. They are never overcooked; only lightly brown on the outside, and creamy in the center.

A most savory omelet we had in France was a Roquefort cheese omelet.

ROQUEFORT CHEESE OMELET

6 *eggs*	1¼ *oz. Roquefort cheese*
Salt and pepper	1 *tbsp. heavy cream*
3 *dashes Worcestershire sauce*	1½ *oz. butter*

Break 6 eggs into a bowl, season with salt and pepper to taste and add 3 dashes of Worcestershire sauce. Beat the eggs well with a fork or wire whisk. In the top of a double boiler over boiling water melt 1¼ ounces Roquefort cheese, then mix 1 tablespoon heavy cream.

Put about 1½ ounces butter in your omelet pan, or skillet, and when sizzling hot pour in the eggs. Make the omelet in the usual way except when it is about half done, or the sides have set, add the Roquefort and cream mixture. Finish cooking omelet, but do not overcook. It should be soft and creamy in the center. This should serve 3 or 4.

I learned a new trick at the restaurant in the Eiffel Tower in Paris. The day we picked to visit the Tower was not a good one, and before we got there it began to snow. Nevertheless we visited the various levels, and I got some pictures. By lunch time both Mrs. Wood and I were practically frozen, and our teeth were chattering. We went to a beautiful restaurant and got a table right by the window, where we had a marvelous view of the city in spite of the snow.

The captain came up and could readily see that we were chilled to the bone. So he suggested a drink for us. It turned out to be a double hot buttered rum, and in moments we were thoroughly warmed, inside and out. Then the captain suggested Eggs Benedict à la Eiffel, which sounded perfect.

Instead of using an English muffin as a base for the Eggs Benedict, they were served in a heated, flaky pastry shell. Put a slice of ham in the bottom, then a poached egg, and top that with the Hollandaise sauce. It was really divine.

Another recipe that I fancied from Charles Francatelli's English cookbook was poached eggs on anchovy toast. It is a delightfully piquant way of serving poached eggs, which are very bland.

POACHED EGGS ON ANCHOVY TOAST

Eggs	*Anchovy filets*
Hot dry toast	*Freshly ground pepper*

ANCHOVY BUTTER

6 *filets anchovies*	*Pinch cayenne pepper*
2 *oz. butter*	*Pinch grated nutmeg*

Poach the number of eggs required, then drain them on a napkin (or paper toweling). Then place each egg on a piece of fresh dry toast spread with anchovy butter, with thin strips of anchovy filets on the anchovy butter. Place a little freshly ground pepper in the center of each egg, and serve.

To make the anchovy butter mash 6 anchovy filets and mix them with 2 ounces butter, and season with a pinch cayenne pepper and grated nutmeg.

From time immemorial Switzerland has been famed for the excellence and high standard of its dairy products. The Swiss peasant cultivates fruit, vegetables and vineyards; he is at the same time cattle-owner and dairy farmer, and the milk, cream, butter and eggs that come from the farms cannot be surpassed anywhere.

Plain meals without meat are a regular feature of the Swiss menu. Vegetables are beautifully done; a great feature of Swiss cookery is fritters—almost anything that can be dipped in batter and fried in olive oil, or deep fat, or butter is relished; all kinds of fish abound in the lakes and rivers, and eggs are fashioned into delectable dishes.

One of the most unusual and picturesque egg dishes comes from the canton of Ticino, in Eastern Switzerland, where the cuisine has an Italian savor. It is called *Zuppa del paes,* and it is really a soup.

ZUPPA DEL PAES
(Egg Soup)

1 *cup consommé (per serving)*	1–2 *eggs*
1 *slice bread*	1 *tsp. tomato purée*
Butter	*Grated Parmesan cheese*

Put a serving (about 1 cup) consommé into small aluminum or earthenware saucepans (these should be just large enough to hold 1 slice of bread), one saucepan for each person. Add to each saucepan a slice of bread fried in butter with 1 or 2 eggs on it, and top the eggs with a small spoonful of tomato purée, and cover the whole with grated Parmesan cheese. Put the saucepans in a hot oven, and when the whites have set, bring the saucepans and their contents to the table.

In Europe we frequently followed the Continental custom of having only rolls or croissants and coffee for breakfast. So, when we ate luncheon, we often had a hearty egg dish of some sort. Two memorable luncheon dishes were Spinach Omelet au Gratin, and Scrambled Eggs on Cheese Toast, both Swiss specialties.

SPINACH OMELET AU GRATIN

7 *oz. (by weight) flour*	1 *oz. butter*
1½ *cups boiled strained milk*	½ *lb. cooked, chopped spinach*
1½ *oz. lukewarm water*	1 *cup sour cream*
4 *egg yolks*	2 *cups grated Gruyère cheese*
4 *egg whites*	*Small chunks butter*

For the omelet mixture combine 7 ounces (by weight) of flour, 1½ cups boiled, strained milk and 1½ ounces lukewarm water, 4 egg yolks, 4 egg whites beaten stiff. With this mixture cook thin omelets in butter in a skillet. When omelets are done spread each omelet with a mixture of ½ pound cooked, drained and chopped spinach, 1 cup sour cream. Roll omelets up separately, divide in half, and place in layers in a fireproof dish, sprinkling grated Gruyère cheese over each layer. Cover the top with grated cheese, add small chunks of butter, and bake for 30 minutes in a medium oven. (You will need about 2 cups grated cheese.)

SCRAMBLED EGGS ON CHEESE TOAST

8 *slices buttered toast*	*Generous pinch chopped chives*
1 *cup dry white wine*	*Generous pinch flour*
1 *oz. butter*	10 *oz. Emmentaler cheese*
Generous pinch chopped	6 *eggs*
parsley	*Pepper*

Butter 2 slices toast for each person and keep hot. Pour into an earthenware saucepan set over a gentle flame 1 cup dry white wine, one ounce butter, a generous pinch each chopped parsley, chopped chives, and flour, and 10 ounces Emmentaler cheese, grated or chopped into fine pieces. Cook, stirring constantly, until mixture is well amalgamated.

Break 6 fresh eggs into a bowl and beat vigorously. Then pour them into the cheese mixture when the latter begins to bubble, and stir the eggs well into the cheese mixture. Season with pepper to taste, and spread the mixture on the toast. This dish must be served very hot, to about 4.

CHEESE

Anyone who is a lover of cheese will have a gastronomical field day in Europe. In practically every country we visited we reveled in the cheeses, not only the well-known cheeses, but those that are indigenous to certain localities.

For the traveler in Europe, as well as those who live in localities where fine imported cheeses are obtainable, I am listing herewith the varieties of cheeses we so thoroughly enjoyed during our travels.

ENGLAND

Stilton	*Cheshire*
Cheddar	*Double Glouster*
	Wensleydale

FRANCE

Roquefort	*Pont l'Evêque*
Port du Salut	*Reblochon*
Camembert	*Caprice des Dieux*

ITALY

Parmesan	*Pecorino*
Gorgonzola	*Ricotta*
Bel Paese	*Mozzarella*
Stracchino	*Caciocavallo*
Fontina	*Provolone*

SWITZERLAND

Emmentaler	*Schabzieger*
Gruyère	*Tilsiter*
Appenzeller-Rasskäse	*Vacherin*

Germans of the Palatinate will meticulously prepare their cottage cheese before drinking any wine. The cheese comes to the scrubbed, spotlessly white table whipped foamy with cream, to which caraway seeds, chopped onion, a little pepper, paprika and salt are ceremoniously added.

In a number of German cities we visited little weinstubes that made a specialty of serving *Handkäse Mit Musik*. The "Handkäse" was a piece of German cheese, sometimes similar to Cheddar; the "Musik" (music) was vinegar and chopped onions. The cheese, vinegar, and onions were all on the same plate. In Frankfurt we had this unusual snack at what was called a cider stube, where both hard and sweet cider was served as the beverage. It was a lot of fun.

Probably the most celebrated cheese in the world is named after the country of its origin, Switzerland. However, the true name of Swiss cheese is Emmentaler, and it is the product of the large farms in the Bernese Valley. Closely resembling Emmentaler is Gruyère, the cheese of the Fribourg Alps in western Switzer-

land. Gruyère has smaller holes than Emmentaler, is not quite
so rich in color, and it is more strongly salted and stronger in
flavor.

In addition to these two famous cheeses, there are scores of
other delicious cheeses produced in Switzerland and every mountain canton has its own special cheeses.

To many people Switzerland is a land of primeval ice and snow,
a paradise for all lovers of winter sports and mountain climbers.
But Switzerland has another aspect of amazing beauty—lush
meadows, an uncountable number of clear and sparkling lakes,
mountain sides completely covered with trees that are greener
than green, quaint and charming villages and cities with flowers
growing everywhere, and always, on the horizon, majestic snow-
capped Alpine peaks.

We visited a number of Swiss cities, but to us Zürich is the
most beautiful and interesting. Situated on the northern end of
lovely Lake Zürich, the River Limmat divides the city in two. It
is a metropolis of science and the arts; it is a city of both ultra-
modern and medieval architecture; the broad, tree-lined Bahnhofstrasse is one of Europe's most famous shopping centers, and
the picturesque, narrow lanes of the old quarter are filled with
historic buildings and churches, fascinating shops, and ancient
guildhalls. To delight the gourmet, both old and new Zürich have
a profusion of wonderful restaurants, all serving intriguing Swiss
food and dishes.

I believe Switzerland's most famous dish is the fondue. It is
to Switzerland what hot dogs are to the United States, fish and
chips to England, and spaghetti to Italy. While it is indigenous
to southern Switzerland, it is to be found in almost every city
of any size in the country. There are four varieties of fondue, but
they differ only slightly, principally in the number of cheeses used,
and the use of kirsch (cherry brandy).

I have never eaten a better fondue in Switzerland than the one
we had one night in an old, raftered restaurant on a narrow little
street near Grossmünster Cathedral. It is called Le Dezaley, and
the people of Zürich flock to it every night. The proprietor, Jean
Combe, gave me his recipe.

SWISS FONDUE

5 oz. piece Emmentaler cheese	3 cups very dry white wine
5 oz. piece Gruyère cheese	2 tsp. potato flour
1 loaf French bread	2 oz. kirsch
1 clove garlic	Salt and pepper

For 2 people get a piece of Emmentaler (Swiss) cheese and a piece of Gruyère cheese, each weighing 5 ounces. Finely grate them and mix together. Also cut a loaf of French bread into 1-inch squares.

Into a large, flat-bottomed earthenware pot, which has been rubbed inside with a split clove garlic, pour 3 cups very dry white wine, and bring to a boil. Then stir in the grated cheese slowly, and keep stirring gently until cheese melts and combines with wine. Have mixed and blended 2 teaspoons potato flour with 2 ounces kirsch, and stir this into cheese and wine mixture. Add salt and pepper to taste and bring to a slow boil. Then put the pot on an alcohol burner, bring it to the table, placing it in the center. Beside it place a basket containing the cubes of bread.

Each participant has a long-handled fork with which he spears a piece of bread, dips it into the pot, swishes it around a bit, then, holding the fork and bread above the pot, he twirls it rapidly for a few moments, then pops it into his mouth.

Copious quantities of chilled dry white wine must go with the fondue. In addition, each person has a couple of ounces of kirsch in a glass beside his plate. Midway through the fondue, half of it is tossed off. The other half is drunk when the fondue is almost finished. The fondue is topped off with a cup of hot black tea, flavored with some prunelle brandy, which in Switzerland is called "Pflumli."

Another famous cheese dish of Switzerland is called Walliser Raclette. A wheel of Walliser cheese about 6 to 7 inches thick is cut in half. The cut side is put on a board in front of a charcoal grill. As the cheese begins to melt the piece is picked up and the melted part is scraped off the cheese onto hot plates. This is served with little boiled potatoes, and makes a wonderful first course.

We had it that way at the Carlton Elite Hotel in Zürich the night of Mrs. Wood's birthday dinner. As yet, I haven't had a chance to try it with cheese that is sold in America. But I imagine that a good Cheddar or Tillamook would work very well. Anyhow, I am going to experiment. Naturally, Swiss cuisine abounds in delectable cheese dishes. During our sojourn in Switzerland we sampled a number of them.

We found cheese toast to be a delightful snack. Here are two recipes for cheese toast, the first in the manner of the canton of Fribourg, and the second in the manner of Vaudoise. Both of these cantons are in western Switzerland, where the cooking is influenced by the French.

CHEESE TOAST À LA FRIBOURG

1 *slice bread*	¼ *-inch thick slice Emmentaler*
Butter	*cheese*
Fried diced bacon	

Fry 1 slice bread in butter for each person. When one side turns golden, turn slices and place on each one a ¼ -inch thick slice of cheese. Cover frying pan and cook until cheese begins to melt and spread. Top each slice with fried diced bacon.

The Vaudoise cheese toast is a little more elaborate, and I think tastier.

CHEESE TOAST VAUDOISE

Round slices bread	*Fresh butter*
¼ -inch thick slices Gruyère	*½ cup dry white wine*
cheese	*Freshly ground pepper*

Cut slices of bread from a round loaf. Spread on side with fresh butter and cover with a ¼ inch thick slice of Gruyère cheese, cutting it a little smaller than the bread, since in the process of melting it is going to spread. Place slices in a fireproof dish containing small chunks of butter and ½ cup dry white wine. Place in a hot oven until cheese melts into a smooth paste. Serve very hot, keeping a pepper mill handy.

Mozzarella cheese is made from milk of the *bufala,* and is white and elastic. It is not imported, although a so-called mozzarella cheese is plentiful in America. Just what the American mozzarella cheese is made from is something I do not know but I doubt that it is made from *bufala* milk! But it is widely used in America in lasagne, and various other dishes.

Mozzarella in Carrozza, in Italy, means literally mozzarella in a carriage. It is as common in Rome and the south of Italy as ham and eggs are in America. I have eaten it, and made it, in America with the mozzarella cheese available, and it is still a delightful dish, either as a first course, as we had it at the Savoy Hotel in Rome, or as a snack with cocktails.

MOZZARELLA IN CARROZZA
(Fried Cheese Sandwiches)

8 slices white bread	¼ tsp. salt
Mozzarella cheese	1 tbsp. dry white wine
Flour	Dash Worcestershire sauce
2 beaten eggs	Olive oil

Cut off the crusts from 8 slices of bread cut about ⅛ of an inch thick. Then cut each slice in half. On 8 half slices of bread put a slice of mozzarella cheese the same size as the bread half slice. Then cover the slices of mozzarella cheese with the other half bread slices, making a mozzarella cheese sandwich, so to speak. Lightly dust "sandwiches" with flour.

In a large soup plate put 2 eggs lightly beaten with ¼ teaspoon salt, a tablespoon dry white wine, and a dash of Worcestershire sauce. Put into the beaten eggs the "sandwiches" and let them soak for about 30 minutes, turning them over once. At the end of their soaking time press sandwiches together to be sure that the cheese is enclosed.

In a large skillet put enough olive oil so that it is about ½ inch deep in the skillet. When the oil is hot fry the egg-coated sandwiches in it until they are golden brown on both sides. Drain on paper toweling, and serve quickly.

13 ≉ DESSERTS

" 'Tis the dessert that graces all the feast,
For an ill end disparages all the rest;
A thousand things well done, and one forgot
Defaces obligation by that blot.
Make your transparent sweet-meats truly nice,
With Indian sugar and Arabian spice;
And let your various creams incircl'd be
With swelling fruit just ravish'd from the tree."

Dr. William King, circa 1700

Desserts can be lovely and sensuous things. The dancing flames
of Crêpes Suzette in a candle-lit dining room, the architecture
and gay colors of an inspired *Gâteau,* the elegance of an English
trifle, its gleaming whiteness emphasized by the red and green
of glacéed fruits, the artistry of a bird of paradise fashioned from
a pineapple—all titillate the eyes as well as the palate. What
odor could be more enchanting than that emanating from an
apple pie fresh from the oven? On a warm evening, what volup-
tuousness there is in the first velvety touch of a luscious ice cream
on the lips and tongue.

Flambéed crêpes (little French pancakes) is the ultimate in
desserts as far as I am concerned. I may have eaten an elaborate
and sumptuous dinner, which has left my taste buds jaded, and
my tummy filled to capacity, but the sight and aroma of crêpes
being prepared and flambéed snaps my taste buds back to attention, and my fork is at the ready even before I am served.

What Mrs. Wood and I thought were most unusual crêpes
were served to us in Brussels at the Auberge de Boendael on the
outskirts of the city.

253

A four-hundred-year-old farmhouse has been transformed into one of the most charming restaurants imaginable. A huge Dutch tile fireplace holding large burning logs brings warmth and cheer into the cocktail lounge where sections of tree trunks three feet wide serve as tables. Off the cocktail lounge is a gay "winter garden," decorated with planters and hung with chintz curtains, where one may have cocktails, or after-dinner coffee and liqueurs. In the main dining room, still rustic in character, is a twelve foot walk-in fireplace, in which are the grills and spits.

Although the Auberge de Boendael is out in the country, its numerous clientele is very cosmopolitan. The night we had dinner there the Nigerian Ambassador and his aides (in colorful native costumes) sat at the table next to us; across from us was the Japanese Ambassador; and a little to one side of us the French Ambassador was host to a large party.

We had excellent martinis sitting before the fire, and the owner, Madame Christine Wilmet-Bocken, ordered our dinner. It started off with a magnificent game pâté, and the entree was spit-broiled chicken, such as we had never tasted before, savory and succulent. Accompanying the entree was a lovely chilled Niersteiner Domthal. And then came the desserts! The first was *Crêpes Auberge.*

Before detailing this, and some of the following recipes for crêpes, I think it might be a good idea to discuss the making of crêpes, and crêpe butter.

CRÊPES
(Thin French Pancakes)

1½ cups sifted flour	2 tbsp. orange curaçao (or
¼ cup powdered sugar	brandy)
Generous pinch salt	1 tsp. grated lemon rind
1 cup milk	5 eggs, well beaten
¼ cup melted butter	Butter

Combine in a mixing bowl 1½ cups sifted flour, ¼ cup powdered sugar, and a generous pinch salt. Slowly stir in 1 cup milk, ¼ cup melted butter, 2 tablespoons orange curaçao (or brandy) and 1 teaspoon grated lemon rind. Next add 5 well beaten whole eggs, and beat the mixture vigorously until it is very smooth, and about the consistency of cream. Cover the batter and let it stand for about 30 minutes.

Grease a 5-inch skillet with butter, and when it is hot put in enough batter to cover the bottom of the skillet with a thin layer (about 2 tablespoons). Let the batter fry for a few seconds, then lift the pan from the flame and tilt it from side to side so that the batter will be of uniform thickness. Cook until one side is brown (about 1 minute), then turn and fry the second side until it is brown. Take out the crêpes, and set aside in a warm place, covering with a napkin. Continue this procedure (greasing the skillet each time) until all the crêpes are made.

CRÊPE BUTTER

½ cup sweet (unsalted) butter
1 cup powdered sugar
Grated rind 1 small orange
Grated rind 1 small lemon

½ cup orange juice
2 oz. liqueur (yellow Chartruese, or Cointreau, or Grand Marnier, or orange curaçao)

Cream ½ cup sweet butter in a bowl until light, then add 1 cup powdered sugar, the grated rinds of 1 small orange and 1 small lemon, ½ cup orange juice, and 2 ounces of a liqueur. The liquids should be added very slowly, while beating, and continue to beat until all is thoroughly blended. This crêpe butter should be made first, and refrigerated while the crêpes are being made and cooked.

The two recipes above are more or less standard, but the crêpe butter, and sometimes the batter, can be varied to suit certain recipes.

And now back to Crêpes Auberge.

CRÊPES AUBERGE

Crêpe batter
Crêpe butter

French vanilla ice cream
Segments of mandarin oranges

The crêpes were made and flambéed in the unusual manner. Then plates were brought to us, each containing a mound of French vanilla ice cream surrounded by segments of mandarin oranges. The crêpes were put on top, and the blazing liqueurs were poured over the whole. To us, it was an entirely new concept of Crêpes Suzette, and the combination of flavors was terrific.

We were still raving over the crêpes when a second dessert was brought. This was called *Parfait Fleuri,* and it brought gasps of amazement from both of us.

PARFAIT FLEURI

Miniature red clay flowerpots	*Grand Marnier ice cream*
Melted chocolate	*Tiny bunch artificial flowers*

Two little miniature red clay flowerpots (such as one starts slips in for the garden) came to the table. The inside and bottom of each pot was coated with chocolate. Then the pot was filled with Grand Marnier ice cream. Stuck in the center of each pot was a tiny bunch of artificial flowers. Even at the table you would swear that you were looking at a tiny pot of flowers fresh from the greenhouse. And of course the deliciousness of the parfait was enhanced by the illusion.

The coating of the bottom and insides of the little flowerpots is tricky, but not difficult if you follow these directions. First of all, put the little flowerpots in the freezing compartment of your refrigerator (or your freezer) a hour or so before making the dessert.

Melt your chocolate in the top of a double boiler, and when it is melted allow it to cool until it is not runny, but of a spreading consistency. Take the flowerpots out of the freezer and pour in enough of the chocolate to coat the bottom. Then with a small spatula, spread the inside of the flowerpot with the chocolate. Smooth the surface, and immediately put the coated flowerpots into the freezer until you are ready to fill them with the ice cream, and serve immediately, sticking a tiny bunch of artificial flowers in the center of the ice cream.

For hostesses who want to end a dinner on a high note of a delicious and spectacular dessert, and furnish a conversation piece at the same time, do try *Parfait Fleuri.*

Wheeler's Vendôme restaurant in London's Mayfair is a charming restaurant, and perhaps the narrowest in London. It is a cozy place, with wooden-paneled walls, and the food is most excellent. The menus are unique, for each item has an explanation of just what the dish is, what goes into it, and the manner in which it is cooked and served. And, of course, the price. You can look the menu over, and even if you are not familiar with the nomenclature, you will know just what you are getting. I don't know when I have encountered a restaurant appurtenance that impressed me more.

Our entree was a delectable *Sole Dieppoise* (". . . steamed, white wine sauce, with button mushrooms, potted shrimps and mussels masked with cream"). The dessert was exceedingly delicious, called Bombe Nesselrode, made with ice cream and chestnuts.

BOMBE NESSELRODE

1 *pint vanilla ice cream*	*Candied cherries*
2 *tbsp. chestnut purée*	*Whipped cream*
6 *marrons glacé (preserved chestnuts)*	*Chestnut purée*
	Candied angelica

Soften 1 pint vanilla ice cream, then blend into it 2 tablespoons chestnut purée, and add 6 marrons glacé (preserved chestnuts), chopped into small pieces. Place in freezing compartment tray, stirring occasionally, and leave until ready to use.

To serve cut into serving pieces and pipe thickly whipped cream around the edge. Fill center with chestnut purée, and top with candied cherries and angelica. Serves 2.

The French are very fond of marzipan, and the people of Auvergne make a dessert with it. Marzipan is sometimes sold as almond paste, and can be bought in American food stores.

CRÊPES MARZIPAN

Crêpe batter	*Marzipan (or almond paste)*
Crêpe butter	*4½ oz. Jamaica rum*

Make the standard crêpe batter and butter, but as you finish cooking each crêpe, spread it with about a teaspoon of marzipan (or almond paste) and roll it up.

Melt the crêpe butter in the blazer of the chafing dish, then put in the rolled stuffed crêpes and heat them through. Then pour over the contents of the blazer 4½ ounces Jamaica rum, set alight. Serve crêpes while rum is still blazing, pouring some sauce over each crêpe.

I detailed in the chapter on meats the magnificent dinner that Madame Prunier gave for us in London. And now here is the recipe for the superb crêpes.

CRÊPES PRUNIER

Crêpe batter	*3 egg yolks*
1 cup flour	*1¾ cups warm milk*
½ cup sugar	*1 cup whipped cream*

Trappistine Liqueur or Benedictine

The filling is made first. In a saucepan mix 1 cup flour, ½ cup sugar, and 3 egg yolks until well blended. Then gradually add 1¾ cups warm milk. Put on a gentle fire and beat continuously until custard is thick. Remove from fire and continue beating for 1 minute. Then add 1 cup whipped cream that has been well flavored with Trappistine Liqueur or Benedictine.

Make your thin French pancakes, or crêpes. Place portions of the custard on each, and roll them. Place the filled and rolled crêpes on a buttered dish and warm in a low oven. Serve them very hot; at the last minute pour on blazing Trappistine Liqueur, or Benedictine.

I had something quite different (to me) in the way of crêpes in the home of a friend in Paris. She called them *Crêpes à la*

Bourbonnaise (after the name of the province in which she was born), and this is the recipe she gave me.

CRÊPES À LA BOURBONNAISE

CRÊPE BATTER

⅔ cup flour	2 egg yolks
1 tbsp. fine sugar	1½ cups milk
¼ tsp. salt	2 tbsp. melted butter
2 whole eggs	1 tbsp. rum

CRÈME PÂTISSIÈRE

¾ cup sugar	⅓ cup flour
6 egg yolks	2 cups milk
	Vanilla bean

APRICOT SAUCE

1½ cups sugar	3 tsp. lemon juice
3 cups apricot juice	¾ cup rum

Sift together in a bowl ⅔ cup flour, 1 tablespoon fine sugar, and ¼ teaspoon salt. Next stir in, one at a time, 2 whole eggs and 2 egg yolks, well beaten, and gradually add 1½ cups milk, and stir until smooth. Then add 2 tablespoons melted butter and 1 tablespoon rum. Blend all well, then strain the batter through a fine sieve, and let it stand for about 2 hours.

In the meantime make the Crème Pâtissière and the Apricot Sauce. To make the crème beat together ¾ cup sugar and 6 egg yolks until the mixture is very thick and lemon colored. Then lightly mix in ⅓ cup flour. When well blended gradually add 2 cups milk heated with a vanilla bean, stirring constantly with a wire whisk. Then place over a very low flame and whisk until it nearly reaches the boiling point. Remove from the fire and cool.

To make the Apricot Sauce, combine in a saucepan 1½ cups sugar and 3 cups apricot juice. Bring to a boil and boil rapidly for 10 minutes. Remove syrup from fire and stir in 3 teaspoons lemon juice and ¾ cup rum.

To make the crêpes put a little butter in a very hot skillet (just enough to butter it well) and pour in a very thin layer of the crêpe batter, about 1 to 1½ tablespoons. The batter should be thin and the pan hot enough so that the crêpe will be "set" and browned on the underside in about a minute. Using a flexible spatula turn the crêpe to the other side and cook until brown. They must be cooked quickly because long cooking toughens them. Place the crêpes on a warm platter as each is done.

Put a generous tablespoon of Crème Pâtissière on each crêpe, and roll each up so that the filling is completely encased in the crêpe. Place them side by side in a shallow baking dish, or in a chafing dish. When ready to serve pour the hot Apricot Sauce over the filled crêpes. Sprinkle liberally with warm rum. Ignite the liqueur and serve the crêpes flaming.

Alfredo made some special crêpes for George and Pat Richardson of San Francisco, and Mrs. Wood and me the night we all dined there. Alfredo made almost as much of a production with crêpes as he did with the fettuccine, and the crêpes, like the fettuccine and the filets of turkey breasts, were superb.

Alfredo's crêpes were filled with a slightly thickened apricot purée, which was seasoned with spices and Grand Marnier. The crêpes, the crêpe butter, and the flambé were all standard.

Another dessert of crêpes that was most unusual and different in flavor was served to us at the famous Zürich night club, the Kindli. The crêpes and the butter were made in the usual way, but the liqueurs that went into the sauce made it marvelous. There was Grand Marnier, Pernod, Kirsch, Chartreuse, Framboise (raspberry cordial), and Cognac. Just a little of each was added, but the combination was delightfully intriguing, and it flambéed beautifully.

"That wonderful object of domestic art, the trifle . . . with its charming confusion of cream and cake and almonds and jam and jelly and wine and froth . . ." is the way Oliver Wendell Holmes, in *Elsie Venner*, described English trifle. To my mind, it is one of the two greatest desserts in the realm of gastronomy.

However, for some strange and unknown reason, English trifle seems to have disappeared from London. I have never seen it listed on the menu of any London restaurant. I have encountered it only once, and that was in the country home of Guy Bracewell Smith. The Smith's cook, Margaret Coleman, made a perfect trifle one week end, and I unashamedly had three helpings!

Charles Francatelli, Queen Victoria's chief cook, has a recipe for trifle in his cookbook written in 1865, and it is practically identical with that in my cookbook, *With a Jug of Wine*. Here is the recipe, which is quite easy to prepare.

ENGLISH TRIFLE

Lady fingers	*Raspberry jam*
1 *sponge cake*	*Macaroons*

1 *cup Madeira*

2 *cups milk*	*Grated rind ½ lemon*
6 *egg yolks*	¼ *tsp. salt*
½ *cup sugar*	2 *oz. brandy*

½ *tsp. vanilla extract*

½ *tsp. lemon extract*	2 *tbsp. dry white wine*
3 *tbsp. maraschino cordial*	2 *cups heavy whipping cream*

Sugar to taste

Slivered almonds	*Candied cherries*

Line the sides of a glass bowl, or china salad bowl, with halved lady fingers standing upright, the flat sides resting against the sides of the bowl. Cover the bottom of the bowl with a 1½ inch thick layer of sponge cake, not too fresh. Spread a generous layer of raspberry jam over the sponge cake, and over the jam place a layer of macaroons. Pour over all 1 cup Madeira, or enough to saturate the cake, macaroons and lady fingers thoroughly. Put in a cold place until wanted.

Make a boiled custard as follows: Scald 2 cups milk. Combine

6 egg yolks, lightly beaten with ½ cup sugar, the grated rind of ½ lemon, and ¼ teaspoon salt. Slowly add the scalded milk to the egg mixture, stirring constantly. Put the whole into the top of a double boiler, and cook over hot (not boiling) water, stirring constantly, until the mixture thickens and will coat a spoon. If you want to make the custard a little richer, use half milk and half cream. Cool, and add 2 ounces fine brandy and ½ teaspoon vanilla extract. Beat well to blend, then place the custard in the refrigerator to chill.

In a glass bowl which has been set in a larger bowl filled with cracked ice, mix together ½ teaspoon lemon extract, 3 table-spoons of maraschino cordial, 2 tablespoons white wine, 2 cups heavy whipping cream, and sugar to taste. Whip the cream until stiff, then place in the refrigerator for a couple of hours.

To complete the trifle, pour the chilled custard into the bowl containing the sponge cake, lady fingers, raspberry jam, and macaroons. Put the whipped cream over the custard, building it up. Sprinkle slivered almonds generously over the whipped cream, and decorate the top with candied, or maraschino cherries.

The last night we had dinner at the Royal Hotel in Naples, the chef, Luciano Timanti, made a dessert for us for which he is famous—Soufflé Royal. I asked for the recipe, but he said it was a secret. However, Signor Chimirri, the manager, persuaded him to give me the recipe, and he graciously assented. In spite of its name, this delicious dessert is not a soufflé.

SOUFFLÉ ROYAL

Sponge cake	*Vanilla ice cream*
Cointreau	*Meringue*
Fruit salad	*Finely chopped orange rind*
Sugar	*Quaker oats*
Lemon juice	*Powdered sugar*
	Chocolate sauce

Place a sponge cake in a round, fairly deep glass baking dish and sprinkle it liberally with Cointreau. On top of the cake place a generous layer of fruit salad (cut up oranges, pineapple, seedless grapes, apples, bananas and pears, which have previously been sprinkled with sugar and a little lemon juice). Top the fruit salad with a good layer of very hard vanilla ice cream. Completely cover the ice cream with a meringue to which has been added some finely chopped orange rind and a sprinkling of Quaker oats. Cover the top of the meringue with powdered sugar and bake in a preheated 450-degree oven until the meringue browns. Serve with a chocolate sauce.

Irish whisky is dear to the heart of the Irishman, and of course anything made with Irish whisky is doubly good. At the Shannon Airport's beautiful restaurant we had a dessert one night called Irish Mist Cream. Besides tasting wonderful it has the added advantage that it can be made ahead. And I can assure you that it will create a sensation among your guests.

IRISH MIST CREAM

1 *pint milk*	2 *oz. sugar*
1 *tbsp. unflavored gelatin*	2 *tbsp. whipped cream*
Pinch salt	1 *egg white*
4 *egg yolks*	2 *oz. Irish Mist*

Heat 1 pint milk in top of double boiler over boiling water, then add 1 tablespoon unflavored gelatin and a pinch salt. Then add the yolks of 4 eggs which have been well-beaten with 2 ounces sugar. Whisk until mixture thickens. Then remove from heat, cook slightly, then fold in 2 tablespoons whipped cream, then the egg white which has been whisked to a snow, and lastly 2 ounces Irish Mist (this is a bottled cordial made with Irish whisky). Place in a wetted mold and cool until mixture sets, then chill. Serve with unsweetened whipped cream and sugared lady fingers.

I have already detailed the charm and beauty of the Caruso Belvedere hotel and restaurant in Ravello, Italy, and the charm and culinary genius of its proprietor, Signor Caruso. His chocolate soufflé is world famous, a culinary masterpiece that is unsurpassed. This is his recipe.

CARUSO'S CHOCOLATE SOUFFLÉ

2 *eggs, separated*   1⅔ *tbsp. unsweetened cocoa*
1 *tbsp. confectioner's sugar*   *Whole preserved black cherries*

Separate 2 eggs, and beat the whites until stiff. Beat the yolks
thoroughly and add, little by little, 1 tablespoon of confectioner's
sugar and 1⅔ tablespoons of unsweetened cocoa. Then fold the
beaten whites into the yolks.

On the bottom of a buttered baking dish spread a thin layer
of whole preserved black cherries. (I see no reason why canned
Bing cherries, drained, could not be used.) Over the layer of
cherries pour the egg-sugar-cocoa mixture.

Bake near the top of a 425-degree oven, where the heat rises
and cooks the top surface, until the soufflé rises. When it has risen
remove it from the oven and serve at once. A small soufflé takes
9 to 10 minutes to cook; one made of 4 eggs (serving 2 persons)
takes about 12 minutes. The center should be creamy.

To many people it is a desecration to cook fresh peaches. Their
perfume and flavor is so ambrosial that something seems to be
lost even when they are gently poached in wine or a syrup. But
this is not true in the case of a peach soufflé.

I know soufflés are supposed to be tricky things, requiring
meticulous care in preparation and cooking. But if you can beat
eggs, and fold them gently; if you have a trustworthy oven; if
you can follow directions, you can make a soufflé.

On the Cunard Line, at least aboard the *Queen Elizabeth* and
the *Queen Mary,* you can ask for almost any dish you desire
(within reason, of course) and it will be served to you that evening, or the following day. The amount and variety of comestibles
carried aboard these huge and luxurious liners is amazing.

One late morning on our way back to America, after having
made a tour of the galleys and storage rooms of the *Queen Mary,*
I asked the head chef if we could have a peach soufflé for dinner
that night. The chef smilingly assented, and sure enough, after a
delicious stuffed Guinea hen as the entree, a lovely peach soufflé

was brought to the table. It was marvelous, and this is the way it was made.

PEACH SOUFFLÉ

8–9 *ripe peaches*	1 *cup warm milk*
1½ *tsp. lemon juice*	¼ *cup sugar*
2 *oz. kirsch*	*Pinch salt*
2 *oz. Grand Marnier*	4 *egg yolks*
3 *tbsp. butter*	5 *egg whites*
3 *tbsp. flour*	*Butter*
	Sugar

Peel and pit enough ripe peaches and force them through a sieve with 1½ teaspoon lemon juice to make 1½ cup purée (about 8 to 9 peaches, depending on size). Then sprinkle the purée with 2 ounces each kirsch and Grand Marnier (or Cointreau). Place the purée in a saucepan and heat just to the boiling point. Then remove from the fire and allow to cool to about lukewarm.

Melt 3 tablespoons butter in the top of a double boiler over simmering water, then blend in 3 tablespoons flour. Cook for a moment, then slowly add 1 cup warm milk, stirring constantly. Then add ¼ cup sugar and a pinch salt and continue to stir until mixture is smooth and creamy. Remove top of double boiler from fire and stir in 4 egg yolks, which have been beaten until light and lemon-colored. To this sauce, add the peach purée and blend thoroughly. Place mixture in a fairly large glass bowl, and allow to cool to be just barely lukewarm.

Now comes the most important step. With a hand rotary beater beat 5 egg whites (which are at room temperature) until they are stiff and creamy (don't use a blender or electric beater). This point is reached when beaten egg whites will stand in peaks, but still glisten. They must not be dry.

With a wooden spoon put about half the beaten egg whites into the peach sauce, and stir thoroughly, but slowly and gently, for about 1 minute. Then *fold in,* carefully and lightly, the remaining egg whites. This should not take more than 15 seconds, and disregard any patches of beaten egg whites that may remain in mixture. Remember, the purpose of carefully mixing and folding the beaten egg whites into sauce is to not let the air bubbles in the beaten egg whites escape. These air bubbles, when heated, cause the soufflé to expand and rise.

Have a 1½ quart ovenproof glass dish, with straight sides, lightly buttered and sprinkled with sugar. Pour your completed mixture into this dish, and put it into a pre-heated 350-degree oven. Let it cook for approximately 30 minutes. Five minutes before that time you can take a peek at it. Open the oven door slowly (don't let any cold air intrude) and move the dish back and forth slightly. If the top crust is golden brown, and it does not shake, or shakes ever so little, the soufflé is done.

However, if it quivers, give it a little more time to cook. But dessert soufflés should be softer inside than entree soufflés.

When soufflé is done, SERVE IMMEDIATELY!

One of our most interesting experiences during our travels was attending the Highland Games at Pitlochry, a town in the heart of the Scottish Highlands. There were foot races, bicycle races, weight throwing, broad jump, hammer throwing, putting the "stone" (which corresponds to America's shot putting), pole vaulting, sword dancing, dancing the sailor's hornpipe, dancing the Irish jig and tossing the claber. This last contest is almost unbelievable unless you have seen it. A man lifts a pole which seemed to me about the size of a telephone pole, runs with it, and tosses it high in the air, so that before it lands, it will have turned end over end. And, of course, there were contests of piper bands.

We stayed at the charming old Dundarach Hotel in Pitlochry, and one night we had a delightful dessert, light, but exceedingly flavorsome.

SPONGE CAKE WITH MARMALADE AND DRAMBUIE

Individual sponge cakes	3 *tbsp. Drambuie*
2 *tablespoons Keiller's orange*	2 *oz. brandy*
marmalade	

For each portion pour 3 tablespoons Drambuie (a Scotch liqueur) over individual sponge cakes on flameproof dishes. Hollow out the center of each and in the hollow put 2 tablespoons Keiller's orange marmalade. Pour around each sponge cake about 2 ounces warmed brandy and immediately set it alight. Serve while brandy is still flaming.

I think the two things most symbolic of Christmas feasting are the boar's head and the plum pudding. The former is, of course, almost wholly English, although it is still a part of the annual Bracebridge Christmas dinner at the Ahwahnee Inn in Yosemite Park in California. But the plum pudding is popular in America, as it has always been in England.

I have often wondered why this rich and hearty finale to the Christmas dinner, with its subtle blend of many flavors, was named "plum" pudding, because it contains nary a plum!

Here are two English recipes for plum pudding which are delicious. One uses rum, and the other uses Cointreau.

RUM PLUM PUDDING

½ cup candied orange peel	1 tsp. salt
½ cup candied lemon peel	1 tsp. baking powder
½ cup candied citron	2 tsp. grated nutmeg
2 cups seedless raisins	¼ tsp. ground mace
2 cups currants	¼ tsp. ground cinnamon
1 cup rum, 151 proof	½ cup chopped blanched
2 cups flour	almonds
½ lb. ground beef suet	4 eggs
1 cup sugar	½ cup warm brandy

In a large bowl put ½ cup each candied orange peel, candied lemon peel, and candied citron (or a 1-pound jar of mixed candied fruits), and 2 cups each seedless raisins and currants. Over this mixture pour 1 cup 151 proof rum, and let mixture stand 1 hour.

Mix 2 cups flour with ½ pound ground beef suet, coating suet well with flour. Mix together 1 cup granulated sugar, 1 teaspoon each salt and baking powder, 2 teaspoons nutmeg, and ¼ teaspoon each ground mace and cinnamon. Combine this mixture with the flour-suet mixture, then stir in ½ cup chopped blanched almonds. Then add the raisin-currant-candied fruit-rum mixture and blend all well. Beat 4 eggs, add to the whole mixture, and mix and blend all well and thoroughly.

Pour the pudding into a well-buttered pan or pudding mold, filling no more than ⅔ full. Cover with 2 or 3 thicknesses of waxed paper, tied securely, or cover with metal foil, and steam for 3 hours. To steam the pudding set pan or mold on a rack in a large pan or kettle having a close-fitting lid. Pour in enough boiling water to come half way up the sides of the mold. Put cover on kettle and boil gently for 3 hours, adding more boiling water as necessary. This makes a 1½ quart pudding—enough for 16 generous helpings.

This is the recipe using Cointreau, and it has a most unusual flavor.

COINTREAU PLUM PUDDING

1 *lb. seedless raisins*	2 *tsp. salt*
1 *lb. currants*	4 *eggs*
½ *cup chopped pecans*	1 *cup sugar*
2½ *cups flour*	2 *cups molasses*
2 *tsp. baking soda*	2 *cups buttermilk*
1 *tsp. powdered cloves*	1½ *cups finely chopped beef*
1 *tsp. ground allspice*	*suet*
1 *tsp. grated nutmeg*	1½ *cups Cointreau*
1 *tsp. ground cinnamon*	2½ *cups fine breadcrumbs*
½ *cup warm brandy*	

Combine 1 pound each seedless raisins and currants, and ½ cup chopped pecans. Dredge these with 1 cup flour. Sift together 1½ cups flour, 2 teaspoons baking soda, 1 teaspoon each powdered cloves, allspice, nutmeg, and cinnamon, and 2 teaspoons salt.

Beat 4 eggs, and add to them 1 cup sugar, 2 cups molasses, 2 cups buttermilk, 1½ cups finely chopped beef suet, ½ cup Cointreau, and 2½ cups fine dry breadcrumbs. To this add the floured raisin-currant-nut mixture, and mix well. Then add the flour-spice mixture, and again mix thoroughly and well.

Pour the pudding into 2 greased 3 pound molds, and steam as

in the preceding recipe for 3 hours. This recipe makes 2 puddings, each serving 12.

In this and the preceding recipe the puddings can be cooled, wrapped in wax paper, and kept in the refrigerator for a week or more. Resteam to heat. In both recipes unmold on a heatproof platter, pour ½ cup warm brandy over puddings, set alight, and serve.

While we were living in Lausanne, Switzerland, Mrs. Wood and I took a bus tour to Mont Blanc. The drive from Lausanne to Chamonix was breathtaking, not only in its beauty, but in negotiating the twists and turns of Alpine roads! The scenery is almost unbelievable during the trip to Chamonix, but the return trip to Lausanne, via Geneva, Switzerland, lacked the grandeur of the Alps.

We missed seeing the Matterhorn, but we did see the Jungfrau in Interlaken. But I think Mont Blanc tops them all. We made the twelve thousand odd feet ascent part way up Mont Blanc via a cable lift, and the views are indescribable.

At Chamonix we had luncheon at the very lovely Hotel des Alpes. A special fish dish was prepared for us, and for dessert we had *Riz à l'Imperatrice,* the classic French rice pudding. Actually, it is not a pudding, but an elegant rice mold garnished with candied fruits, and its base is surrounded with current jelly slightly diluted with brandy.

RIZ À L'IMPERATRICE
(Rice Molded with Candied Fruits)

½ cup raw converted rice	¾ cup hot milk
1¼ cups milk	Small piece vanilla bean
¾ cup finely chopped candied	1 tbsp. unflavored gelatin
fruits	2 tbsp. cold water
2 oz. kirsch	1 cup heavy cream, whipped
4 egg yolks	Red currant jelly
½ cup sugar	Brandy

In top of a double boiler over boiling water, cook ½ cup converted (enriched parboiled long grain) rice in 1¼ cups milk until milk has been absorbed, or rice is tender (about 35 minutes). Then pour into a mixing bowl. While rice is cooking marinate ¾ cup finely chopped candied fruits (available put up in jars in fine food stores) in 2 ounces kirsch.

In top of a double boiler over boiling water combine 4 egg yolks, ½ cup sugar, ¾ cup hot milk, and a small piece vanilla bean. Cook, stirring constantly, until thick and smooth. Then stir in 1 tablespoon unflavored gelatin which has been softened in 2 tablespoons cold water. Then add the marinated candied fruits, cooked rice, and 1 cup heavy cream, whipped. Blend well, then turn the whole into a decorative ring mold, and chill in refrigerator for at least 4 hours.

To serve, unmold rice onto a chilled platter, and garnish with fancy shapes of candied fruits and citron. Surround base with red currant jelly, melted and diluted with a little brandy, and whipped to smoothness. This serves 6.

Prunus Persica, meaning Plum from Persia, is the Latin name for that most delicious of all fruits, the peach. Oddly enough it was once believed to contain a deadly poison, which probably accounts for its delayed appreciation by the Western World. However, it delighted the palates of the Chinese centuries before the Christian era, and the *tao,* as they called the peach, was to them a symbol of longevity.

With fresh peaches one can make a surprising number of ambrosial desserts. French chefs are noted for their ways with peaches, and it was Escoffier who devised that world-renowned Peach Melba.

I have a trio of French recipes for peaches. The first one comes from Normandy.

PEACHES FLAMBÉED WITH CALVADOS

4 *fresh peaches*	½ *cup of syrup peaches*
2 *cups cold water*	*cooked in*
½ *cup sugar*	*Few small strips orange peel*
¼ *stick cinnamon*	4 *oz. Calvados (or applejack)*
Peel of 1 lemon	*Vanilla ice cream*

Cook 4 whole peaches with the skin on in 2 cups cold water, ½ cup sugar, ¼ stick cinnamon, and 1 lemon peel. Cover, bring to a boil, and simmer 15 minutes. When cool, remove the peaches from the syrup, peel, cut each peach in half, and remove pits. Place the peach halves in a chafing dish with ½ cup of the syrup and heat. Then add a few small strips of orange peel, and 4 ounces of heated Calvados or applejack, and set aflame. To serve, pour the flaming ingredients over individual dishes of vanilla ice cream. This serves 4.

We had this marvelous combination of fresh peaches and raspberries at the Auberge du Père Louis, a restaurant I have mentioned before.

POACHED PEACHES AND FRESH RASPBERRIES

6 *ripe peaches*	2 *oz. Grand Marnier*
2 *cups water*	*Fresh raspberries (or frozen)*
2 *cups sugar*	*Whipped cream*
Piece vanilla bean	*Kirsch*

First peel 6 ripe peaches (the easiest way to peel peaches is to quickly plunge them into boiling water, remove, and place in a bowl of ice water), halve them, and remove the pits.

Make a syrup by combining 2 cups water, 2 cups sugar, and a piece of vanilla bean, and allow it to boil for about 10 minutes. Poach the peach halves in this syrup until tender, then remove them and allow to cool. To the syrup add 2 ounces of Grand Marnier, cook until it is reduced to the consistency of thick syrup, then remove vanilla bean, and allow syrup to cool.

To serve fill peach halves with fresh raspberries, pour syrup over them, and top with whipped cream flavored with Kirsch.

The following recipe for poached peaches flambéed was given me by an American friend who has lived in Paris for many years. She said that it was a specialty of the great Café de Paris, which was on the Avenue de l'Opéra, but is, alas, no longer in existence. She told me that she was a friend of the chef, Paul

Billon, and he wrote out this recipe for her, which she says she frequently serves.

PÊCHE ET FRAMBOISE, FLAMBÉ
(Peaches and Raspberries Flambéed)

6 *firm but ripe peaches*	½ *cup fresh raspberries*
1 *cup water*	*Juice 1 orange*
1 *cup sugar*	½ *cup poaching syrup*
Grated rind 1 lemon	4 *oz. kirsch (or brandy)*
2 *oz. butter*	2 *oz. Cointreau*

Vanilla ice cream

Select 4 firm but ripe peaches. Peel them (if they do not peel easily plunge them into boiling water, quickly remove them and plunge into ice water. Then the skin will come off easily), halve them, and remove the pits. Keep the peeled halves in ice water while you make the poaching syrup.

In a large shallow saucepan mix 1 cup water with 1 cup granulated sugar and add the grated rind 1 lemon. When the sugar is dissolved stir over a low heat for a few minutes, then add the drained peach halves. Poach them for about 10 minutes in the gently boiling syrup, then lift the halves out with a strainer to a serving platter.

In the blazer of the chafing dish over the direct flame melt 2 ounces butter. Then add ½ cup fresh raspberries, crushed, the juice of 1 orange, and ½ cup of the syrup the peaches were poached in. Stir and cook for a few minutes until bubbly, then put in the peach halves, cut side down. Cook for a few minutes, basting with the sauce. Finally, pour in a mixture of 4 ounces of Kirsch (or brandy) and 2 ounces Cointreau (or curaçao) which has been heated, and set the whole aflame.

In each of 4 individual dishes put a scoop of vanilla ice cream. Top each scoop with 2 peach halves, cut side down, and ladle the sauce over the top.

The dessert served at Guy Bracewell Smith's dinner on July 4th, 1962, featuring fruits, was *Quartiers de Pêches Flambées au Kirsch*. It was the creation of Chef Viguers, of the Park Lane Hotel.

QUARTIERS DE PÊCHES FLAMBÉES AU KIRSCH
(Peach Quarters Flambéed with Kirsch)

8 *peaches*	4 *oz. kirsch*
3 *cups heavy simple syrup*	*Sugar*

Ice cream

Peel and pit 8 peaches, and cut into quarters. Poach in a heavy simple syrup (about 3 cups). Then remove the peach quarters to a metal serving dish. Reduce the syrup to a light caramel, and pour over peaches. Warm about 4 ounces kirsch, pour over peaches, sprinkle with sugar, then set alight. Serve in shallow bowls, and add a generous portion of ice cream to each bowl. This recipe serves 4.

With the exception of the apple, what fruit would you guess to be cultivated more extensively than all other fruits in all parts of the world (tropical and sub-tropical lands excepted)? I made three guesses, but they were all wrong. It is the pear.

Pears have been cultivated ever since the remotest periods of antiquity. They are mentioned in the oldest Greek writings, and those gourmets of ancient times, the Romans, cultivated them extensively. Today there are some 5,000 varieties of European pears, and around 1,000 varieties of American pears.

For a light and most gratifying dessert, pears are ideal. They have a distinct, yet rather bland and mild flavor, but they blend perfectly with foods and liquids that are distinctly flavored, and they make excellent carriers for flavors that are sharp.

During their season fresh pears are far superior for use as desserts. They may be used "as is," poached in a simple syrup flavored with a piece of vanilla bean (or vanilla extract), or baked.

No meal in Italy is complete without fruit, no matter how much you have had before. The day we had luncheon at the Ristorante Onda d'Oro on Capri an Italian family of four had the table next to us. They had had an exceedingly substantial meal consisting of soup, pasta, and an entree. Then a large fruit basket was brought to the table, and, so help me, each one of the four had an orange, an apple, and two pears!

We had two wonderful pear desserts in Italy. One was baked pears, with their cavities stuffed with macaroons, nuts, and port wine. Incidentally, I learned that it was the Italians who invented macaroons, which are called *amaretti*.

BAKED MACAROON-STUFFED PEARS

6 *firm ripe pears*	3 *tbsp. chopped pecans*
4 *tbsp. dry sherry*	1 *tbsp. grated lemon rind*
½ *cup crumbled macaroons*	¾ *cup port wine*

6 *tbsp. honey*

Peel 6 ripe but firm pears, cut them in half lengthwise, remove the core, and arrange them in a baking dish.

Combine 4 tablespoons dry sherry, ½ cup crumbled macaroons, 3 tablespoons chopped pecans, and 1 tablespoon grated lemon rind. Divide this mixture among the cavities of the pear halves. Pour ¾ cup port wine around the pears and bake in a 350-degree oven for 10 minutes. Then remove them from the oven and pour 1 teaspoon honey over each pear and return pears to oven and bake 5 to 10 minutes longer, or until pears are tender.

In Florence one night we dined at the Ristorante Oliviero, which is a very plush place. There are three or four dining rooms, and each one has a charming intimacy. It is the sort of restaurant that might make you think that you were in Paris, or New York.

We had a delicious pear dessert, one that was typically Italian.

ITALIAN STUFFED PEARS

Fresh pears	*Candied ginger*
Ground almonds	*Strega liqueur*
Powdered sugar	*Marsala wine*

Peel the number of pears required, cut them in half lengthwise, and remove the cores.

Combine ground almonds, powdered sugar, and candied ginger, which has been finely chopped. Then moisten the mixture with Strega, so that it will all hold together. Stuff the cavities with this mixture, place the pears in an ovenproof baking dish, and pour around them Marsala wine. Bake in a moderate (350 degrees) oven until pears are tender. These can be served either hot or cold.

The next four recipes for pear desserts come from France. The first, Pears Cardinal, we had at Drouants, in Paris.

PEARS CARDINAL

4 *firm, ripe pears*	1 *cup sugar*
Cold water	1 *1-inch piece vanilla bean*
Lemon juice	1 *pint fresh berries (see*
1 *cup water*	*recipe)*
2 *oz. Cointreau or 1 oz. kirsch*	

Carefully peel 4 ripe yet firm pears and cut them in half lengthwise, and remove the core. Immediately drop them in cold water containing a little lemon juice to prevent them from turning brown.

In a saucepan combine 1 cup water and 1 cup sugar and a 1-inch piece vanilla bean. Boil for 5 minutes, then put the pear halves in the syrup and poach them gently until they are tender, but not soft. Then let them cool in their syrup, drain them, and then chill them.

To serve them, you have a choice of procedures, depending upon the time of year. During the berry season, you can mash a pint of fresh strawberries with 2 ounces of Cointreau, or mash a pint of fresh raspberries with ¼ cup of granulated sugar and flavor with about 1 ounce of kirsch. When berries are out of season use frozen strawberries or frozen raspberries. Defrost them, and add about 2 ounces kirsch, or cognac. Don't use a sweet liqueur because frozen berries are already sweetened.

Place 2 pear halves on chilled dishes, pour the berry sauce over them, and serve. If you wish, you can force the berry sauce through a fine sieve before pouring over the pears. Serves 4.

This recipe is somewhat similar to the preceding recipe, except that it uses ground almonds, and from that it gets its name.

PEARS AMANDINE

4 *firm, ripe pears*	*½ cup ground, toasted*
Cold water	*almonds*
Lemon juice	*Brandy*
1 *cup water*	*Frozen strawberries or*
1 *cup sugar*	*raspberries*
1 *1-inch piece vanilla bean*	

Prepare and poach 4 pears as in the preceding recipe, let them cool in their syrup, then remove them, and drain.

Put enough toasted almonds through the finest blade of the food chopper to make about a generous half cup. Moisten them with enough good brandy so that you get sort of a paste. Distribute this paste equally among the cavities of the pear halves.

Defrost a package of frozen strawberries (or raspberries) and then force them through a fine sieve. Spoon this over the pears, chill thoroughly, and serve to 4.

One of the loveliest hotels we stopped at during our travels through France was the Plaza Hotel in Nice. It faced out on the Jardin Albert I, and our balcony had a marvelous view of the Mediterranean. Due to an injury to her knee that happened the second night we were in Nice, we stayed at the Plaza for six weeks. The Hotel is luxuriously furnished, the service all through the hotel is perfect, and the food was superb. I'll never forget our Christmas dinner in the dining room, with our table right in front of a roaring fire in a huge fireplace.

One of the delectable desserts we had at the Plaza was *Poire Hélène,* a dessert that is a Continental favorite.

POIRE HÉLÈNE

4 firm, ripe pears
Cold water
Lemon juice
1 cup water
1 cup sugar
1½ oz. unsweetened chocolate
1 tbsp. butter

½ cup boiling water
¾ cup sugar
¼ cup corn syrup
Few grains salt
½ tsp. vanilla extract
2 oz. brandy
Vanilla ice cream

Chopped pistachio nuts

Prepare and poach 4 pears as in the preceding recipes and let them cool in their syrup, then drain them, and chill.

Make a chocolate sauce as follows: melt 1½ ounces unsweetened chocolate and 1 tablespoon butter in a double boiler. Stir in ½ cup boiling water, ¾ cup sugar, ¼ cup corn syrup, a few grains salt, and cook until smooth. Add ½ teaspoon vanilla and about 2 ounces brandy.

To serve, place 2 chilled pear halves on a bed of vanilla ice cream. Sprinkle the pear cavities with chopped pistachio nuts, and pour over all the hot chocolate sauce.

In Dijon, France we had the celebrated *Poires Dijon*. This dish gets its inspiration from the famous black currants of Dijon. However, in America, dried currants will do very well.

POIRES DIJON

6 firm, ripe pears
Butter
½ cup chopped currants
Brown sugar

1 tsp. grated lemon rind
1 tbsp. chopped pistachio nuts
1 oz. Cointreau
¾ cup Madeira wine

Peel 6 ripe but firm pears, cut them in half lengthwise, remove the core, and lay them, cavity side up, in a buttered baking dish.

Combine ½ cup chopped currants, a sprinkling of brown sugar, 1 teaspoon grated lemon rind, 1 tablespoon chopped pistachio nuts and about 1 ounce Cointreau. Divide this mixture among the cavities of the pear halves. Pour around the pears ¾ cup Madeira wine (or sweet sherry), cover, and bake in a 325-

degree oven for about 40 minutes, or until the pears are tender, but not soft. Serve at once.

We enjoyed this delicious pear dessert in The Hague, Holland. The ginger really adds a provocative touch to the gentle delicacy of pears.

PEARS WITH A GINGER SAUCE

4 *large, firm ripe pears*	1 *tsp. ground ginger*
4 *small lumps butter*	4 *tbsp. sugar*
Brown sugar	1 *tsp. grated lemon rind*
1 *cup sweet sauterne*	1 *tbsp. lemon juice*
	2 *oz. brandy*

Peel 4 large firm pears, cut them in half lengthwise, remove the core, and arrange them in a baking dish, cavity side up. In each cavity put a small lump of butter, and sprinkle over each pear a little brown sugar. Pour around the pears 1 cup sweet sauterne, cover, and place in a 350-degree oven and bake about 20 minutes, or until tender, basting occasionally with the liquid. Then remove the pear halves carefully to a hot dish and keep them warm while making the sauce.

Pour off the liquid from the baking dish into a saucepan, adding more sauterne, if necessary, to make 1 cup. Add 1 teaspoon ground ginger, 4 tablespoons sugar, and 1 teaspoon grated lemon rind. Stir until sugar is dissolved, and bring mixture to a boil. Then simmer gently for about 15 minutes, stirring occasionally. Just before serving stir in a tablespoon lemon juice and 2 ounces fine brandy. Blend well, then pour over pears and serve.

"Doubtless God could have made a better berry, but doubtless God never did," is the way Dr. Boteler characterized strawberries as reported by Izaak Walton in *The Compleat Angler*.

I think one of the reasons luscious red, ripe strawberries are such a miracle of goodness to the palate, aside from their unique, tangy flavor, is that they are the first of spring and summer's fresh fruits. If you were brought up in a small town I am sure you can never forget the enchantment of those church strawberry festivals, with their rich, yellow ice cream, homemade cakes, and, best of all, strawberries that looked like giant, edible rubies, and, of course, strawberry shortcake!

The French call strawberries *La Petite Reine des Desserts*— the little queen of desserts. They prepare them in ways that enhance their superb flavor, instead of overpowering them with too pronounced flavors.

FRAISES CHANTILLY

Cut strawberries in half, and stir them into whipped cream sweetened with vanilla extract, or cordial.

FRAISES PARISIENNE

Mix whole strawberries with whipped cream, and enough sweetened purée of strawberries to give a pink color.

FRAISES AUX CHAMPAGNE

Sprinkle whole strawberries with sugar, chill them, then serve in glass compotes with champagne poured over them.

Strawberry tarts have the same importance to the French as strawberry shortcake has to Americans. A baked pie shell or individual tart shells, made with rich pastry dough, is filled with either a custard, or rich crème, and is then topped with strawberries.

We had a magnificent strawberry tart one night at Maxim's in Paris. I have never eaten a more delicious one.

TARTE AUX FRAISES
(Strawberry Tart)

3 *tbsp. butter*	2 *egg whites*
1 *tbsp. cornstarch*	½ *cup heavy cream, whipped*
2 *tbsp. flour*	2 *tbsp. kirsch*
¼ *cup sugar*	*Baked pie shell*
1 *cup milk*	*Whole ripe strawberries*
2 *beaten egg yolks*	3 *tbsp. currant jelly*
½ *tsp. almond extract*	2 *tbsp. brandy*

Melt 3 tablespoons butter in top of double boiler and blend in 1 tablespoon cornstarch, 2 tablespoons flour, and ¼ cup sugar until smooth. Add 1 cup milk and cook over boiling water, stirring constantly, for 10 minutes. Add small amount of hot mixture to 2 well beaten egg yolks, then add them to the hot mixture and cook 2 minutes longer, stirring constantly. Remove from heat and stir in ½ teaspoon almond extract. Put top of double boiler into pan of cracked ice and stir the cream to cool it quickly. Then fold in 2 egg whites stiffly beaten, ½ cup heavy cream, whipped, and 2 tablespoons kirsch.

Turn the cream into a baked pie shell which has been brushed with kirsch. Cover the filling with rows of whole ripe strawberries. Glaze the strawberries with 3 tablespoons currant jelly melted and thinned with 2 tablespoons brandy. Serves 5 to 6.

The provinces of Limousin and Auvergne in central France are not particularly noted for gourmet food, but the region has a dessert specialty that is utterly delicious. It is a black cherry *flan* (custard) called *La Clafoutis*.

But it is not necessary to travel to these central provinces to savor the delight of *La Clafoutis*. It is wonderfully made at Le Grand Comptoir, a restaurant I have mentioned before, one of the best bistros in the central markets area.

LA CLAFOUTIS
(Cherry Custard)

5 *tbsp. flour*	2¾ *cups milk*
Pinch salt	¼ *cup cherry brandy*
5 *tbsp. sugar*	2 *lbs. black sweet cherries*
½ *cup cold milk*	*(unpitted)*
3 *eggs*	*Powdered sugar*

Put 5 tablespoons flour, a pinch salt, and 5 tablespoons sugar in a bowl and mix well. Then mix in ½ cup cold milk, stirring until smooth and without any lumps. Next beat in, one at a time, 3 eggs, then slowly add 2¾ cups milk combined with ¼ cup cherry brandy.

Cover the bottom of a well-buttered cake tin or baking dish with about two pounds of black sweet cherries, *unpitted* (the pits in the cherries contribute to the flavor of this dish). Pour the custard mix over the cherries and bake in a 325-degree oven for about 30 minutes, or until a silver knife inserted in the middle of the custard comes out clean. While still hot, sprinkle the top with a little powdered sugar. Serve either hot or cold, to about 4.

The dessert we had at our dinner at Movenpick's restaurant at Dreikönighaus, in Zürich, was a superb *Cerises flambées Merveille*. I believe the literal translation of that would be "Marvelous Flambéed Cherries," but that doesn't tell the whole story. It is really a flambéed cherry and raspberry sauce over ice cream.

CERISES FLAMBÉES MERVEILLE
(Cherry and Raspberry Sauce, Flambéed, over Ice Cream)

3 *tbsp. sugar*	2½ *oz. fresh raspberries*
5 *oz. light dry red wine*	2 *tsp. warmed kirsch*
30 *red cherries*	*Sugar*
	Vanilla ice cream

In a flambé pan (or chafing dish pan) mix together 3 tablespoons sugar and 5 ounces light red wine. Let this simmer until sauce thickens. Then add 30 red cherries and stir once slightly. Then carefully add 2½ ounces red raspberries. Pour over all 2 teaspoons warmed kirsch and set alight. During the process of flambéeing sprinkle a little sugar over the mixture.

To serve, in the middle of a cold plate place a scoop of vanilla ice cream. Decorate with the fruits around the ice cream, and top all with the sauce.

Leoni's Quo Vadis restaurant on Dean Street, in London's Soho District, is, I believe, the oldest and best known Italian restaurant in the city. We found the service excellent, and the food to be very good. Our dessert was most unusual, and was called Orange Bambolina. It was typically Italian.

ORANGE BAMBOLINA

1 *orange*	1 *tbsp. cold Sabayon sauce*
Fruit salad	*Ice cream*
Grated nuts	*Meringue*

First, cut off the top of an orange about an inch or so from the top, and with a pointed knife and a spoon scoop out the flesh, being careful not to damage the orange skin shell.

The preparation of the filling (which they call "fruit salad") can be as varied as one wishes: strawberries, raspberries, grapes, orange segments cut up, bananas, pineapple chunks, or any combination of these desired. A small quantity of grated nuts (pistachio, walnuts or pecans) is mixed with the fruit salad.

To make the Bambolina fill the orange shells about ½ full with the fruit salad. Add to this about 1 tablespoon of cold Sabayon sauce to each orange. Fill up the orange shells with any flavor of ice cream you prefer, or even a mixture of ice creams.

Make a meringue sufficient for the number of servings desired, and over the top of each stuffed orange put the meringue in a pyramid shape about an inch high. Put the whole under the broiler until meringue is nicely browned, then serve at once.

We had a very similar dessert at the Hotel Monaco, in Venice. To my mind the outdoor dining terrace of the Hotel Monaco is one of the loveliest places on the Continent to eat. The Grand Canal, with its gay traffic, lapped at the edge of the terrace, and on the particular night we ate there a huge British cruiser was anchored on the other side of the canal from us, and was brilliantly floodlighted, a truly breath-taking picture.

ORANGE SURPRISE

1 *orange*	½ *oz. orange curaçao*
Vanilla ice cream	½ *oz. Strega*
Fruit salad	½ *oz. kümmel*
	1 *oz. warmed brandy*

Cut about ⅕ off the top of an orange, and remove all the meat, using a sharp knife and a teaspoon. Fill the orange shell ¼ full with vanilla ice cream, and keep very cold until ready to serve. Cut the orange meat into small pieces, and mix with small pieces of pineapple, peaches, apricots, candied citrus fruits, crystallized ginger, or any combination you prefer, using only enough to fill up the orange shell with its ice cream filling.

Put the mixture of fruits in the blazer of a chafing dish which is warmed. Pour over the fruits ½ ounce each of orange curaçao, Strega and kümmel, and mix all well. Then light I ounce of warmed brandy, and pour over the contents of the blazer. When the flame dies out ladle the flambéed fruits into the orange shell containing the ice cream, and serve. This recipe serves 1. Multiply above amounts for additional servings.

Europeans seem to be exceedingly fond of pineapple. On a great many of the menus we collected I find it listed under desserts as either *Ananas,* which is the French designation, or as *Ananasso,* the Italian name.

Mr. Stone, the manager of the restaurant in the Park Lane Hotel in London, made a delicious pineapple dessert for us one night, preparing it for us at our table. I can't recall that he had a name for it, so I'll just call it Fresh Pineapple à la Stone.

FRESH PINEAPPLE À LA STONE

Fresh pineapple slices   *Maraschino cherries*
Granulated sugar   *Kirsch*

Pierce the fresh pineapple slices with a fork, then lightly sprinkle them with sugar. On each pineapple slice place at regular intervals 4 maraschino cherries. Then over each slice pour 1 ounce kirsch, and serve.

Pies as Americans know them are rarely found in Europe. Little tarts are frequently encountered in France, as they are in America, and are wonderful. But a large 8- or 9-inch pie is a great rarity.

One of the most awe-inspiring sights in Switzerland (a land

that abounds in breath-taking views) is the Rheinfall, directly north of Zürich, near the old city of Schaffhausen.

The Rheinfalls are the most powerful in Europe. The river, 500 feet wide at this point, plunges from a height of 70 feet, and great sheets and masses of water foam upward more than 50 feet in the air. From the courtyard of Laufen Castle (which has been turned into a restaurant) you go down a staircase to the level of the falls. There is a little kiosk with colored windows, and you get a view of the huge masses of water in red, blue, green, and yellow.

The castle serves excellent food, and on Saturdays and Sundays it is jammed with tourists, who partake of sausage sandwiches (terrific!) and beer, or cups of excellent Swiss coffee, or a delectable luncheon or dinner on an out of door terrace. One of the specialties is an apple pie that is most unusual and delectable. The sliced apples in the pie are covered with a smooth, creamy filling, and there is no top crust to take away the eye appeal.

LAUFEN APPLE PIE

*Pie crust to fit 8- or 10-inch pan
    or plate*
1 *tbsp. crushed, toasted
    almonds*
1 *tbsp. fine, dry breadcrumbs*
4 *cups sliced tart apples*
*Pflumli (Swiss prune brandy)
    or Calvados, or applejack*

2 *whole eggs*
2 *egg yolks*
2 *cups whipping cream*
1 *cup sugar*
2 *oz. kirsch*
2 *tbsp. melted butter*

The American housewife can use her own favorite pie crust recipe. Roll it out on a lightly floured board ⅛-inch thick. Line a deep 10-inch pie pan or plate, trim the edge, and sprinkle evenly over the pastry in the bottom of the pan 1 tablespoon each of crushed toasted almonds and fine, dry breadcrumbs.

Have ready about 4 cups thinly sliced tart apples. Arrange the apple slices in the pie pan, making even layers. Sprinkle each layer of apples lightly with Pflumli, or with Calvados, or applejack. Then put in a 350-degree oven and bake for 5 minutes. In the meanwhile combine 2 whole eggs and 2 egg yolks, and beat lightly. Then add 2 cups whipping cream, ½ cup sugar, and 2 ounces kirsch. Stir until sugar dissolves. Pour half of this mixture over the apples (which have been baked for 5 minutes), and bake about ½ hour, or until firm. Then pour in the remaining egg-sugar-cream-kirsch mixture, and bake again until a knife inserted near the edge comes out clean (about ½ hour). Remove pie from oven and pour 2 tablespoons melted butter evenly over top of pie. Sprinkle top with ¼ cup sugar and return pie to oven. Bake 5 minutes longer, or until top is crusty and golden. Let pie cool somewhat before cutting.

I detailed in the chapter on soup the marvelous Green Turtle Soup we had on the California Zephyr on our way to Chicago, New York, and Europe. But Chef Walter Blockman came up with another superlative dish, a dessert, which he called Cherry Cream pie. When he told me that he had used a commercial pudding or pie mix and canned cherry pie filling, I was amazed.

CHERRY CREAM PIE

Baked pie crust for a 9-inch   *Regular package vanilla*
       pie tin   *pudding and pie filling*
              Canned cherry pie filling

Get a regular package of vanilla pudding and pie filling and prepare according to directions on package. Prepare and bake your own favorite pie crust for a 9-inch pie tin. Pour the pudding and pie filling into the baked pie shell and let cool until set. Top with the cherry pie filling and thoroughly chill.

The following two recipes are not desserts, but are breakfast dishes. One is for pancakes, and the other for waffles.
At the lovely Old Ground Hotel in Ennis, Ireland, where we spent a week, we had for breakfast one morning some of that heavenly Irish bacon, and Kilkenny pancakes. The latter are really something, as they have for one ingredient—Irish whisky!

KILKENNY PANCAKES

6 *tbsp. sifted flour*	2 *eggs*
1 *tbsp. sugar*	1½ *cups milk*
½ *tsp. grated nutmeg*	¼ *cup Irish whisky*
Pinch salt	¼ *tsp. baking powder*

To 6 tablespoons sifted flour add 1 tablespoon sugar, ½ teaspoon nutmeg, and a pinch of salt. Mix in 2 well-beaten eggs, 1½ cups milk, and ¼ cup Irish whisky. Beat the batter thoroughly. Let stand 40 minutes in a cool place, then add ¼ teaspoon baking powder. Lightly grease your skillet or griddle, and fry thin like French pancakes. Serve with sugar and lemon.

This is the recipe for Dutch waffles which we had one morning for breakfast at the Krasnapolsky Hotel in Amsterdam, Holland.

DUTCH WAFFLES

¼ *lb. sugar*	1 *tsp. ground cinnamon*
2 *oz. butter*	2 *oz. cream (sweet) sherry*
4 *eggs*	*wine*
4 *tbsp. flour*	*Melted butter*

Cream together ¼ pound of sugar and 2 ounces of butter. Beat in 4 eggs, 1 at a time, adding a tablespoon of flour for each egg. Then stir in 1 teaspoon of ground cinnamon and 2 ounces of cream (sweet) sherry wine. Bake in a waffle iron and serve piping hot. These waffles are sweet, and all that should go over them is plenty of melted butter.

While dessert is the sweet finale to a meal, yet paradoxically, it is not the end, for to most people coffee must follow. A demitasse, alone or accompanied by a lovely liqueur, is the epilogue. In France, we loved a demitasse accompanied by a fine marc, and in Italy, a caffè espresso accompanied by Strega was almost a must. And, in Ireland, it was Irish coffee. But the finest Irish coffee

we had was not in Ireland (it originated at Shannon Free Airport,
if I am to believe Stanton Delaplane), but in the home of two very
dear friends in London, Victor and Frieda Goldman.

Victor Goldman is one of the top anesthesiologists in the world.
He is head of the department of anesthesiology at the University
of London, and he travels all over the world lecturing on his
specialty.

Mrs. Wood and I were frequent visitors in his lovely home in
London. The Sunday luncheons that Frieda and Victor gave were
gastronomic delights. There were always marvelous martinis in
the living room; then we went downstairs to the beautiful dining
room, where a superlative meal was served, with exquisite and
properly selected wines. Then back upstairs to the living room,
where Victor made and served Irish coffee. It was so wonderful
that I invariably peeked around to see where the leprechauns,
who must have assisted him, were hidden.

Victor is a very generous person, and when I asked him for
his recipe, he gave it to me without hesitation.

VICTOR GOLDMAN'S IRISH COFFEE

Boiling water
1 *large teaspoon Demerara*
  sugar

⅔ *glass HOT coffee*
⅓ *glass Irish whisky*
Cream

Pour boiling water into Waterford Irish whisky glasses and let
stand until glasses are very hot. Then pour out the water and
place in each glass a large teaspoon Demerara sugar (this is a
West Indian sugar which is brown and has a wonderful flavor).
Fill the glass ⅔ full with *very hot* coffee, and stir until sugar is
dissolved. Then stir in ⅓ glass Irish whisky. Float heavy cream
on top, and serve at once.

I think it is eminently fitting that this *Jug of Wine* book of
European recipes should end with a wonderful recipe for a
punch using that delightful German springtime beverage, May
wine, or as the Germans call it, *Mai Wein*.

MAY WINE PUNCH

½ oz. dried woodruff
4 bottles German Riesling wine
1 bottle champagne
2 oz. Benedictine liqueur

4 oz. brandy
½ lb. fine granulated sugar
1 pint sparkling water
1 pint fresh hulled strawberries

Place ½ ounce dried woodruff (see page 53) in a quart Mason jar, and pour over it 1 bottle German Riesling wine. Seal jar tightly and let steep for 8 hours. When ready to serve pour herbed wine into a punch bowl, and stir. Then add 3 more bottles of chilled Riesling, 1 bottle chilled champagne, 2 ounces Benedictine, 4 ounces fine brandy, and stir again. Next add ¼ pound fine granulated sugar dissolved in 1 pint chilled sparkling water, and stir. Finally add 1 pint fresh strawberries, hulled. Then, in center of punch bowl, place a pitcher shaved ice. This keeps punch chilled, but will not dilute it. Serves 12 generously.

And now, Good appetite, *Bon appetit,* and *Buon appetito,* and *auf wiedersehen!*

INDEX

302   INDEX

Printed in the USA
CPSIA information can be obtained
at www.ICGtesting.com
LVHW091130150724
785511LV00001B/52